Contents

THE GREAT WAR
EXPLAINED

Dedication

When I go to Ypres, I visit Tyne Cot Cemetery at Passchendaele, the largest British military cemetery in the world. Two identical headstones stand side by side, each marking the grave of 'A Second Lieutenant of The King's Shropshire Light Infantry'. I was just such a one myself once, and I am proud to have worn the cap badge that they wore. This book is dedicated to them and to the many tens of thousands of soldiers who died in that war but who have no marked grave.

THE GREAT WAR EXPLAINED

EXPLAINED

A Simple Story and Guide

Philip Stevens

Pen & Sword
MILITARY

First published in Great Britain in 2012
and reprinted in this format in 2014
By Pen and Sword Military
an imprint of
Pen and Sword Books Ltd
47 Church Street
Barnsley
South Yorkshire S70 2AS

Copyright © Philip Stevens, 2012, 2014

ISBN 978 1 78346 186 8

Printed and bound in England
by CPI Group (UK) Ltd, Croydon, CR0 4YY

Typeset in Times New Roman by
Chic Graphics

Pen & Sword Books Ltd incorporates the imprints of
Pen & Sword Aviation, Pen & Sword Family History, Pen & Sword Maritime,
Pen & Sword Military, Pen & Sword Discovery, Wharncliffe Local History,
Wharncliffe True Crime, Wharncliffe Transport, Pen & Sword Select,
Pen & Sword Military Classics, Leo Cooper, Remember When,
The Praetorian Press, Seaforth Publishing and Frontline Publishing

For a complete list of Pen and Sword titles please contact
Pen and Sword Books Limited
47 Church Street, Barnsley, South Yorkshire, S70 2AS, England
E-mail: enquiries@pen-and-sword.co.uk
Website: www.pen-and-sword.co.uk

CONTENTS

Preface

I first met Philip Stevens in early May 2006 in that most English of locations, the boundary of the cricket pitch. He was watching his son play cricket (rather well) for Wellington College. He introduced himself and said he was one of a party of forty-five Wellington parents coming with me to the battlefields of the Somme and Flanders two weeks later, and would I like him to interject relevant information at different locations? I assured him that that would be delightful, making a mental note to myself as I rushed onto the next parental boundary deckchair that he was obviously a troublemaker and one to watch. By that stage I had taken forty-five parent or pupil trips to the battlefields from five different schools, and felt that I could walk from Verdun to Passchendaele with my eyes closed, knowing every inch of surviving trenches and the story behind each.

How, how wrong I was. Halfway through the first day of the trip, as I was breezily telling the assembled parents about the mysteries of Vimy Ridge, Philip started his machine gun patter of information. Never have I heard any guide speak with such authority, animation and enthusiasm. I was awed, as were all present.

Philip became a regular adjunct on my annual trips to the trenches, and he became simply stronger and stronger. Comparisons were made with David Rattray, the captivating oral historian of the Anglo-Zulu war murdered in January 2007, or indeed Richard Holmes, the brilliant military historian who died in April 2011 and who was such a good friend of Wellington College. Those who heard Philip begged for him to write a book about the war so a wider audience could benefit from his insights and brilliant mind.

Thus was this book born, nicely in time for the hundredth anniversary of the outbreak of the war.

We have lacked a single volume history introducing the war in all its dimensions, written by someone who has served in the army, with a profound knowledge of the war, and with the gift of communicating this complex knowledge for the general reader.

It is twenty-five years since I myself first took parties to the First World War battlefields. I was stunned then, as are all first time visitors, by the galaxy of sights available for all to see. I counted myself lucky to have gone at that time, rather than some years later, when I imagined that interest would have faded as veterans died, and the Second World War loomed ever larger in popular consciousness. If anyone had told me that twenty-five years later, interest in the First World War would have doubled or trebled along with the numbers of visitors, I would have thought them quite mad. Yet, it is the case.

The First World War moves the young and not so young beyond their understandings. Truly, it is the most strange of all wars. This book will shape and inspire the fascination that all have in it. It is the essential starting point for all who want to make the pilgrimage to understanding the First World War. It will also be a humbling re-education to those who, like me, thought they knew it all.

Dr Anthony Seldon
Wellington College
July 2011

Foreword

This is not a learned history of the First World War; I started to write this book as a story, after guiding a battlefield tour when a question was asked – 'Where can I find a beginner's guide to why we are here and what we are seeing?'

The tutors in the Military History Department at the Royal Military Academy Sandhurst taught me a love of their subject that has been a defining part of my whole adult life. In 2006 Dr Anthony Seldon, Master of Wellington College, led the Trenches Trip for Wellington parents that made me think that I had something to write about. I thank him for writing the preface.

This is a story about people. This was a war of millions, during which generals accepted casualties in tens of thousands, often in a day or a morning, but each casualty was an individual. When I write about the mass of men I always think of individuals: Colonel Driant at Verdun, Private Parr at Mons, Noel Chavasse and the Liverpool Scottish, the small group of Devon men at Mametz.

Not all generals were incompetent buffoons, and just as I did, you should form your own opinions. As the greatest historians of the twentieth and twenty-first centuries still cannot agree about whether some of the most studied generals of all time were competent or fools, I think we need not wait upon their deliberations to make up our own minds.

Robert Burness and I enjoyed many visits to battlefields together. I am sorry that I cannot give him a copy of this book in memory of the many 'Bottlefield Tours', so named by his daughter Julia, that we enjoyed together.

In 2006 James Osborne and his family led me to study the 7th Battalion, Royal Sussex Regiment's action at Aveluy Wood in 1918. James's father won his medal there as one man's personal contribution to winning the war; this book is a reminder that the history of the First World War is part of almost every family's history as well.

Marney Brosnan produced maps for this book despite working amid the damage and loss caused by the Christchurch earthquakes. Roni Wilkinson found many pictures that are new to me and perhaps to you. I thank them both for their help.

Finally, I am grateful to many friends and members of my family. If you wondered why I am so dedicated to studying a war that happened a long time ago, I hope that when you have read this book you will say 'I know now'.

Timeline of the War

1914

28 June	Archduke Franz Ferdinand assassinated
1-4 August	The main countries declare war on each other
4 August	Germany invades Belgium, Britain declares war
Mid-August	British Expeditionary Force (BEF) deploys at Maubeuge on Franco-Belgian border
23 August	Japan declares war on Germany
	The Battle of Mons and start of retreat to the Marne
6 September	Allied counter-attack at the Marne, German retreat begins
19 October	First Battle of Ypres begins
	Entente to war with Turkey

1915

22 April	Second Battle of Ypres begins
7 May	Sinking of RMS *Lusitania*
25 September	The Battle of Loos and French attack in the Champagne
19 December	Sir John French sacked, Sir Douglas Haig becomes Commander-in-Chief

1916

21 February	The Battle of Verdun begins
31 May	Battle of Jutland, the only major fleet battle of the war
1 July	Assault phase of the Battle of The Somme begins
27 August	von Falkenhayn dismissed, Hindenburg and Ludendorff take over German command
15 September	Tanks appear on the Somme battlefield at Flers-Courcelette
24 October	Fort Douaumont recaptured by the French at Verdun
Mid-November	The Battle of Verdun closes, both sides exhausted
13 November	The Battle of The Ancre, twelfth and last battle of the Somme campaign
18 November	The Battle of The Somme officially closes
6 December	Asquith government falls, Lloyd George becomes Prime Minister
12 December	First German peace proposal

TIMELINE OF THE WAR

1917

1 February	Germany resumes unrestricted submarine warfare
	USA breaks off diplomatic relations with Germany
12 March	Russian Revolution begins
17 March	Germany withdraws Western Front to Hindenburg Line
6 April	USA declares war on Germany
9 April	Battle of Arras, Vimy Ridge captured
16 April	French disaster on Chemin des Dames
	First French Army mutinies
7 June	Firing the mines on Messines Ridge
19 July	Vote for peace passes in *Reichstag*
31 July	Third Battle of Ypres begins, summer rains begin
4 October	Second Battle of Passchendaele, part of Third Ypres
10 November	Third Battle of Ypres ends
17 November	Armistice between Russia and Central Powers
20 November	The Battle of Cambrai begins, first massed tank battle

1918

3 March	Treaty of Brest-Litovsk between Russia and Central Powers
21 March	Final German offensive, the *Kaiserschlacht,* begins as *Operation Michael* opens on the Somme
26 March	Foch becomes Allied Generalissimo
9 April	Second German attack, Ypres region
27 April	Third German attack, Chemin des Dames
1 July	Fourth German attack, The Marne
18 July	Foch's reply – *Tout le Monde á la Bataille*
12 September	The Americans clear St Mihiel Salient
2 November	The last Allied assault begins
3 November	Austrian Armistice
9 November	The Kaiser abdicates
11 November	BEF arrives in Mons, exactly where they had started in 1914
	German Armistice

1919

28 June	The Treaty of Versailles

The war ends legally, five years to the day after the assassination of Archduke Franz Ferdinand

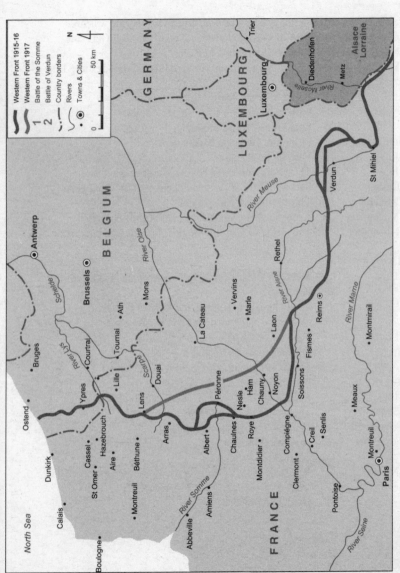

The Western Front – the main arena of the war.

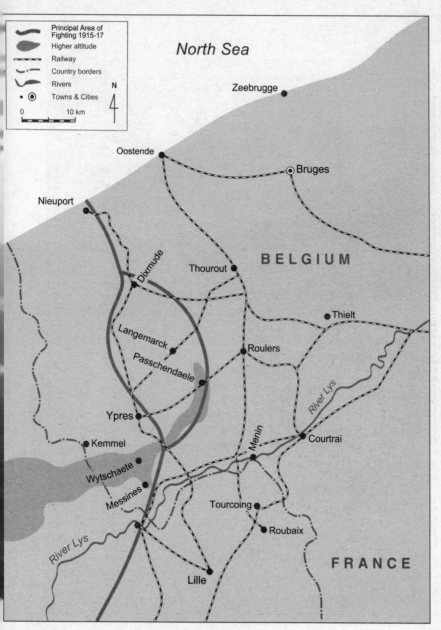

North Sea

Principal Area of Fighting 1915-17
Higher altitude
Railway
Country borders
Rivers
• ⊙ Towns & Cities

0   10 km

N

Zeebrugge •

Oostende •

⊙ Bruges

Nieuport •

Dixmude

BELGIUM

Thourout

Thielt •

Langemarck •

Roulers •

Passchendaele •

River Lys

Ypres •

Kemmel •

Courtrai •

Menin

Wytschaete •

Messines •

Tourcoing •

Roubaix •

River Lys

Lille •

FRANCE

The Ypres Salient – a major battle took place here every year except 1916.

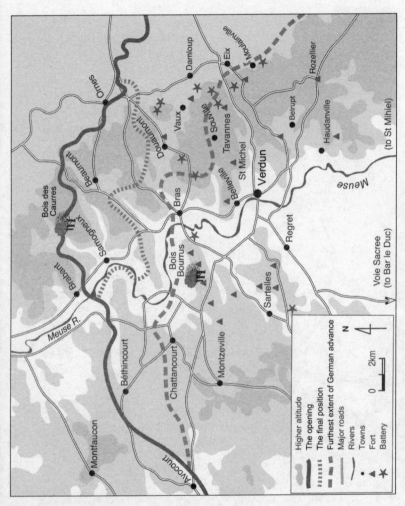

Verdun – a defining battle of French history and of The Great War.

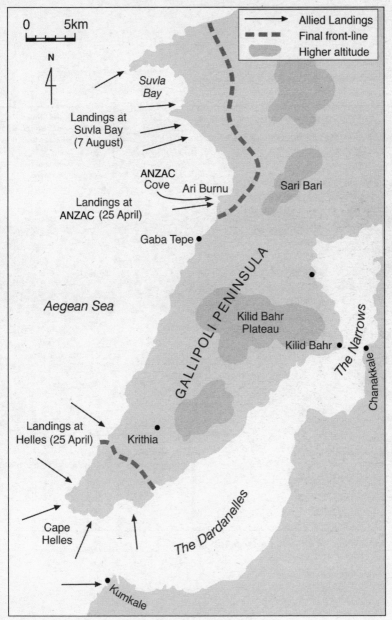

Gallipoli – the forging of Australia and New Zealand.

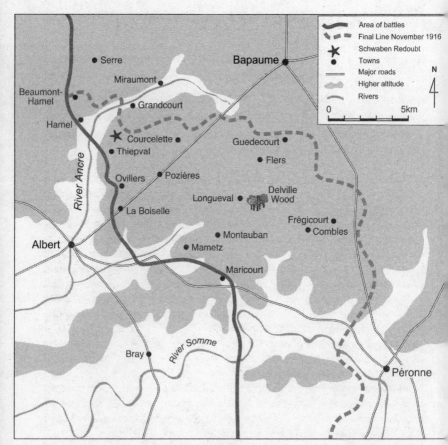

The Somme – a by-word for the futility of war.

1

Why Was There a War?

After a fight in the playground, Teacher wants to know 'Who Started It?' After a fight on the scale of this war, the question takes some answering. However it can be argued that it all starts with one man.

Bismarck

Otto, Prince von Bismarck, the most obvious playground bully, had been dead for sixteen years before the war started. He became Chancellor of the Kingdom of Prussia in 1862 in dangerous times. The previous twenty years had been unsettled in Europe. In England the Corn Laws were increasingly seen as a food tax, a bar to foreign trade and a cause of price instability. Rising levels of national unrest forced final repeal in 1846. Eighteen forty-eight was 'The Year of Revolutions', with anti-monarchical uprisings and revolutions across Europe caused by a variety of economic and social grievances. France and England then fought Russia in the Crimea, with no real reason beyond suspicion of Russian ambitions in the Balkans. In Africa, India and beyond, the maritime powers continued to develop existing colonies and stake out new ones. In the 1860s America was to be busy with its own Civil War, where the Gatling gun introduced industrialised killing for the first time and the railway facilitated the first genuinely mobile war of citizen armies.

Bismarck strode into the European playground at an opportune moment. By character and ability he was the outstanding politician of the day, and his political philosophy appealed to the King of Prussia and his army. In simple terms Bismarck wanted a strong and united Germany, with Prussia as its main constituent state and himself as the dominant political personality. In the decade after becoming Chancellor, he fought Denmark for possession of territories, then Austria in 1866 to establish leadership of the Germanic nations. He rounded off the territorial expansion by humiliating France in the Franco-Prussian War, taking Alsace and Lorraine as the spoils of war. In 1871 he completed the programme with the creation of a united German federation, with the King of Prussia as Kaiser, and himself as Chancellor of the Empire.

From 1857 onwards the Prussian army was the iron tool wielded by Bismarck, The Iron Chancellor. After the unification of Germany, the Kaiser was Commander-in-Chief, but in reality General Count Helmuth von Moltke led the army. He was a profound thinker about military affairs in every aspect and created many modern concepts of military management, such as a general staff and staff training. He was also a considerable fighting general during Bismarck's local wars of expansion.

The new Germany was a latecomer to the world of overseas territories and colonies. All the major powers had long-established empires. The King of Belgium was effectively the private owner of the Belgian Congo, and Disraeli had flattered Queen Victoria by arranging for her to be crowned Empress of India. In German thinking, the new and largest nation in Europe should also have colonies, and it was wrong that all the best places had already been taken. A restless desire to develop a proper empire, with colonies and possessions, became a fixed point in German political ambitions.

Kaiser William II was a particularly unfortunate successor to the throne created by Bismarck. William was the not-quite-absolute monarch of the largest nation in Europe, the nearly-absolute Commander-in-Chief of the largest, most professional army on the continent, and in both roles his powers outran his abilities. His grandfather, the first Kaiser, had been the nominally absolute monarch for seventeen years, but always under Bismarck's tutelage. The old Kaiser William I died in 1888. His son Frederick was fifty-seven and Frederick's only son William was less than thirty. Frederick the Third of Prussia, but the First of Germany, came to the throne a sick man and died of throat cancer in that same year.

The new Kaiser William II, still only aged twenty-nine when he came to the throne, was very aware of his standing as Queen Victoria's oldest grandchild and pre-eminent monarch amongst her descendants. He considered that the Queen's oldest son, his uncle Edward Prince of Wales, was an idle pleasure-seeker. It irritated him greatly that this elderly, fat *roué* was generally seen as the first gentleman and prince of Europe. By the time Queen Victoria died William had been Kaiser for twelve years, and although he had actually been the grandson holding her in his arms as she died he knew that King Edward VII would usurp his pretensions to primacy in the world of royal courts. Even the Kaiser of Germany could not hide the reality that the King-Emperor, the old Queen's eldest son and his senior by eighteen years, was a person of greater significance than the Kaiser of the still-new German Empire that still lacked anything reasonably to be called imperial possessions.

> Kaiser William II was impatient, jealous and extremely conscious of his status. His left arm was withered and all but useless, a humiliating handicap for the Kaiser of Prussia and all Germany. He over-compensated for this handicap in his militarism, constant need for ever more elaborate uniforms and decorations, and demand for physical excellence in those around his court.

Players, Alliances and Plans

Austria-Hungary was crumbling as an ageing empire, but as a client state of Germany was anxious to preserve Germanic leadership, not least in the troubled regions of Germany's and her own homelands. Austria-Hungary's Hapsburg Emperors would have difficulty containing developing independence movements in parts of their empire without Germany's support, especially among the minority population linked by language, history and culture to a meddlesome Serbia next door.

Further towards Asia, the Ottoman Empire had lasted for 500 years of prosperity, but by the beginning of the twentieth century had been declining for over a hundred years, a crumbling and corrupt regime with little but force to hold it together and little enough force to ensure that aim. The empire supported the German and Austro-Hungarian axis, not least because these powers shared the same apprehensions about military and political threats from Russia.

Russia itself was another empire in decline, ill at ease with itself and its neighbours. War was an occasional hazard, especially with the Ottoman Empire, and for over fifty years Russia had been subject to attempted revolution at home. Concessions were given but led only to more demands. Church and State held an uneasy arbitrary grip on the mass of an agricultural peasant population, bound to the concept of Mother Russia and the Czar as Father of The People.

France, in particular, had defined her European ambitions. Above all other aims stood the national ambition to get back the provinces of Alsace and Lorraine, taken by Germany as the spoils of the Franco-Prussian War of 1870-71.

Great Britain was the perpetual stumbling block in the way of any European nation with international ambition. Britain controlled the largest empire the world had ever known and had the military strength, mostly naval strength as befitted a maritime empire, to protect its possessions. British naval policy was simple: the British merchant marine represented 60 per cent of the global shipping fleet, and the British Empire about half of the civilised world. The Royal Navy should therefore be similarly dominant. As a rule of thumb, the tonnage of the Royal Navy should be twice that of the next largest navy. Germany set out to challenge this doctrine, driven by the Kaiser and his jealous guardianship of his own heritage. This dual policy committed Germany to land armies on the continental scale as well as naval forces on the global one.

Within the British Empire, the Dominions of Australia, Canada, India, New Zealand and at least part of South Africa would be counted into British plans.

In the Far East another empire was in the ascendant. Japan was emerging from medieval isolation, had beaten Russia decisively in the naval war of 1906. The defining battle was the naval Battle of Tsushima, in which Japan captured or destroyed thirty-four of Russia's thirty-eight ships, killing or capturing over 10,000 Russian sailors for the loss of three small torpedo boats and 116 dead. Japan was an important customer of Tyneside ship-builders, especially for fighting ships, and this was thought to give a pro-British advantage to Japanese inclinations in the event of a European war. In the event, Japan would play little or no part in the war when it did come.

To the west the United States of America wanted to be left alone to heal the still-open wounds of the Civil War and continue the process of turning a group of states into a single nation, whilst developing an industrial base to compete with the world. There was little appetite for military power, beyond that needed to cope with a quarrelsome border relationship with Mexico.

Thus five Western empires, a number of European nations and the USA had more or less set out their positions for the war that many thought must come.

Formal alliances became the fashionable tools of international diplomacy. Germany and Austria-Hungary naturally allied themselves as the Central Powers; France and Russia allied themselves in a mutual defence pact to take effect in the event that the Central Powers might attack one or the other. Simultaneously, Russia appointed itself as the protector of the small Baltic Slavic states and declared its interest in their freedom from external pressure. The Ottoman Empire, in its death throes, dithered between the two main blocs, before eventually coming down on the side of the Central Powers. Italy was expected to join the German–Austrian alliance in the event of a European war. Belgium was neutral, her neutrality respected by all, and guaranteed by the Treaty of London of 1839. Most of the smaller countries around the edge of Europe were also neutral and of little significance in the political posturing of the Great Powers. Great Britain alone held herself aloof, pursuing the historic role of supporting the weak against the strong, preferring a balance of power rather than any single dominant power in Europe.

A remarkable diplomatic achievement served to increase German fears of encirclement by land and sea. The British and French governments had been moving closer together since the Crimean War of 1853-56, when they had fought on the same side against Russia in the fight for spoils and influence in areas where the Ottoman Empire was no longer able to maintain its imperial control. Since then, Britain and France had also fought side by side in the Second Opium War against China in 1856-60. A new treaty, The *Entente Cordiale*, was signed in 1904. It was not a military agreement and was little more than an expression of hope of friendship and cooperation. The public of both nations believed the Entente to be the work of the new king, Edward VII, whose gallant manners, roving eye and status as Queen Victoria's son made him as popular in smart French society as they made him awe-inspiring in British. His ability to speak easily to all politicians probably did help bring the Entente into the world but he was by no means the only, nor the most significant, midwife at its birth.

The Entente certainly made no formal military commitment to France. However, senior British military figures agreed that the small British army was destined to fight alongside the French when the inevitable European war would occur. Military planning was effectively centred on the deployment and employment of a British Expeditionary Force (BEF), in the event that France would go to war with Germany. Naturally the officers responsible to the Imperial General Staff, the leadership of the army, for this planning were very conscious of the need for secrecy. Indeed they saw no need to tell their pacifically inclined Liberal political masters that they were undertaking no other preparation for a European war.

The new century unfolded: tensions arose within and across borders, and all countries were naturally writing war plans. Great Britain and France might have no sure idea about whether, how or where the BEF would be employed when they got to France, but Ferdinand Foch had no doubt about how the French Army would be employed. As pre-war Commandant of the *École Supérieure de Guerre* (ESG), the French Staff College for training future senior officers, he had exercised a very considerable influence over thinking in the higher reaches of the army. In the event of war, France would advance immediately and with unstoppable courage into the lost provinces and re-take them. *La Revanche*, Revenge, was the doctrine and *L'Attaque á l'Outrance* was the instrument, literally the extravagant application of force to achieve the objective. Foch's disciple Colonel Grandmaison was chief instructor of G3, a special third year of study at ESG for a few selected high flyers marked out for accelerated promotion to the higher levels of command. He advocated the heroic concept, the courage of the French private soldier, the *poilu*, who would advance with panache, his courage defending his breast against the German machine gun. Yes, he really did write and speak like that, and in the years immediately before the war delivered a series of lectures with such oratorical brilliance that those who heard them accepted his doctrines with almost religious fervour. Grandmaison suffered for his own military beliefs by dying on the battlefield in 1915.

Meanwhile, over the years since 1911 the French planning staff had been led by the army Chief of Staff, Joseph Joffre, in constantly refining and elaborating on the execution of *La Revanche*. Each major refinement was written as a new model plan for the conduct of the inevitable war, and by 1914 the numbering system had taken the process to Plan XVII. For the benefit of anyone who doubted the new French philosophy of war, the opening sentence of Plan XVII made the position clear – 'Whatever the circumstances, the Commander-in-Chief intends to advance, all forces united, to attack the German armies.' By August 1914 Joffre was ready to put his theories, and Colonel Grandmaison's interpretation of them, to the test. The French First and Second Armies would advance headlong into the occupied provinces in a series of actions that would later be known collectively as The Battles of The Frontiers.

Foch little knew that as a Corps Commander (1913), then Army Commander (August 1914) then Commander of the Northern Group of Armies (October 1914) he was to play a significant role in the unfolding of Plan XVII.

Germany knew that they could not win decisively a war fought simultaneously on two fronts, against Russia in the east and France in the west. From the mid-1890s onwards General Count Alfred von Schlieffen, Chief of the German Great General Staff, directed his planning staff to solving this problem. As successor to Helmuth von Moltke he had at his disposal the largest, most professional army in Western Europe, and was confident in their ability to win a European war. In essence, he planned that a small force in the east would hold that frontier for a few weeks, against a slow and ponderous Russian mobilisation and advance, whilst an overwhelming force, gathered in Western Germany, would strike a blow to knock France out of the war in six weeks. The German attack would not go across the Franco-German border; the French Army would be there in strength, indeed it suited Schlieffen's plan that the French would actually advance into the lost provinces and meet powerful German home defence at some distance from French supply lines. The German Army would march to the sound of a greater drum, to conquer countries not provinces.

So, the German Army planned that on the outbreak of war they would indeed advance not southward directly into France, but westward, into neighbouring neutral Belgium. The Belgians might grant free passage, but if they would not then the pitifully small Belgian forces would be swept aside. The great fortress cities like Liege would be by-passed and later captured, but speed of advance would be the key to success. After advancing westwards almost to the North Sea, the Germans would turn south, sweep down the gap between Paris and the sea, swing round south-eastwards below Paris and then turn north to take the French Army from behind. With her capital surrounded once again, as in 1870-71, and with her army crushed between the German home defences and the German Army behind, France would surrender within six weeks and free the German Army to transfer east in time to deal with Russia.

For fifteen years von Schlieffen and his successor, Helmuth von Moltke 'The Younger', nephew of the great architect of the Prussian army, refined the plan and prepared its implementation. The Schlieffen Plan, the Great Memorandum, as it was officially know, was never a completed work, always a work in progress. All major civil engineering projects were planned with a thought for their potential contribution to the greater work. As one example, railway building was considered as part of the plan to move an army west to fight France and then east to fight Russia. Four-track railways ran east to west across Germany, ending always just within the borders, at stations with sidings and platforms built to handle armies on the move. Military warehouses were built and filled with the necessary stores. The male population underwent national service, in a system that ensured that all men could serve usefully, in the front line, in reserve, as troops guarding communications or as home defence forces, until past their fortieth birthdays.

Throughout Europe war was seen as inevitable. The tensions between the Central Powers and the Triple Entente were ever-present and varied only in their degrees of intensity from time to time. But there was no obvious sign of any probable event that would actually set the whole series of war plans in motion. When the event came it was so small in international terms that it scarcely registered on the politicians' antennae.

The Black Hand Movement

The Serb people were a divided race. The independent nation of Serbia adjoined the eastern edges of the Austro-Hungarian Empire, between Albania on the Adriatic and Bulgaria on the Black Sea. A sizable Serbian population lived across the border within Austria-Hungary as reluctant subjects of the empire. The wilder fringes of the desire to liberate Serbian peoples from the Austrian yoke had formed the Black Hand Movement, a secret body dedicated to ending Austrian rule by any possible means. The Serbian government probably knew of the movement and rather agreed with its objectives, tolerating the movement's existence even if only to the extent of ignoring it.

In June 1914 the Austrian heir presumptive was the Archduke Franz Ferdinand. He was unhappy, charmless and despised at court, and only became heir to his uncle, 84-year-old Emperor Franz Josef, through the suicide of the Emperor's own son Crown Prince Rudolph at Mayerling. (Franz Ferdinand's father, the Emperor's younger brother, renounced his claim to the succession.)

Franz Ferdinand was happily married to Countess Sophia von Chotkowa und Wognin, but resented strongly the ruling of his uncle the Emperor that she was not sufficiently noble to be permitted royal honours or titles. Her husband might indeed be about to become Emperor, but she could never be his Empress, and her own birth placed her in the lower ranks of the rigid court hierarchy. However, outside the imperial court Franz Ferdinand was Inspector General of the Forces, the senior military figure of the empire, and in that role at least his wife would be accorded the respect that he wanted for her. Their wedding anniversary was on 28 June, and he ensured that on that date he would be away from Vienna with the army in Sarajevo, who could be relied upon to provide the ceremonies and recognition that the date deserved. With processions, High Mass in the cathedral and a reception for the leading local dignitaries his wife would have no cause for complaint about her treatment on this day.

The Black Hand saw this visit as an ideal opportunity to achieve a blow for freedom. At least four, and perhaps as many as seven separate assassination plans were prepared, and if one might fail another must succeed. Each assassin was to place himself at a different point on the route that would take the official visitors from the railway station to the civic hall. The first assassination attempt was made, a homemade bomb thrown at the car carrying the Inspector General and his wife. It missed and failed to kill the intended victims but seriously wounded members of the party in the car behind. After being driven at speed to the civic hall, Franz-Ferdinand decided to visit the wounded in hospital, and Sophia insisted on joining him. In the chaos of the still-crowded streets, the driver missed a turning and drove the royal party into an impassable alley. He started to reverse the car into the main road again, watched by a few passers-by, one of whom was a despondent Gavrilo Princeps, a nineteen-year-old student. He had been one of the would-be assassins, now walking away from the original route and the place where he had been waiting to shoot the passing targets. The driver of the Archduke's car was unfamiliar with its workings, and stalled the engine as he tried to engage reverse gear. Princeps now found that the same targets were beside him and stationary, so he drew his revolver and shot both the Archduke and Countess.

The Austrian government saw the assassination as a chance to force Serbia to cease sponsoring Serb nationalist groups inside the empire's lands, and as June turned into July they increased this pressure, ending with a ten-point ultimatum. This covered Austrian supervision of the Serbian police investigation into the assassination and went on to dictate the whole nature of Serbia's relationship with the empire. The paper was written so provocatively as to force Serbia to reject it and so give the empire a cause for war. Serbia did not reject the paper, accepting nine points exactly as they were presented and wanting only a minor change to the tenth. Using this single point of dispute Austria-Hungary started to mobilise the armies and prepare to enforce its will on Serbia.

This mobilisation order set in motion the chain of events that would lead to war. Russia mobilised, declaring that Mother Russia would fulfil its role as Protector of the Slavic Nations and stand by its client state of Serbia. Almost simultaneously, treaty obligations caused France to mobilise in support of Russia, and Germany to mobilise in support of Austria-Hungary and as a precaution against being attacked on two sides. Britain had anticipated events. The Royal Navy Review at Spithead, the eastern approach to Portsmouth, took place in late July, and acting with no authority except that of his office as First Lord of The Admiralty, Winston Churchill decided that after the review's finish the Fleet should not disperse to peace-time locations and manning levels but should remain assembled ready for war-time dispositions. The government endorsed this decision and formally announced precautionary mobilisation on 2 August.

In the background there were increasingly frantic rounds of diplomatic efforts. Different factions within different nations wanted different outcomes, and some factions changed their minds from day to day about what they wanted to happen. Mobilisation was a preparation, getting ready for war, but was not intended to lead to war without further opportunities for negotiation and compromise. The Kaiser, Wilhelm II of Germany was keen that that mobilisation would drive the nations to negotiate and compromise, not to fight. By the end of July he was confident that compromise was being accepted and he decided that he could safely take his annual summer cruise to Norwegian waters on the royal yacht *Hohenzollern*. In his absence, the situation deteriorated, and the military options were found to be no options at all. The years of planning for mobilisation and the lightning-swift timetable of the Schlieffen Plan had created such elaborate arrangements that to try to halt mobilisation would effectively leave Germany unprotected and open to attack by any other country that did not suspend its own moves.

War actually broke out on 1 August. Because of the numbers of nations involved, and because some countries were at war with only one or two of the opposing groupings of nations, not everyone went to war at the same time, so declarations of hostilities sped back and forth across Europe for the next few days.

Germany immediately began to implement the Schlieffen Plan. By day and night long trains packed with troops and supplies ran westward from all over Germany to the Belgian border. At the Rhine bridges, trains ran to a tight timetable, trains crossing at two or three minute intervals, night and day.

As soon as Germany invaded Belgium the next four years became inevitable, but at that moment neither Germany nor France could be sure that Great Britain would join the war; the Entente was not binding on her in this context. However, the Treaty of London of 1839 was consulted. It was one of the international agreements that had brought Belgium into being. Under Clause VII Great Britain stood co-guarantor of Belgian territorial integrity. Therefore the British government presented Germany with an ultimatum. Germany must withdraw from Belgium or be at war with Great Britain as well as France and Russia. Germany did not withdraw, so Great Britain and the Empire declared war against Germany on 4 August. Germany's political leaders were almost unable to believe that Great Britain would declare war because of the Treaty of London. 'You would go to war over a scrap of paper?' asked the incredulous German Chancellor Bethmann-Hollweg when British Ambassador Sir Edward Goschen was collecting his diplomatic *Laissez-passer* to return home on declaration of hostilities.

2

1914 – The War Begins

The Home Front

Upon the declaration of war, Herbert Asquith's Liberal government appointed the legendary soldier Field Marshal the Earl Kitchener of Khartoum as Secretary of State for War. Kitchener had fought in many of the wars and skirmishes of the last twenty years. He had been commander-in-chief of the Egyptian army and had been knighted, created successively baron, viscount and earl in recognition of his military achievements. Both in the closed military world and in the eyes of politicians and the public, Kitchener was a recognisable and admired personality.

Kitchener was the obvious but unfortunate choice for Secretary of State for War. The peace-minded Prime Minister Herbert Asquith was not strong enough to control Kitchener, who attended meetings of the Cabinet and other war committees dressed in full dress uniform, complete with the large stars of the four great orders of chivalry and the badge of the Order of Merit that he had collected over the years. Kitchener, with his personal presence and reputation, would clearly be the dominant figure in the councils of war. Asquith himself, known aptly but behind his back as 'Squiffy', was scarcely a match for him. Squiffy preferred gossiping with a group of female friends to the business of making war, and preferred a drink to either.

Over ten years before the war, in a much-needed series of reforms, the army had created the now-familiar concept of a small regular army supported by a larger territorial force, which could take its place in the line of battle if needed. Behind that stood larger numbers of home defence forces, less ready to take part in war and largely exempted from any risk of being sent to fight overseas. Kitchener was famous for some extraordinary flashes of brilliance that occasionally seemed close to stupidity, but which usually turned out to be accurate. In his new appointment he recognised that this war would be an affair of years, lasting far longer than the three or four months that were generally expected. Therefore he also saw the need to raise armies on a scale that had never been contemplated by the pre-war planners, and that vision led to his third part of this intuitive process; the existing arrangements could never cope with the needs of this new scale of war. As a result he bypassed the existing arrangements and set about raising a citizens' army from scratch. The regular army and territorials would hold the line until the new citizens' armies could be recruited, equipped and trained.

In the national fervour that followed the outbreak of war, men flocked to enlist. Enterprising recruiters appointed themselves to raise battalions. In the north, in particular, local rivalries developed, between Leeds and Newcastle, Manchester and Liverpool, to raise battalions, regiments, artillery units and the like. The whole of Tyneside watched the local rivalry between the Irish and Scottish communities to see which would be first to raise an entire battalion from among its members and declare its numbers complete. The two communities achieved so much more than the original plan to raise a single battalion each that two brigades were formed, each of four battalions. One consisted of four battalions of the Tyneside Scottish and the other of four battalions of the Tyneside Irish. In the mill towns like Salford and Accrington, the ports like Grimsby, and a dozen other places, the promise was that pals who joined up together would stay together and fight together. The Glasgow Tramways Battalion, the Public Schools Battalion of The Middlesex Regiment, four Public Schools Battalions and The Sportsmen's Battalion of the Royal Fusiliers and many others recruited on this promise. Even the London Stock Exchange raised a complete battalion of 1,200 men to join the London Regiment. Above all the concept of joining up together and serving together appealed in the close-knit communities of the mill towns, where the battalions were unofficially, and sometimes even officially, called 'The Pals'.

Hull raised three club-like battalions of the East Yorkshire Regiment – The Commercials, The Traders and The Sportsmen – with strict entry criteria. Men unable to gain entry to these select battalions were able to join a fourth, 'T'Others'. We shall meet them and others like them again.

Many of these overnight units had to look after themselves. Few experts expected the war to last more than months, so most recruits were more anxious about missing the chance to 'do their bit' than about the risks of war. To begin with, the 'New' army had no officers, training staff or even premises for the flood of volunteers. Equipment was non-existent. Men would be asked to volunteer to be officers or serjeants. A local landowner or the local council would set about providing the very basic equipment that would enable the unit to hold together. It would be August 1915, almost a year later, before the War Office could take over responsibility for many of these units.

> **The British spelling 'serjeant' was the standard one until 1946, when the more familiar 'sergeant' replaced it. The Rifles, formed in 2006, have revived the old spelling.**

The lack of official support meant that many units had to send their recruits home again for the time being. Few were pleased to be sent back to work on the railways, farms or in factories or mines from which they had seen joining up as a chance of adventure and escape.

These units, The New Army, would get their chance to do their bit, to 'Biff The Bosch', not in 1914 and 'Home for Christmas', but in late 1915 and 1916.

The Battle of The Frontiers

As soon as war broke out the French launched their planned attacks on the frontier. Plan XVII was under way. The blue frock coats and brick-red pantaloons of the French infantry marched behind regimental bands, with young officers at the head of each regiment, proudly holding regimental colours aloft. The cavalry had polished their silvered *cuirasses* (breast plates) and brass helmets with enormous dyed-red horsehair plumes.

The plan involved five separate French invasions into the lost provinces of Alsace and Lorraine, and each achieved initial success. The Germans seemed anxious to avoid standing to fight, and retreated back towards Germany itself. Towns that had not seen a French military uniform in forty years were quickly back within France's embrace. History does not record whether the townsfolk were as pleased to see that in essence the French idea of the equipment to wear to war had not changed in the forty year interval.

The advances were exactly as the Great Memorandum had predicted, indeed exactly as Plan XVII had so indiscreetly advertised. The French successes simply led them on, into the deep buffer zones in front of the Germans' true defensive positions. The German counter-attack, starting in the third week of August, was a model of planning and execution, and within a day or two the French armies were back where they had started the war.

The blow to France was as great as Schlieffen and his successors could have wished. France's Western armies had lost 200,000 men in one month, and 75,000 of them were dead, almost before the war had begun. Contemporary writings note the shocking discovery that the élan, bravery and colourful uniform of the French private soldier were not, after all, sufficient to overcome the machine gun.

It was obvious that at this stage towards the end of August the two plans, Schlieffen and XVII, were developing in very different ways. Schlieffen was unfolding as expected, even if a little delayed, as we shall see, by the modestly greater resistance than had been expected of the Belgian fortress cities and the totally unplanned resistance put up by the BEF. For France, Plan XVII was ruined and there was no other plan for defeating Germany.

From Mons to the Marne and Back Again

The British Expeditionary Force (BEF) was a little smaller than expected when it reached France; at the last minute the British government decided to keep back one third of the force to defend against a possible German invasion. As a result only 100,000 men set off from Britain to reinforce the left wing of the French armies that already numbered over a million men under arms.

The pre-war plans had decided that the BEF would assemble at Maubeuge, on the Franco-Belgian border, beside the main road from Paris to Brussels. Maubeuge suited the commanders of the BEF very well, the Belgian Army's cavalry school was at Mons, only a few miles away, and an army commanded by cavalrymen was naturally interested in the opportunities for cavalry work. However, even as the war was breaking out, the government and military planners could not actually be certain what the BEF would do when it got to Maubeuge.

Field Marshal Sir John French commanded the BEF. (French, Haig and other senior figures are given sketched backgrounds in Appendix I.)

The force's two army corps were commanded by Lieutenant General Sir Douglas Haig and Lieutenant General Sir James Grierson respectively. The latter died of a heart attack after the BEF had been two weeks in the field and was replaced by Sir Horace Smith-Dorrien.

Sir John French disliked Smith-Dorrien and made it clear that he had preferred another nominee. The roots of this dislike went deep. About ten years earlier, after Smith-Dorrien took over command at Aldershot from French, he had changed the training emphasis for cavalry from lance drill and swordplay, and the traditional knee-to-knee cavalry charge. He believed that the real importance of cavalry in the next war would be their ability to get to the battle quickly, dismount and fight as infantry. Sir John was a man fully capable of bearing a grudge for ten years against the man who had so openly discarded the principles on which he, the senior of the two, had based his own training priorities.

The BEF in 1914

This was the force that set off for France in August 1914:

Commander-in-Chief Field Marshal Sir John French

Army Troops
>   **One cavalry regiment**
>   **One infantry battalion for headquarters defence**
>   **Five infantry battalions defending lines of communication**
>   **Six batteries of heavy artillery, each of four or six guns**
>   **Five aeroplane squadrons**

Cavalry Division
>   **Four brigades, each of three cavalry regiments**
>   **Two brigades of horse artillery, each of twelve guns**
>   **One field squadron of Royal Engineers**

I and II Corps
>   **Each corps of two infantry divisions**

1st, 2nd, 3rd and 5th Divisions – each division consisting of
>   **Three infantry brigades, each of four battalions**
>   **One cavalry squadron**
>   **Three brigades of field artillery, each of six guns**
>   **One brigade of medium howitzers, of six guns**
>   **One brigade of heavy artillery, of four guns**
>   **Two field companies of Royal Engineers**

In 1914 no medical establishment existed beyond each battalion or regiment's Regimental Aid Post, consisting of a regimental medical officer, his assistants and a few bandsmen acting as stretcher-bearers.
**   The way an individual soldier fitted into the army that ended with two million men is given in Appendix II.**

By mid-August the BEF was deployed and advancing north towards Brussels. The Germans were coming south from Brussels to meet them. The Schlieffen Plan was running behind schedule; the Belgian Army had put up unexpected resistance, and the fortress city of Liege had proved stubborn, holding out against the special siege artillery that had been designed to destroy fortifications. The King of Belgium commanded in person and used his resources carefully. He refused to leave the country when offered the chance by his British allies and achieved vital success in slowing the German advance enough to dislocate the timetable. The Germans knew that the BEF was ahead of them, but also knew that numbers were few in relation to continental armies. Many on the German staff reminded each other of Bismarck's remark during an early continental scare in which Britain had looked like being involved: if the British Army landed and attacked Germany he would send a patrol of Berlin policemen to arrest it.

> The siege guns used in the destruction of the fortresses at Liege and elsewhere were 43-ton monsters with crews of 200 men per gun. They were called Big Berthas, previously a nickname given to the wife of Gustav Krupp, Chairman of the company that manufactured them. It took six hours to assemble the gun on arrival on its firing site.

On 21 August patrols ahead of the two armies met north of Mons. The 4th Battalion of the Middlesex Regiment was in the forefront of the BEF's unopposed advance and had stopped the previous evening on the banks of the Canal de Mons et Conté, a mile or so to the right of where it crosses the main road to Brussels. During this day they halted to await information about German presence in the area. Amongst the battalion was a group of bicyclist scouts, including Private John Parr. These bicyclists formed the eyes of the battalion, trained to observe, and assess what they observed, to shoot quickly and accurately and to get information back to the battalion in the best possible time. Parr and a fellow scout were sent forward, to investigate a bridge over the canal. As they came to the bridge, the two scouts came under fire. Parr was well ahead of his companion; as trained scouts they always rode at some distance from each other. Parr took shelter in a ditch and waved his colleague back, indicating that he would stay to observe whilst his companion reported the presence of the Germans to the battalion. Parr came under fire in his ditch and was killed without having the opportunity to return fire. He was the first British soldier to die in action in a Western European war since Waterloo, ninety-nine years previously. He was sixteen years old, the first of many who would manage to join the army as adults, escape detection and die before reaching the legal minimum age for enlistment. On his gravestone his age is recorded as twenty, but it is actually unarguable that John Parr, formerly of 52 Lodge Lane, North Finchley, was sixteen years old when he died on 21 August 1914.

On the following day, just a mile or so to the west, just outside Mons, the

Royal Irish Dragoons, a cavalry regiment, were also edging forward, northward. They were aware of Germans in the area but had no precise knowledge of exact whereabouts or numbers. Patrols were sent ahead to reconnoitre the route. Very shortly after leaving Mons and starting along the main road through the woods, a strong patrol of two troops, about sixty men, met a small German patrol coming the opposite way on a similar mission. Corporal E Thomas fired a shot. This was another 'first', the first shot fired in battle by a British soldier in continental Europe since Waterloo. The squadron drew sabres and charged, and the Germans withdrew. The cavalry war had begun, although it could hardly have been guessed that it was almost the only true British mounted cavalry action during the whole war. Two hours later the first casualty of the war in the air occurred when German artillery shot down a British reconnaissance plane.

At the same time as the BEF was groping northward into contact with the German *First Army,* the German *Second* and *Third Armies* were making progress southward towards the French Fifth Army, which stood on the right or eastern side of the BEF. The French Commander, Lanrezac, had his army in an exposed position where his left flank depended on the tiny BEF, his front faced the *Second Army* across the River Sambre, and his right flank faced the *Third Army* across the River Meuse. The two rivers merge at the northern tip of Lanrezac's position and he was therefore placed in a narrow neck of land overlooked by the Germans on two sides and thinly protected on a third. He was sure that his best option was to fall back towards more defensible positions. However, Joffre was still excited by the gains being achieved by Plan XVII and issued imperative orders that Lanrezac should attack the advancing Germans and drive them back just as the more easterly French armies were doing.

The Fifth Army was unable to complete preparation for this attack, because on 21 August the German *Second Army* attacked first. They quickly achieved some remarkable local success, throwing two bridgeheads across the Sambre. It has always been a highly risky undertaking for an attacking army to establish itself on the far side of a defended river, but the *Second Army* managed this well. Bringing overwhelming superiority of numbers to the point of attack the Germans forced on Lanrezac exactly the retreat that he had proposed. The *Third Army* attacked across the Meuse on the following day but desperate defence on the right flank enabled Lanrezac to complete his retreat in some good order. In doing so, he was able to re-establish some defensive coherence and avoid the destruction of his army that would have left Paris exposed to the German armies' advance.

Despite lack of numbers, the BEF played a significant part in the events unfolding to its right. Sir John French undertook to hold fast for twenty-four hours to give Lanrezac time to establish his new defensive positions, and was as good as his word. However, cooperation on the tense 22 August could not always be taken for granted. About three miles from their hard-pressed infantry colleagues on their right flank, a French cavalry division of colonial troops, about 12,000 men, sat and waited for orders. None came, so the divisional general did nothing to help his neighbouring unit resisting the far greater numbers of the *Third Army*. The Divisional Commander was to be one of the first of over seventy-five French generals relieved of command and posted to a notional job at the military garrison city of Limoges. Later in the war this process of sacking generals and posting them to notional commands would be described by the invented verb '*Limoger*', which is nowadays the standard French slang verb translated as 'to sack'.

During these three days Lanrezac had managed a skilful transition from preparing to attack into conducting a retreat in the face of overwhelming numbers. He had saved France from the disaster of giving Germany a direct and undefended route into Paris. Joffre only saw Lanrezac's failure to attack when instructed and relieved him of his command. Lanrezac immediately retired from military service and played no further part in the war.

War had come suddenly in this peaceful corner of Belgium, and on Sunday 23 August, the local villagers, dressed in their Sunday-best clothes, made their way to church, oblivious to the battle around them, and on occasion actually passing between the front lines of the opposing armies. As they passed by, the villagers were unaware that they were in no-man's-land, where nobody would go willingly, and few would go voluntarily, for the next four years.

During this period the legend of the Angels of Mons became a perceived reality. Journalist Arthur Machen wrote a fanciful morale-raising article for the *London Evening News*, describing how soldiers of the BEF had seen the apparition of St George in the sky over the battlefield, summoning the spirits of the dead bowmen of Agincourt to repel the advancing Germans. The credulous public were already becoming aware of the scale of the losses being suffered by the BEF and many were only too willing to believe the tale. The tale was re-published in a spiritualist magazine at a time when many in Great Britain were turning to spiritualism and séances as they attempted to contact lost sons, husbands and fiancés, giving another impetus to the totally imaginary tale. Although Machen himself tried to kill the tale, it had taken on a life of its own and would be widely quoted as a truth for years to come.

Back in the realms of reality the pressure of German numbers, superior artillery and planning began to tell, and after the initial retreat by the French

Fifth Army, the French and British began to fall back, constantly seeking a foothold to steady themselves, and constantly being dislodged. It was vital that the BEF would not become separated from the larger French forces, and so the retreat developed to the south-east and away from the coast, but staying north of Paris to cover the approaches to that city. It was equally important to the Germans to drive a wedge between the BEF and the French, so they had to follow the retreat, effectively abandoning the Schlieffen Plan in favour of the more modest objective of separating the armies of their opponents. The Allies' retirement was soon a full-scale retreat. Travelling by day and night the armies fell back 125 miles, past Paris, over the Rivers Somme, Aisne and Oise. As they fell back, the whole French Army, the Fourth, Ninth, Sixth and Fifth Armies, and the Second and BEF on the very left of the retreating line, all fell back. The line pivoted anti-clockwise in an arc centred on the Argonne Forest and Verdun. A great door over 100 miles wide was swinging open to let the German invaders into France.

During the retreat, a desperate defence of ground by Smith-Dorrien's Second Corps at Le Cateau was not supported by Haig's First Corps. During the following night at Landrecies Haig undoubtedly panicked and led a precipitate retirement by his corps, leaving Smith-Dorrien dangerously exposed. Smith-Dorrien recognised that he was better placed to fight a holding action, to obtain breathing space, than to continue in headlong retreat. He also had the professional skill to fight one of the most brilliant defensive battles since Wellington's peninsular campaigns, to save the day. Relations between the Commander-in-Chief and his two Corps Commanders sank to low levels after this near-disaster for the BEF. The Commander-in-Chief Sir John French decided that Sir Horace Smith-Dorrien had wilfully disobeyed orders to maintain the retreat, and his simmering dislike became an open feud.

As the Germans advanced they moved further and further from their lines of supply, and their flanks became more vulnerable to attack from the side. Over 25,000 men were needed simply to keep the railways in France and Belgium working and more than that number were needed to guard them. Maintaining momentum became increasingly difficult, and opposing them the French Commander-in-Chief, General Joffre, was prepared to continue to retreat eastwards and wait for the right moment before turning from retreat to attack. The moment came in early September, helped by examination of papers in the notecase of a senior German staff officer killed during the retreat. Amongst them was a highly confidential and pessimistic report on the state of affairs in the ranks of the invading armies. To the south of the diverted German advance, Paris was strongly fortified, and General Gallieni, the Military Commandant of the Paris region, had substantial forces at hand. He commandeered the Paris omnibus fleet, several hundred private taxis and every other available vehicle to create a mobile counter-attack force. On 5 September the French and British forces attacked the exhausted and under-supplied Germans. Leaving their defensive positions on the River Marne, they moved north-west against the front of the German armies, and Gallieni launched his improvised mobile army ferociously at the exposed right flank of the Germans. The German advance collapsed and became a hurried withdrawal to less exposed areas, pivoting around Verdun as before. Over one million men set about driving the Germans back along the roads they had travelled as invaders only days before. The door was closing again and Germany had lost all chance of achieving their war objectives.

The famous Kitchener poster 'Your Country Needs YOU' was first displayed in England on this first day of The Battle of The Marne. Actually, most of the men who would join up voluntarily at this stage of the war had already done so and this, the most famous advertising poster of all time, did not boost the slowing flow of new recruits. Margot Asquith, the Prime Minister's wife, disliked Kitchener and used the poster to cruel effect after his death: 'If Kitchener was not a great man, he was, at least, a great poster.'

As their retirement slowed the Germans began to stabilise their presence in France. Whilst they took up the strongest possible defensive positions, the French set about the process of constant attack intended to drive the Germans out of France altogether and restore Alsace and Lorraine. Rather than attack head-on, each side sought to reach north, pass the exposed flank of the other, pass forces round the end of the opposing forces and roll-up the enemy line along its length. For the rest of the year this process continued, and there were numerous instances when one side reached the end of the opponents' line only to find the opponents also arriving just in time to hold them back. By Christmas the 'Race for the Sea' was over, both sides reached the sea together and the nature of the war changed into the form that would be familiar for the next three years.

The First Battle of Ypres

To end the year the First Battle of Ypres was fought in November. The city of Ypres represents the last strategic strongpoint between Belgium and the Channel ports. If the Germans could control the city they could threaten Calais and Boulogne, forcing the BEF to depend on ports as distant as Le Havre and Cherbourg for supply. If the French, Belgians and British could control Ypres they could threaten the railway junction at Roulers, only ten or so miles further into Belgium. Without Roulers, Germany could not maintain control of the Belgian coast and its maritime threat to the North Sea.

German forces had passed through Ypres in August 1914 during their advance to Mons. They arrived again in October, and in a throwback to an earlier custom of war had fined the city 75,000 gold francs for failing to welcome them properly with the ringing of church bells and other ceremonies. The Burgomaster was taken hostage as a security for payment. Defending Ypres itself against an attack from the western, or British, side would not be easy, so the Germans withdrew to the ridges of high ground that lie in a semicircle around the north, east and south-eastern sides of the city. As so often in the war, the Germans were willing to give up ground if by doing so they could achieve defensive advantage. The semicircle around Ypres can be thought of as the right-hand side of a clock-face.

The BEF arrived in Ypres hard on German heels and immediately set about establishing a line beyond the city beneath the German-occupied ridges. The French occupied the northern part of the arc around the outer edges of the city, from *midnight* to *three o'clock*; the BEF took the southern part as far as *half-past five*, and the French occupied the last piece, from *half-past five* onwards. Here as everywhere along this new line of German defences, policy dictated that the lines must be as close to the German positions as possible, to ensure that the invaders would not have any chance to move further forward into Allied sovereign territory. Thus, the Allied positions beyond Ypres formed a perfect salient, a bulge projecting from the Allied line into the German lines, and so forming a pocket overlooked from three sides by the Germans on the higher ground.

Further to the north-west the Germans now renewed their efforts to clear the coast and roll the line forwards to the Belgian coast and down towards Calais. Having brushed past the Belgian army based on Antwerp during their first visit, the Germans set about the business of clearing the threat to their flanks, opening the coast to threaten the North Sea and finally knocking Belgium out of the war. Antwerp was invested and the Austrian siege guns, firing a shell 42 centimetres in diameter, were wheeled out again. They were not actually 'wheeled out'; each gun travelled as a single railway train. Ten 30-ton cars carried the parts of the gun and its shells that weighed almost a tonne each, whilst extra cars carried the cranes needed to assemble and dismantle the gun, and other carriages carried the crew to work the complex construction. The fortresses surrounding Antwerp fell one by one, and the city itself by 9 November. Meanwhile, until the city would fall, the Germans had their own besieging force to shield them from any attack out of Antwerp, and another screen holding back the BEF and French in the Ypres area. Between these screening forces the main German forces moved on along the coast, and reached the River Yser in mid-October.

Nieuport lies at the mouth of the Yser and here the Belgian Army stood again to oppose the Germans. The Royal Navy sent a flotilla to lie offshore and provide artillery cover for the Belgians. Three of the ships had just been built by Vickers for the Brazilian navy and were bought from them at the outbreak of the war. These lightly armoured but heavily gunned ships caused serious damage to the advancing Germans. Far more powerful, accurate and heavy than any field artillery, they excelled in their primary role as anti-artillery weapons. The Germans made little progress under this threat from the sea, about which they could do nothing, but resistance in front of them was slowly failing. The Belgian Army, outnumbered, running short of ammunition and other supplies, was close to losing any ability to offer further opposition. The King took the grave decision to hold up the Germans by flooding the land lying below sea level, ahead of the German advance. Labourers worked to block drainage culverts, and over a week of exceptionally high tides at the end of the month the engineers ran in reverse the established sequence of working the locks and sluices at Nieuport. They were opened to let the incoming tide flood the low-lying land, and closed during the ebb tide to stop the waters from retreating, until the whole country from Nieuport to Dixmude was flooded. An impassable lake running north to south, nearly 30 kilometres long and 5 kilometres wide, had made the country impassable.

The gap between the lake and the sea at Nieuport could not be forced, certainly not whilst the remnants of the Belgian Army were entrenched there and supported by the Royal Navy. To continue the move along the coast, Germany would have to swing inland, force a way through Ypres and then regain the coast road. The First Battle of Ypres would be the result of this necessity.

The battle was a desperate struggle. Germany needed to pick up momentum, to complete the Great Memorandum's business in the west before Russia could recover from two shattering defeats at Tannenberg and Lemberg in late August and early September. Germany launched a succession of violent attacks on the ill-sited BEF and French ahead of them. On 29 October they broke the line, at Gheluvelt on the road from Ypres to Menin, on the *four o'clock* axis, about 5 miles from Ypres centre. A bayonet charge by the Worcestershire Regiment, through the wood where the victorious Germans were re-forming before moving forward again, closed the gap again in the nick of time. In the north of the salient the Germans launched a major attack in the area of Langemarck. The attacking units were largely reserve regiments, composed of men who had completed their period of compulsory full-time service and were now serving part-time as trained and more or less battle-ready reinforcements.

Facing this onslaught were battalions of the original BEF. As pre-war regular soldiers they were highly trained riflemen, expected to be able to maintain a steady aimed rate of fire of eight to ten rounds per minute, and increase this to at least fifteen accurately aimed shots for the 'mad minute' that might be needed at the crisis of an enemy attack. There would be several such minutes at Langemarck in October 1914.

After this attack bodies were piled chest-high where the rear ranks of the advancing Germans had been shot as they tried to climb over the bodies ahead. The Germans gave the attack a sombre name, the *Kindermort*, the Slaughter of the Innocents, but this reflected the fact that there were some young students from university cadet units in the ranks, not the more dramatic legend of wholesale slaughter of almost totally untrained volunteer troops drawn from the university population. The German war cemetery at Langemarck contains the bodies recovered from this battlefield and is a gloomy reminder of the battle that provided its first harvest of bodies. The cemetery provides a last resting place for most of the German bodies actually recovered from this part of the Ypres Salient, about 44,300 of them. Many times that number were never recovered, but simply lost in the mud or blown into fragments as the battle lines moved back and forth over the next three years.

There were well-documented unofficial truces on Christmas Day of 1914. Troops left the safety of their trenches, cautiously at first, but in increasing numbers. Gifts were exchanged; the BEF troops had each received a gift box of cigarettes and sweets bought with funds raised by Princess Mary, the seventeen-year-old daughter of King George and Queen Mary, and the contents were exchanged for the stronger tobacco provided by the German authorities. The standard BEF rum ration made a fair exchange for German schnapps, and German pre-war spiked helmets were the most desirable exchange gift of all; everyone wanted to take one home. The experience caused alarm at senior levels; if the soldiers came to fraternise like this they might not want to fight! Fierce artillery barrages were used to ensure that nobody would want to repeat the truce on Boxing Day or afterwards.

To mark the changing nature of the war, on Christmas Day Sir John French announced changes in the military hierarchy. The BEF would now become two armies. Sir Douglas Haig would command the First Army; Sir Horace Smith-Dorrien would command the Second Army. These two were promoted from Lieutenant General to General, and the commanders beneath them also enjoyed a step-up in rank. We may presume that Smith-Dorrien's promotion was forced on French by his superiors in London.

At the end of this first year, more accurately five months, it was time to take stock of progress. The BEF had set out in early August and was soon reinforced by more troops arriving from India and further afield. The small BEF had suffered 86,000 casualties in just over four months of fighting. In all, eighty-four infantry battalions had been in action by the year-end. Each had started out at full strength, 1,000 men each, of whom thirty were officers. At the end of December the old professional army no longer existed and the war would not be over by Christmas. The muster rolls showed that just ten of the eighty-four battalions still counted more than half their original 1,000 members. Sixty-five battalions could muster between 100 and 500 of their starting manpower. Nine battalions could each parade fewer than 100 men of the original BEF. Having started in August with nearly 80,000 rifles, the BEF could not now put 20,000 of the original infantry into the line. As Kitchener had planned, the Territorial and Reserve forces were taking the strain, with the regular army units re-filled by reservists re-joining their old units and Territorial units coming into the line. The process of taking a unit out of the line, replenishing its numbers, re-training and making it fit for renewed action came to be called 'fattening up', probably with some awareness of biblical references to killing the fatted calf as a sacrifice.

The rifle was the principal personal weapon of every infantryman, by a wide margin the commonest weapon of the war.

The BEF relied on the Lee-Enfield .303 rifle, introduced in 1895, later modified and developed through a number of versions into a reliable, accurate and robust weapon. A magazine held ten cartridges, and was light enough and reliable enough hardly to impede the rate of fire when one magazine was changed for another. A trained soldier could fire rapidly and accurately. At First Ypres the pre-war infantryman was trained to fire fifteen accurately aimed shots in one minute. This 'mad minute' caused many Germans to believe that the BEF had many more machine guns than was actually the case.

The rifle and machine gun were designed for ammunition to be interchangeable, an important matter in the need to ensure that both weapons could be supplied with the amounts of ammunition that the war demanded.

In all armies, the realities of warfare made clear that the highly accurate long-barrelled rifle was a cumbersome weapon for trench warfare, and shorter-barrelled versions were needed. These appeared as the war progressed.

Other weapons are considered in Appendix IV.

The Eastern Front

German plans for the east were more defensive in the early months. The Schlieffen Plan presumed upon slow Russian mobilisation and manageable threats for some weeks, giving plenty of time for the lightning conquest of France before switching the main body of the German armies eastward where the destruction of the Russians' infinitely larger resources of manpower would be accomplished by superior training and equipment. As the Russians were capable of mobilising ten armies, given time, the Plan made some important assumptions about what the Russians could achieve in the limited time available before the German switch from west to east would take place. The Schlieffen Plan provided only a single army for the defence of East Prussia to begin with, envisaging nothing more than a slow falling back into East Prussia, pending the arrival of reinforcements. Unfortunately the Russians had not read the Great Memorandum. They mobilised faster than expected and made early incursions towards East Prussia and the Slavic regions within Greater Germany. Within days they had two full armies half-way across Eastern Prussia, only 40 kilometres from the great naval bases of the Konigsberg area in the north and past Warsaw in the southern area of this advance. Even further south they were pressing against the Carpathian Mountains and threatening Budapest, the second city of the Austro-Hungarian Empire.

German command in East Prussia was in the hands of 66-year-old General Maximilian von Prittwitz. He achieved some early but small success against the Russians but became nervous about his predicament. He saw himself becoming pinned down by one Russian army whilst a second advanced around his southern flank and encircled him. He proposed to withdraw his *Eighth Army* from East Prussia altogether, both to get behind the encircling movement and better to defend Germany proper. This suggestion involved abandoning the Prussian heartland of Imperial Germany as well as the vital base at Konigsberg, and scarcely fitted in with plans for the defence of exactly those areas. He was dismissed from command and von Moltke replaced him with another equally elderly and actually retired soldier, General Paul von Beneckendorff und von Hindenburg.

Hindenburg and his Chief of Staff Erich Ludendorff were not daunted by the scale of the task that they faced. The first orders were to halt the withdrawal by the *Eighth Army*, and in a matter of days Hindenburg had approved a plan already prepared by von Prittwitz's staff. A thin covering of troops was kept in place to hold the Russian First Army in the north whilst a powerful offensive against the Second Army in the south led to the Battle of Tannenberg. The Russians committed 150,000 men to this battle. Ninety-five thousand were taken prisoner, and over 30,000 were killed or wounded, the latter all too often amounting to the same thing on this front. The 95,000 prisoners provided a much-needed addition to the numbers of men needed in Germany for agriculture and other work normally done by men now away at the front. The sixty trainloads of captured war matériel taken back to Germany provided invaluable metal and other physical assets for a Germany that was already under tight blockade from the Royal Navy. The Second Army had ceased to exist. Records are almost non-existent but the total number of Russians who went on to fight again was probably less than 10,000.

Hindenburg immediately re-deployed his troops. The Prittwitz staff plan that he inherited envisaged a double strike that would destroy both wings of the Russian advance into East Prussia and by the end of the second week in September that result had indeed been achieved, with the First Battle of The Masurian Lakes. The Russian Second Army was in pell-mell retreat towards Russia's own frontier and the protection of the border fortresses.

Although Hindenburg took all the credit, his predecessor's staff had actually created the blueprint for one of the most remarkable dual battles in history. In the space of three weeks, on battlefields some 400 kilometres apart, a German army had utterly destroyed one larger army and then routed another. East Prussia was cleared of the Russian incursion and it would take until the latter years of the Second World War for them to return.

Hindenburg had been helped to some degree by the transfer of two good army corps from the west to the east. He had not wanted them, he was confident of clearing the Russians out of East Prussia without them, but von Moltke had been worried enough by von Prittwitz's pessimism to send them anyway. If left in the west and used effectively, these corps would probably have been enough to turn the balance in the German advance from the Belgian frontier and the sweep to the west and south of Paris. As it was the two corps added a little to the blow against Russia, an enemy who could in truth afford the loss of men in their tens of thousands, but that little was at the expense of being unavailable to contribute to destroying the army of Great Britain, who certainly could not afford such losses.

3

1915 – The Year of Trial

In the early weeks of 1915 the War Office in London and Sir John French at his headquarters waited for the new forces now being formed, equipped and trained. Once these men were ready, a swift attack could break the German defensive line and lead to a cavalry breakthrough and advance to the Rhine. The initial recruitment campaign had borne far more fruit than expected, and the New Army, Kitchener's Army, was being prepared for the battles to come. In reality, recruitment had run so far ahead of the War Office's ability to manage it that equipping and training the New Army was proving to be less important than simply feeding and housing it.

Whilst the recruitment and training went on, it was vital that the offensive spirit be maintained. However, Sir John French was not the only person who realised that the nature of the war had changed when the Race for the Sea had ended in a dead heat. In London Winston Churchill was the leading advocate of trying other options to prosecute the war. He wanted to consider invading Germany through the north German state of Schleswig Holstein, or persuading Italy to join the war and give access to the southern flank of Austria-Hungary, or invading Turkey and so gaining access to the landmass of the Central Powers from the south-east. In effect these were all plans to take the war into Germany by out-flanking the line that now ran across Europe from Switzerland to the sea.

The option selected was to force a passage through the Dardanelles and threaten Constantinople with bombardment from the sea. The Turkish capital would thus surrender. An invasion army would be landed somewhere in western Turkey, and would march to take control of the surrendered city. This campaign would knock Turkey out of the war.

Gallipoli

The Gallipoli peninsula lies in the western or European edge of Turkey, a 50-mile tongue of land that juts into the Aegean Sea. The Dardanelles is the long, narrow channel, nowhere more than about 5 miles wide and in places less than 1 mile wide, that lies between the peninsula and the land-mass of Eastern

Turkey. It gives access from the Mediterranean and Aegean Seas to the Sea of Marmora, and the Black Sea beyond. Therefore the sea route could open the southern route to Russia. Under Allied control it would be possible completely to surround and cut off Germany, Austria-Hungary and their allies from outside supply.

The first attempt to break through the Dardanelles to Constantinople took place in February, involving several elderly British and French warships that could be spared from more important duties in other theatres. The first advance up the Dardanelles ended in something close to panic when one of these elderly vessels struck a mine. A second attempt in March was more successful, in that some Turkish shore defences were severely damaged, and a solitary submarine broke through the minefield to sink a Turkish warship within sight of Constantinople itself. However, the main advance was never able to penetrate the heavily mined waters, past the still-formidable shore batteries. Turning away from the shore the Anglo-French squadrons ran in line abreast onto a string of mines laid north to south down the middle of the channel. Three battleships were sunk, several more ships were more or less seriously damaged and the assault was called off. It was clear that another approach would be needed.

Politicians in London and military planners in the area decided that a landing on the outer, Aegean side of the peninsula itself was the right answer. The best intelligence available suggested that the Turks would not be able to resist a number of simultaneous landings along the outer side of the peninsula. Once the peninsula was secured, an overland expedition could capture Constantinople. The Mediterranean Expeditionary Force (MEF) was hastily brought into being and General Sir Ian Hamilton was appointed to command the expedition and sent post-haste from London to Alexandria in Egypt to prepare.

Lord Kitchener originally named the Mediterranean force 'Constantinople Expeditionary Force' but Hamilton noted that this might perhaps reveal the secret purpose of the assembly of troops and give Turkey time to prepare for its arrival.

From the beginning the campaign was dogged by poor planning, complacency and incompetence. At sixty-two years old, Sir Ian Hamilton was apparently frail but was a decorated officer with great experience, twice recommended for the Victoria Cross. His experience of war covered Afghanistan, the First Boer War, the Nile Expedition, Burma, India and the North-west Frontier, the Second Boer War and the Russo-Japanese War. In the Second Boer War alone he had seen action in ten battles and fourteen skirmishes. He had been wounded in the arm and was effectively one-handed. Walking any distance was difficult as the result of serious injury in a fall from his horse. However, he was an acknowledged fighting soldier, and senior enough to expect a field command in the war even if not thought capable enough to have a command on the Western Front. All these factors made him an ideal commander of an expedition that had more in common with colonial fighting than with what was happening in France and Belgium.

Hamilton's force was assembled using troops to hand in Egypt, from where the expedition would be launched. The key elements of the MEF were:

- A British regular army division, the 29th, commanded by Major General Aylmer Hunter-Weston. The division was nicknamed The Incomparable and was formed of pre-war regular units brought together from garrisons and outpost scattered around the Empire.
- The Royal Naval Division, formed of Royal Marines and sailors not needed to man ships and therefore available to be trained as infantry. Many thought that this was Churchill's private attempt to have a hand in managing the land war rather than a serious attempt to employ under-used sailors.
- The French Oriental Expeditionary Corps, including troops from the French African colonies being trained for European warfare.
- The Australian and New Zealand Army Corps, the ANZACS, two divisions, one from each country of about 18,000 men each. They were all volunteers and were in Egypt training to be brought into the BEF.

The scope of this book does not run to a detailed account of the disaster of the landings by British troops in the south of the peninsula and further north by the Australian and New Zealand troops. However, some account is needed because the failure of the Gallipoli campaign was given as important proof, for any who needed proof, that the war must be fought and won in France and Belgium, against Germany, and that other theatres and operations could never be more than distractions from the main business of the war.

Several weeks now passed whilst the MEF prepared for its invasion. The second naval advance had taken place and failed on 18 March. The Gallipoli landings actually started six weeks later, on 25 April. There had been a false start when it was realised that the ships carrying the equipment needed for a landing on enemy shores had been loaded so incompetently at the docks in Alexandria that they could never be unloaded into small boats lying offshore under the guns of an enemy coastline.

The Turks had not wasted the six weeks' warning. Their energetic German adviser Liman von Sanders had driven a programme of building roads to permit

Turkish troops to move to any point of danger. He had improvised mines that could be used to cover approaches to beaches. He had arranged for beaches and tracks leading from them to be made impassable by erecting barbed wire entanglements. He had deployed his Turkish allies' forces to cover the most probable landing sites whilst ensuring their ability to move to meet landings that might take place elsewhere. Both the Turkish commanders and he recognised that the spine of hilltops that ran along the peninsula held the key to the attack or defence of the region, and disposed the Turkish forces accordingly. Later, von Sanders wrote: 'The British allowed us four good weeks of respite. This respite was just sufficient for the indispensable measures to be taken.'

The landings met with mixed fortunes. The main landing on the morning of 25 April was at the southern tip of the long tongue of land. The Incomparables landed at Cape Helles, at this southernmost point, and met stiff opposition. However, a few miles round the corner, on the Aegean side of the peninsula, the diversionary landing found no resistance and 2,000 men got ashore unhindered. Unfortunately the plan made no allowance for the main landing to be held up and the diversion to become the main event. One British officer led his men to the edge of Krithia, a deserted village on the very peak of the spine of hills running down the peninsula. The village was a key objective and the limit of the first day's objectives for the main landing force. However, finding Krithia empty and having no orders to the contrary, the diversionary force commander turned back and took up the positions that his own part in the plan set out for him. Later in the day, the main landing force had moved the 4 or 5 miles that they needed to get from the beaches to Krithia, but the Turks had moved to cover the position. In the end, no member of the Allied forces would ever enter the village that had been empty and for the taking only hours before. The following day saw the evacuation of the troops who had landed so close to Krithia and had the place for the effort of walking into it.

Further up the Aegean side, the ANZACS landed in the teeth of violent opposition. They were to cut the peninsula at its neck, to prevent reinforcements and supplies from reaching the hard-pressed Turks and to ensure that any fleeing Turks would not escape. This was defenders' country and any attack was bound to be expensive. However, even the defence sometimes paid a terrible price. The Turkish *57th Infantry Regiment* faced one ANZAC assault off the beach on that first morning. The engagement was so ferocious that after the battle not a single member of the regiment was found alive. There has never been a *57th Regiment* in the Turkish army since that day.

As spring turned to summer the attempt to force the passage to Constantinople was driven on. Attacks led to Allied casualties, and Turkish counter-attacks led to even greater losses. On 19 May a Turkish force of over 40,000 sought to overwhelm the ANZAC positions by sheer weight of numbers. After the attack they admitted to over 3,000 killed and over 10,000 wounded. The defending Australians of ANZAC suffered a little over 600 casualties, about 160 killed and 450 wounded. However, all attempts to break out of the beachhead at the southern tip were clearly failing and the attacking emphasis switched to the ANZAC beachhead. Extra troops were brought in to reinforce the ANZACs and a series of attacks seemed to start with promise but end in disappointment. The Turks always seemed to be able to get just enough men into place to prevent any breakthrough onto that vital ridge that dominates the peninsula.

By late August, the attempt to bring down Turkey by a naval incursion through the Dardanelles or a land attack along the peninsula was over. Bulgaria had entered the war alongside Germany and the threat of German artillery arriving through that country to support Turkish infantry was too imminent to be ignored. In addition Serbia was directly threatened by the German, Bulgarian and Turkish alliance and needed Allied support. The Gallipoli campaign was more or less suspended and Allied efforts were diverted to a new Mediterranean front, based on landings in Salonika, a port city in southern Serbia. The force was never large enough to play a decisive role in the Balkan element of the war, and one German commentator called the Allied occupancy of southern Serbia as 'the largest prisoner of war camp in history'. Large numbers of troops were indeed committed to doing nothing, except die from disease, and did so for most of the rest of the war until mid-1918 when they were able to break out and press back the crumbling Austrian presence in the country.

The Gallipoli adventure was abruptly ended at the end of 1915. General Sir Charles Monro had replaced Sir Ian Hamilton in command in October, and recommended closing the campaign and evacuating the peninsula. Lord Kitchener himself went out to see what was going wrong. He saw enough to enable him to persuade the War Office that the campaign could not succeed in achieving even the smallest part of its objectives. In all, 44,000 British, Australian and New Zealand troops had been killed, 97,000 had been wounded and 145,000 had died or been rendered invalid by disease. The only success of the campaign was its ending. Hamilton had stated that to end the campaign without defeating the Turks first would cost casualties of 50 per cent of his force. Monro achieved the remarkable feat of taking every man off the peninsula without losing a single life to enemy action.

In the Gallipoli campaign in 1915, 196 pairs of brothers were killed. Two sets of three brothers were killed. Of that total of 398 killed, only thirteen have marked graves, the rest are commemorated on the Chunuk Bair, Helles and Lone Pine memorials.

> Of the 196 pairs, at least seventy-two pairs were killed on the same day. One of the sets of three brothers was all killed on the same day. Of the seventy-two pairs killed on the same day, twelve were killed on the same date, 7 August 1915.
>
> At least 1,100 other servicemen killed during Gallipoli had a brother (plus one sister) killed on other fronts during the war.

Neuve Chapelle and Afterwards

Back on the Western Front, 1915 began with a redistribution of areas of responsibility. The BEF was brought together around the Ypres Salient, and the French Army that had been in the middle of the BEF's line moved further south. The Belgians held the line north of the salient, facing the Germans across the flooded plain of the Yser. Two weak French divisions held a reduced segment of the Salient itself, from *midnight* until *two o'clock*. The BEF held the rest, with the 1st Canadian Division placed from *two o'clock* to *three o'clock* and British troops from that point round to the southern end of the salient.

Although the war could not be won in 1915, a policy of aggressive pressure on the German armies in France and Belgium was to be maintained, and a series of offensive operations were undertaken along the front. Most were intended either to drive the Germans out of strong fortified positions that might be used as start-points for their own attacks or to force them to give up ground.

The first of these limited offensive actions took place in March. The village of Neuve Chapelle lies about 18 miles south of Ypres, where the eastward bulge of the Ypres Salient ended. The Germans had made a strong fortified zone to exert pressure on this weak part of the British line, and as the trench lines moved to and fro this zone formed a miniature salient of its own. This time it was a German bulge into British defensive lines. It threatened the supply lines and rear areas on which the Ypres Salient depended for its maintenance. The village and German lines were opposite the junction of two corps of Haig's First Army. Haig's operation to 'pinch out' the German bulge in his line would be carried out by three British brigades of 7th and 8th Divisions and the Garwhal Brigade of the Indian Corps, newly arrived. The attack was devised according to principles that would form the basis of all major operations by the BEF for the next two years. A methodical bombardment of German positions would be followed by a charge to take the first and second German lines whilst their occupants were sheltering from the shellfire. The whole process would then be repeated to take the reserve lines and make it possible to break through and threaten the whole German presence in Belgium.

1915 – THE YEAR OF THE TRIAL

The north end of the German bulge was anchored by The Quadrilateral, a self-contained system of trenches and strongpoints designed to be defensible even if the trench line on either side would be overrun. The heaviest British bombardment of the war so far opened the attack in the early hours of 10 March. Three hundred artillery pieces were lined up behind the 2 miles of the front to be attacked, and fired a thirty-five minute bombardment before the BEF troops 'went over the top' in the first British set-piece attack of the era of trench warfare. By nightfall the German trenches had been taken, and it appeared that the hoped-for opportunity to break out into the land behind the trench lines had come about. Preparations were made for the second day's action, crossing the small brook that runs behind Neuve Chapelle and fighting on through the woods beyond. However, the Quadrilateral had not fallen, and the Germans worked throughout the night to create a new trench line, defended with machine guns and barbed wire, that would mean that the whole initial attack programme would have to start again from the beginning in order to clear this new line.

Fierce fighting lasted through 11 and 12 March, with the BEF consolidating its gains and the Germans reinforcing their new defensive lines. Just before midnight on the third day, Haig ordered a halt to the battle, changing the emphasis to building defences intended to withstand the increasing of German counter-attacks. Neuve Chapelle village was in British hands, but the Quadrilateral was not, and for the next several months different ends of this system of trenches formed segments of both British and German front lines.

The battle seemed to demonstrate that although it was not difficult to break into the German trench lines, it was impossible to break through them. Having the better of the railway system, the Germans could always get more reserves to the point at risk than the BEF could do. Additionally, any troops advancing beyond their own front line always had to cross ground that they had destroyed themselves in preparatory bombardment. This greatly impeded bringing up the supplies and reinforcements needed to maintain their advance.

The battle demonstrated something else: the cost of a set-piece battle against German defences. Sir John French's Despatch written immediately after Neuve Chapelle listed the human cost:

- 190 officers and 2,337 other ranks, killed.
- 359 officers and 8,174 other ranks, wounded.
- 23 officers and 1,728 other ranks, missing.

It was generally true of the roll call after most actions that few of the men whose names appeared on 'missing' lists were still alive.

The list made clear that officer casualties, killed or wounded, were disproportionately high in relation to the ratio of officers to men.

Remembering that the battlefront was not longer than 2 miles, it can be calculated that the BEF suffered more than one death or wounding for every single yard of the front, for each day of the battle.

The lessons of the Battle of Neuve Chapelle would be worked out over the coming months. More and heavier guns were needed, with vastly more shells available so that bombardments could last for hours rather than minutes. More men must be at hand, especially cavalry, to provide instant reinforcements who could maintain the impetus of the initial breakthrough. The analysts of the Battle of Neuve Chapelle were unwittingly writing the blue-print for the Battle of The Somme in 1916, seeking to create better and longer bombardments and make more and more men available, without questioning whether the basic principles of these methods might be flawed.

Second Ypres and St Julien Crossroads

Six weeks after Neuve Chapelle the Germans launched an offensive at Ypres. They did not especially intend this attack to result in the capture of Ypres, but wished to bring the front lines closer to the city perimeter, where they could exert greater pressure on the roads behind the city along which all supplies had to travel. Intelligence reports suggested that the Germans also intended to use this attack as an opportunity to test out new poison gas weapons. Prisoners captured at Neuve Chapelle reported that large containers were being moved into the German forward positions. Air reconnaissance was ordered but no evidence of such activity could be seen from the air, and the intelligence reports were largely discounted.

The attack began with the Germans discharging gas onto the gentle northerly wind on the morning of 22 April. The release points were along the north side of the Salient, and again using the clock-face, were heavily concentrated from *midnight* to *two o'clock*. The greenish clouds of chlorine gas rolled down from the slightly higher ground and swept into the trench systems of the French 87th, Territorial Division and the 45th (Algerian) Division. These unprepared forces could not hold ground in the face of this totally new weapon, and both divisions fell back in disarray, leaving the Canadians with their northern or left flank utterly exposed. As the Germans advanced, so the Canadians had to fall back. The small village of Pilckem, in the middle of the French sector, started the day over a mile behind the French front lines, but by nightfall it was the same distance behind the German front. The German attack was so much more immediately successful than planned that they had few reserves to hand and so the attack ran out of momentum. The Germans dug in where they had reached, 2 miles from the city centre of Ypres instead of 4 miles, as they had been that morning.

On the following day the Canadians were in the forefront of counter-attacks, trying to drive the German lines back out of the segment *midnight* to *three o'clock*. However, during the morning of 24 April, after being delayed by contrary winds, the Germans released a second gas attack in front of the Canadians and forced them back a mile or so, which they covered in a desperate retreating action. The combination of the delay in releasing gas and the Canadians' stubborn retreat enabled the Northumbrian Division to march hard and fast from the other side of Ypres and plug the gap left by the broken French forces.

> **The Canadians, with some basic chemistry knowledge somewhere in the ranks, realised that a piece of urine-soaked cloth would diminish the effects of chlorine sufficiently to enable a man to stay in the fight. Uric acid reacts strongly with chlorine to form urea crystals. A soldier would still be destroying his lungs and eyes, but he could buy time for the reserves to get forward.**

The Germans contented themselves with artillery bombardment into the shrunken Salient on 25 April, and during that evening the Canadians were withdrawn from the line. The village of St Julien was at the heart of this fighting, and the Canadian National War Memorial at St Julien records Canadian losses of 1,700 dead and 2,500 wounded in the battle, about one quarter of the men of the division.

The Northumbrian Division was a Territorial Army formation. It was formed exclusively of pre-war Territorial units from the north-east. Of the division's three infantry brigades one was the Northumbrian Brigade, formed of four battalions of the Northumberland Fusiliers. Another brigade consisted of four battalions of The Durham Light Infantry. The divisional artillery, supply train, medical services, signals companies and engineers were also entirely north-eastern units. The first units had left England for France on 15 April, and the last of the main body travelled on 19-20 April. Newcastle Central Station had been the main point of departure, and the division had travelled by train to Southampton. After a sea crossing by ferry to Boulogne and then by local train to the assembly areas behind Ypres, the last units arrived at 0500 on the morning of 21 April. That day and the next were spent in unpacking and checking equipment, but by 23 April the division already had units in action in support of the hard-pressed Canadians. The German advance was ultimately stopped, and shortly afterwards this part of the 1915 Ypres Offensive had run its course. The Northumbrian Brigade of this division had lost over 1,900 officers and men, from a total strength of just about 4,000, in the first three weeks of their war.

The Ypres Salient was now a misshapen bulge into German lines. Most of the *midnight* to *three o'clock* segment had been lost, and what was left was open to enemy shelling at short range from three sides. The Germans had brought up plentiful supplies of artillery, machine guns and infantry to hold the new positions that gave them such an advantage in this particular struggle.

The BEF simply could not let this new situation pass without a push to recover at least some of the lost ground. Lieutenant General Herbert Plumer, commander of V Corps of the BEF's Second Army, launched two separate counter-attacks on 26 April, which the Germans held off with small local gas release at about lunchtime. Plumer was careful of his men's lives and by late afternoon he decided that the cost of recovering the lost ground was too great. The cost of trying unsuccessfully was about 1,500 dead and 2,500 wounded in the day.

Noel Chavasse MC

The fighting at Ypres would die down but never cease in the intervals between the four named Battles of Ypres. The British and French relentlessly sought to press the Germans back to the Rhine, and the Germans still sought the opportunity to destroy the BEF in the Ypres Salient. In April, around the village of Hooge, only a couple of miles from Ypres city centre, fierce fighting was constant as the BEF retreated to the new defensive line and the Germans pressed home their advantage. The Liverpool Scottish, a part-time Territorial Army battalion, was one of the first to fight in France, as part of one of the earliest brigades sent to France in August 1914. In the early hours of 16 June the battalion, reduced to twenty-three officers and 519 other ranks after earlier battles, attacked the German positions at Hooge, at about *four o'clock* on the clock-face and less than 3 miles from the city centre. The battalion was relieved two days later, and after stragglers had been able to rejoin the ranks the roll call established that two of the twenty-three officers were on parade. The other twenty-one were killed, missing or wounded. Of the other ranks, 379 of the 519 were similarly absent. It was later established that, as usual, the missing men, one in five of the strength on 14 June, were almost all killed. This was a terrible blow to Liverpool; the battalion was an elite military unit in the city, and represented the city's civic pride. Their battalion had been one of very few considered good enough to serve alongside the regular army units from the beginning of the war. Fewer than 20 per cent who went to war at the start now remained.

A third officer serving with the battalion survived, Lieutenant-Surgeon Noel Chavasse of the Royal Army Medical Corps. In recognition of his gallant work for the wounded under fire he was awarded the Military Cross. A few weeks later he would write home a graphic account of how the battalion, strengthened by drafts of fresh men, had carried out an attack through Sanctuary Wood, adjacent to Hooge. The wood had long been a place to which men who had become separated from their units could make their way, knowing that they would be treated there as stragglers and not deserters, but the recent German attacks had made it a dangerous location, just on the edge of the trench-lines. Several battalions' medical posts were sited in the wood, and Chavasse used whatever shelter he could find to establish his own Regimental Aid Post there among them.

The Costs of Second Ypres

The most obvious cost is the loss of life and toll of wounded. Seven infantry divisions and two cavalry divisions fought in the Salient during this period. Allowing for new drafts brought in to replace men killed or wounded, that nominal size of force indicates that about 150,000 to 200,000 men of the now large BEF fought during Second Ypres. The casualty roll is given at a little under 60,000, about 35 per cent of those taking part, not including French or Algerian casualties. The battle lasted almost exactly a month on a maximum front of 9 miles, suggesting that, including French and Algerians, the casualty rate was about one person for every 8 yards of the battlefront, every day for that month.

Sir Horace Smith-Dorrien's Second Army had fought Second Ypres, and he spoke with particular knowledge when he proposed that much of the Salient be abandoned for a more defensible position. At last Sir John French had the chance he had been seeking. The proposal to abandon ground was dangerous to morale and tantamount to cowardice. French seized the opportunity to dismiss Smith-Dorrien from his command. Lacking the courage to dismiss Smith-Dorrien face to face, French asked Robertson, his Chief of General Staff to do the deed for him.

'Wully' was famously careful with words, speaking little at the best of times and even less at others. Asked by French to break the news tactfully to Smith-Dorrien that he was to be dismissed, Wully marched into Smith-Dorrien's office, announced 'Orace, you're for 'ome,' and marched out again. Plumer, variously known as Plum, Plum Jam or Daddy to his troops, would take over as commander of Second Army, and apart from one short break remain in command at the Salient for the rest of the war. His first action was to propose reducing the bulge of the Salient to more defensible perimeters. Sir John French at once accepted from Plumer the proposal for which he had dismissed Smith-Dorrien.

When the battles of Neuve Chapelle and Second Ypres were done, Sir John French was wary of being criticised for the failure of Neuve Chapelle to deliver the results that he had encouraged people to anticipate. He chose the correspondent of *The Times*, Colonel Repington, as his conduit for laying the blame at the feet of politicians who had not tried hard enough to ensure adequate supplies of shells to the battlefield. So it was that as the last struggles of Second Ypres were ceasing the Liberal Government fell and was replaced by a coalition. David Lloyd George was to be Minister of Munitions, responsible for resolving the shells crisis. Winston Churchill would have to go from the Admiralty, distrusted by the Conservative Party, who refused to enter the coalition if he remained. His defection from the Conservatives to the Liberal Party some years before the war still rankled. Later in the year he would leave government altogether and join the army, serving on the Western Front in command of an infantry battalion until recalled by a new Prime Minister, Lloyd George, to serve as his successor as Minister of Munitions.

Artois and Champagne

Meanwhile, the French were also pressing forward. For ten continuous months the French Tenth Army battered the German positions north of Arras. A salient jutted some three miles into the French line, and the Germans had used four or five villages along the edge of the salient as anchor points for its defence. Extremely strong and well-planned defensive redoubts were built on each site, linked by several lines of well-constructed trench systems. The German commander of the Sixth Army, Crown Prince Rupprecht of Bavaria, may have been appointed to his command as a royal figurehead, but he was also a capable and studious professional soldier who would in time be recognised as one of the more formidable army commanders of the German war. He built his positions in this salient to withstand the heaviest attacks, and they duly held up against three separate Battles of The Artois in late 1914 and 1915. Over the year the French made very modest gains, as little as a mile over a narrow front during the three specific battles, but the cost was terrible. During the six weeks of the second battle alone the French suffered over 100,000 casualties. Local commander Philippe Pétain made great advances on the first day of the Second Battle of The Artois but the reserves, not expected to be used to exploit a breakthrough so soon, were too far back to be available when needed. The moment came and went unexploited, just when launching the reserves into the attack might well have secured the French Moroccan Division's brief capture of Vimy Ridge and given France domination of the Plain of Douai behind it. In the end it would be spring of 1917 before the Canadians would capture these strategically important heights.

Joffre was keenly aware of the drain of resources, and particularly the shortage of artillery and shells, caused by the Artois and other offensives. He decided to play down the importance of the fortified city of Verdun, and the fortresses, gun batteries and emplacements that surrounded it, a long way to the east. He did not feel it necessary to reveal this decision to his political masters. As the year went on, men and guns were drawn from the Verdun area to reinforce the armies fighting elsewhere. In 1909 Joffre had been one of the generals who had argued that the French Army should never encumber itself with heavy artillery, which would hamper and slow down the advances to which all French military planning was directed. Only in 1911 was the French government able to force the army to accept any build-up of heavy artillery capability. Now, only four years later, Joffre was justifying stripping the frontier fortresses of their artillery, saying that heavy guns were vitally needed, and better used, elsewhere.

As the Artois battle around Arras was in progress, a new French offensive for which the guns had been needed opened in September, in the Champagne region. The French launched their attack east of Reims, in the 15-mile gap between that city and the Argonne Forest. As was so often the case, the Germans held the advantage of the better ground, and the French attacks were pressed forward against all odds. The Battle of Champagne lasted for six days, and achieved gains of up to 2 miles in the middle of the attacking front, or as little as nothing at all at the edges. Casualties ran at 25,000 per day for the six days, and the offensive petered out, never having threatened the vital lateral railway line that ran parallel to the German lines and about 4 miles behind them.

Loos

The start of the Battle of Loos was timed to coincide with the French Champagne offensive, and indeed the two offensives were the first stages of a larger plan to punch two holes in the German lines and break up the whole centre of the German lines from Switzerland to the sea. Loos lies in the heart of a densely populated area, south of the March battlefield at Neuve Chapelle and north of Lens and Vimy. The German lines were strong and followed the usual pattern of being anchored with strong local fortifications. Short of artillery and of the shells to shoot from what guns he did have, Sir John French decided to employ gas for the first time. There was not enough gas to cover the frontage to be attacked, originally 3.5 miles but extended to over 8 miles by the time of the actual assault. On the day, too little gas was available to cause the sort of effect that Sir John French had forecast. The gas discharge lasted little more than twenty minutes, half the time that the gas experts had asked for. The wind was inconsistent and in places wafted the discharge into the trenches where the British infantry were waiting to go 'over the top'.

Under the circumstances, the attack achieved mixed results, and more than might have been expected. In a few places, German resistance collapsed as completely as had French resistance at Ypres when faced with gas for the first time. In other places, the gas blew back into British trenches and the attacks never really started. However, by nightfall on the first day the BEF had achieved some notable gains, several miles in places, including the town of Loos itself and the major Hohenzollern Redoubt at the north of the frontage attacked. Ominously, the attack had not reached the fortified second German line or the slag heaps of mining spoil behind this line that the Germans had used as raised platforms for artillery spotting and fire control. Tunnelling upwards through the slag heaps and building concrete observation bunkers, with openings looking out over the Allied lines, had been simple work for the well-equipped and industrious German mining companies.

It was not the first time on either side that breaking into the first lines of the enemy trench systems and beyond them was a great deal less difficult than holding the gains and exploiting them. For the BEF, the shortage of shells and poor management of the reserves did nothing to help the cause. Although shells were actually becoming more plentiful, the huge increase in quantity was largely cancelled out by their poor quality. The British armaments industry was expanding faster than its competence. Importing shells made in America and Japan was not proving to be successful, except in enabling politicians to boast about how things were better than they had been only months before. Communication difficulties, especially between the artillery and their observers, made matters worse. The Germans used their overview from the slag heaps and their railway superiority effectively, and three days after the break-in that promised so much the BEF were back exactly where they had started, and the Germans were back in Loos and the Hohenzollern Redoubt.

Sir John French did not survive this failure. The Government knew that the army commanders in France considered him a dangerous liability. Sir Douglas Haig in particular had used his friendship with the King to report on French's many shortcomings, reminding His Majesty that he himself stood, of course, ready to serve his country in whatever capacity his services might be required. Sir John French was relieved of his command and appointed Commander-in-Chief of Home Forces. This role enabled him to try from time to time to interfere in the conduct of the war, but fortunately without real effect. Sir Douglas Haig was appointed as his successor in command of the BEF and despite setbacks and political efforts to unseat him would hold that position for the rest of the war. Shortly afterwards, Sir William Robertson also returned to London, but in very different circumstances. He was to be Chief of the Imperial General Staff, professional head of the army and eventually a Field Marshal, the only man in history to have served in every single rank of the army, from the lowest to the highest. He was to serve well in the coming years, covering Haig's back when political attacks from the government threatened to bring Haig down as Haig had brought down French.

RMS *Lusitania*

Surface ships of the German *Kaiserliche Marine* had ceased to offer an acceptable option for disrupting British trade after the Battle of The Falkland Islands in December 1914. During that battle Admiral Graf Spee's squadron of eight ships had been destroyed and six ships sunk. The captain of one of the two surviving ships subsequently scuttled it after being trapped against the coast of Chile some months later. After these costly attempts to use surface raiding ships during the early years of the war, Germany had decided to use submarines, *Unterseebooten* shortened to U-boats, in two roles. These vessels would be the principal weapon to counter-attack against the Royal Navy's blockade of the North Sea and English Channel, and the principal weapon to attack British and neutral ships bringing supplies to British ports.

In December 1939 another German surface raider, the *Graf Spee*, named after Admiral Graf Spee, would fight a similar action in the same waters, further north. After the indecisive Battle of The River Plate this ship too would be scuttled by her captain.

In February 1915 Germany announced that in future all British shipping in the waters around the British Isles would be considered combatant and liable to be sunk without warning. This was effectively a denial of the old 'cruiser rules', under which merchant ships would only be sunk after giving passengers and crews time to leave the ship in safety. The announcement brought heavy condemnation from the USA, where many prominent citizens considered that their right to travel freely was more important than the war, and where many merchants resented any interference in their ability to profit from the war. In the later days of April that year, the German Embassy in Washington placed advertisements in American newspapers, warning of the dangers of transatlantic travel in British ships. Only days later, on 1 May 1915, the Cunard ship RMS *Lusitania* left New York on her regular transatlantic run to Liverpool. Despite the warning advertisements, about seventy American citizens had sailed in her.

The Admiral commanding the war staff in London ordered two destroyers to escort *Lusitania* for the most dangerous part of the voyage, the run along the south coast of Ireland and up to Liverpool. The senior destroyer commander telephoned Cunard in Liverpool to ask for *Lusitania's* course, so that he could arrange a rendezvous. Cunard refused to give the details, and by the time proper channels had become involved it was too late; *Lusitania* was running eastward along the south coast of Ireland and into the path of a German U-boat. Their paths crossed on 7 May; 1,198 passengers and crew were killed, of a total complement of 1,959.

The sinking of the *Lusitania* caused international outrage. Reaction in America was so strong that the new policy was abandoned. The German navy reverted to the old cruiser rules. However, the American body of support for the war was given a propaganda coup, a concrete reason for their calls to join the war against the Central Powers.

The Year's Result

Nineteen-fifteen was a year of trial, of new tactics, new weapons and even new theatres of war, in Gallipoli, Greece and Mesopotamia, where the British suffered shattering reverses in the year at the hands of the Ottoman armies. In truth there can be no aspect of the war in this year where it could realistically be claimed that France and the British Empire had advanced their war objectives to any degree remotely commensurate with their expenditures of life and resources. Nonetheless, planning for 1916 began in December in a mood of optimism. All the mistakes of the year could be rectified, by better planning, better equipment and especially by the availability of more men, more guns and more shells. The Western Front generals agreed that the war must be fought on the Western Front; all other theatres were side-shows and drains of resources from the only place that mattered.

Out of all the facts and opinions that have always surrounded the First World War, one of the least appreciated is that in 1915, in the Battles of Artois and Champagne alone, the French nation suffered the deaths of over one-third of a million men. Marginally fewer had died in 1914, and so after allowing for other fighting, France would enter the third year of the war having lost 1.1 million men before 31 December 1915. *La Génération Perdue* was becoming a grim reality.

Appendix VI shows the numbers that lead to the broad suggestion that sixteen million lives were lost as a direct result of the war, with a further twenty-two million suffering injury.

As a side-script to the year's events, American outrage at the deaths of their neutral fellow-countrymen in the *Lusitania* was inexorably dragging America into the war. President Wilson, anxious to avoid becoming embroiled in any war, especially a European one, declared that it is sometimes braver not to fight than to fight. Large numbers of his fellow Americans disagreed, and some set off to join in the war in whatever way they could. The American Press, alert to the news value of these independent efforts, followed the trail to Europe, and their writings about the heroics of their boys began to change American public opinion. Pro-German regions like Minnesota and Wisconsin, homes of large immigrant German populations, lost the public ear, and the pro-Allied voice became louder and more insistent. The fact that the British Empire was financing the huge expansion of America's industrial capability to provide matériel for the war was also a strong point on her favour.

4

1916 – The End of the Beginning

Plans for the 1916 campaigning season were ready by Christmas 1915. The French and BEF would break through in the west and win the war. The Russians would destroy the German armies in the east and enjoy some large territorial gains at the expense of Austria-Hungary, who would thus be knocked out of the war. Nobody seemed to know what the Germans would do, other than sit in the defensive lines and await their fate. The Wellingtonian belief in looking over the hill to divine the enemy's intentions was not much considered during these planning conferences.

The British and French planned a joint offensive. It would be launched towards the western end of the Western Front. General Joffre, the French Commander-in-Chief, suspected British commitment and insisted that the offensive be launched as a joint Anglo-French initiative. He decided that the point where the BEF and French armies stood side by side, to the east of the town of Albert, in the *département* of the Somme, would be the centre of the line of attack. This great offensive would take place after mid-summer and there would be ample time to prepare to fight this battle to knock Germany out of the war. The lessons of 1915 had been learned and new methods applied. Numbers of troops would be greater than ever before, there would be more artillery, more shells, more gas and more cavalry ready to exploit the opportunity that would follow the infantry's breaking through the German defensive systems and 'Ride to The Rhine', the aim of every cavalry-minded officer. The Germans attacked first.

Verdun – *Le Minceur*, The Mincing Machine

At 0700 on 21 February 1916, a German shell fired from some miles away to the north landed in the courtyard of the palace of the bishop of Verdun. It was the first of the 2.5 million shells that had been brought forward into ammunition dumps to be fired in the opening days of the attack. *Operation Gericht* had begun.

The German word *Gericht* can be translated as 'retribution' or in a much older usage, 'killing ground'. General Erich von Falkenhayn was German Chief of Staff, having replaced von Moltke on the latter's breakdown. In his memoirs after the war von Falkenhayn wrote that he wanted to attack and threaten to capture somewhere of such symbolic significance that the French would accept any sacrifice necessary to prevent the Germans from capturing it. It would not be necessary actually to break through the French lines, but enough to threaten to do so. The intention was to 'bleed France white', not to capture territory. Falkenhayn reasoned that if he could force France out of the war Germany would win; he saw the French Army as the sword in England's hand and thought that Britain would not fight on alone in a continental war in which no vital British interests were involved.

Verdun was a good choice for such a purpose. The city had meekly surrendered to the Prussians in the 1792 revolutionary war, it had been the last fortress city to surrender after the fall of Paris during the Franco-Prussian War, and before this war much had been proclaimed of its fortifications and ability to withstand any assault. Von Falkenhayn was certain that France could not allow Verdun to fall into German hands for a third time in just over 100 years. Militarily, the place meant little; it offered only limited access to the open land in north-east France whence Paris could be threatened, but that same lack of good communication meant that Germany could attack for as long as they wished before breaking off the engagement, knowing that France could not launch any counter-offensive there to threaten German-held territory. It helped that Verdun was closely surrounded on three sides, west, north and east, by German forces, placing the city in a salient at least as perilous as that of Ypres. The last point in favour of an attack on Verdun was that the Kaiser's son, Crown Prince Friedrich Wilhelm, commanded the German *Fifth Army* in the region. Von Falkenhayn was never blind to the advantages of ensuring the goodwill of his nominal Commander-in-Chief; a triumph for the Crown Prince would certainly add to the credit of its architect.

What was 'Verdun'? It is a small city, a major frontier point, and the crossing point of the Meuse on the road between the Roman Empire's Gallic capital in Paris and the Roman frontier fortress and garrison city of Metz. Thus even before the wars of the eighteenth and nineteenth centuries, Verdun had been a key fortress city in its own right, but the Fortified Region of Verdun came to full flowering in the late nineteenth century. A fortified region was created around the city, anchored on twenty major fortresses and another forty minor works. Each fort or work overlooked some of its neighbours and was overlooked by others. Each major fortress contained artillery to break up enemy attacks from a distance, and every work was able to defend its neighbours with machine-gun positions that formed an interlocking system of mutual defence against closer-range attacks. In addition there were trench systems, concrete shelters and stores of all kinds, and light railways and tramways for local transportation of stores and munitions. As technology developed, so were the defences upgraded; fortresses that had originally been built of masonry were encased in thick concrete carapaces, the latest guns were installed as they became available, and the French newspapers wrote at length about the impregnability of the region. By the beginning of the Great War, Verdun was generally seen as the most impassable of the possible routes of a German advance into France.

In 1916, a particular feature of the Verdun Fortified Area was its poor communication with the rest of France. The River Meuse runs north through the centre of the area, and through the city itself. As in so many other places in France, where stretches of the river itself were not navigable, a canal had been built alongside, meaning that there was a navigable waterway running northwards from below St Mihiel, 30 kilometres to the south, and on into Belgium and The Netherlands. Unfortunately for the defence of Verdun, by late 1914 both the river and canal were both overlooked by German positions to the south-east of Verdun. When the Germans created the St Mihiel Salient in 1915 the nose of it actually projected beyond that town and across the river and canal. Beyond Verdun the river runs northwards, through the hills on which the fortified area was based. It neatly divided the salient into two separate potential battlegrounds before disappearing into the German frontline and defended areas beyond. The river and canal system was therefore blocked at either end of the region and useless to the French as a means of transport of troops and supplies into the fortified area.

Apart from the waterways, there was a small railway junction in Verdun, where two single-track railways came in from the south. One rail route from St Mihiel followed the northward line of the river and canal and like them was rendered useless when the Germans crossed all three. That left one single-track line as a transport resource to supplement the roads. North of Verdun the railway separated into three branches that fanned out to the north and east, into territory now in German hands. There were roads, of course, but in this remote corner of France they were compacted chalk and stone, not metalled and certainly not expected to act as the main arteries for a battle on the scale of the one now erupting. In any event, one of the only two roads that were worth the name also ran alongside the river to St Mihiel and was therefore overlooked by the Germans before also ultimately running into the German positions. In effect, once the Germans had crossed the Meuse at St Mihiel in 1915, the whole Verdun area was to be serviced by one single track railway line and one un-metalled road.

Von Falkenhayn did not expect German troops to launch a major offensive devised solely on the principle that more of the defending enemy would be killed than attackers. Therefore the German Army staff presented *Gericht* as a blow to capture Verdun and use it as a jumping-off ground for a greater offensive that would sweep through the weakened French armies and capture Paris from the east. Railway branch lines were built to bring forward all the supplies that *Gericht* would need. Artillery positions had to be made ready. Ammunition dumps were created to store the 2.5 million shells weighing almost 50,000 tons. Shelter, hospitals and other facilities had to be provided for the assault troops. Regimental colours and standards and band instruments were brought out of storage and the attacking forces looked forward to the fall of Verdun and the victory parade that would take place in the city's streets.

These preparations could not be hidden from the French defenders. From the Regional Commander General Herr downwards came calls for more artillery, more machine guns and more men. Unfortunately Joffre's attention was wholly focussed on the coming Franco-British offensive planned for the summer, and when asked for more resources he was more inclined to see the Verdun area as a 'quiet' sector. From there he could take men, guns and resources for other tasks, and he continued to discount the possibility of a German threat to Verdun that might affect his own plans. As the build-up to the assault continued, with only the actual start time in doubt until the last moment, the French in the salient were acutely aware of their weakness, conscious that they were not heeded in the high places and they prepared to resist as best they could.

The first day of *Gericht* created an unlikely hero. He was needed, to distract France's attention from the disgraceful lack of attention to the defence of Verdun. Emile Driant was not an easy officer to command or control. He had married the daughter of General Boulanger, a highly political general who had cherished ambitions to be the next Napoleon for the end of the nineteenth century. Driant was thus seen as an imperialist in a republican army. In 1905 he had retired from the army in disgust at the national failure to fortify the northern borders, and had been elected to the Chamber of Deputies as member for the northern city of Nancy.

From that position he was outspoken, in criticising lack of preparation for a modern war, in demanding a national policy based on recovery of the lost provinces and in crying out the need for France to regain her pride and leadership of European politics. He was fifty-nine when war broke out, but despite that had re-joined the army as a captain in a staff post at Verdun headquarters. He swiftly arranged to be posted to an active field unit and promoted, so that by the end of 1915 he was a lieutenant colonel commanding two battalions of light infantry Chasseurs reservists, about 1,200 men in all, stationed at the northernmost point of the Verdun Salient, the Bois des Caures. In this relatively quiet sector of the French front line he could see around him all the neglect, abandonment and distraction about which he had been writing and speaking for the last ten years. He used all his political connections to highlight the certainty of a German attack in the north-east and the lack of preparation for such an event. By the end of 1915 he was openly critical of Joffre's command, but his connections were powerful. Even Joffre, who had so far dismissed over seventy-five of the generals who had been commanding the armies, corps and divisions at the beginning of the war, felt unable to dismiss or discipline this reservist, over-age and outspoken and relatively junior officer. Driant used his year in the Bois des Caures to build the defences of his own segment of front line as best he could. He had no illusions about being able to hold off an attack in strength, so built a series of mutually supportive strongpoints and command posts, ensuring that an attacker would find a series of individual obstacles, each of which would briefly delay the inevitable advance and give time for the unprepared forces behind him to prepare in their turn.

When the bombardment began, in the clear frosty morning of 21 February, the fruits of German preparation were harvested. Over 1,200 pieces of German artillery covered the whole sector on the right, eastern bank of the Meuse with hundreds of thousands of shells. Even so, lack of resources prevented the Crown Prince from similarly attacking the left or western bank simultaneously. However, taking the left bank to protect his right flank would only be essential if Falkenhayn really intended to capture Verdun and press on; his more limited plan did not need the French defences on the left bank to be overrun. Over 100 miles away, men felt the ground tremble beneath them, and in the eastern salient itself all command of the military situation instantly passed from the generals at the rear to the junior officers and serjeants in the front line, who in turn could only exercise command over soldiers almost within touching distance. The noise and intensity of the bombardment made any wider exercise of control impossible.

Driant and his lightly armed troops waited for the assault that must follow. The German fire plan ensured that the concrete strongpoints and trenches of the front line were battered by 10,000 tons of artillery shells in the first twenty-four hours of *Gericht*. At 1600 on the first day the bombardment moved on, beyond the strongpoints of the Bois des Caures and onto the areas of defended woodland behind. Out of the clouds of smoke and the debris of the wood ahead of Driant's force emerged the first of 20,000 men of the German *18th Corps*. Well-trained, these soldiers did not arrive in neat lines, but in small and elusive groups, carrying grenades and small mortars to provide very local capacity to attack strongpoints. The Germans also had flame-throwers available in numbers in a French-opposed sector for the first time. The principle of using fire in warfare is as old as history, but the Germans were the first to devise flame-throwers for use on the modern battlefield. On their first appearance against soldiers who had not experienced them, flame-throwers always terrified opposing defenders, and helped greatly to add momentum to any advance. Naturally, once the initial shock of their appearance had passed, *flammenwerfer* operators attracted heavy weights of rifle and machine-gun fire to themselves. The German soldier carrying 10 litres of petroleum liquid on his back was slow, easily identified and frequently on his own; no soldier wanted to be near that amount of fuel when it took a direct hit from a rifle bullet. With a range of only about 25-30 yards, flame-throwers were not much more than a morale booster in these early stages. Their real value would come later, in neutralising bunkers and shelters from greater distance than a grenade could be thrown.

Fighting in the Bois went on all that night and into the following day. Colonel Driant's 1,200 men were in the way of this overwhelming attack, and held up the Germans, despite their smaller numbers, the weakness of their defensive position and lack of artillery support. On both sides of these positions defence was less resolute, and Driant's men were increasingly in danger of being surrounded and cut off from reinforcement or re-supply. In the afternoon of the second day, 22 February, after thirty hours of continuous fighting, Driant's men had run out of ammunition and were trying to hold off the advancing Germans by throwing stones at them. He decided to gather his force and withdraw from the now overrun wood. Trying to lead his men to safety he himself was hit in the forehead, and pausing only to murmur '*Oh La! Mon Dieu!*' he died.

Of Driant's 1,200 men, 118 came out of the wood, the rest were lost, few of their bodies ever recovered. The Germans buried Driant where he fell, and sent messages to his family through Switzerland to assure them of his proper burial and telling them that his grave was well signed. It is right to ask what degree of heroic defence moved the Germans to make so much of the death of one man in a war that had already killed millions.

Suddenly the vital importance of Verdun was recognised. The Germans had said that they would take the city and inflict a great defeat on France. Joffre and his generals discovered that their government and public had not adjusted to the new doctrine that fortress cities no longer mattered, mainly indeed because they were unaware that this doctrine existed. France could not tolerate the loss of Verdun; however irrelevant it might be to French defensive strategy, Verdun had become a symbol of French determination to resist and win. By mistake, Verdun had become a city that both sets of generals had to win, and the generals who lost the struggle could expect no sympathy or strategic understanding from their unforgiving political masters.

Before the French could rally to hold back the German advance, they suffered one of the most shattering blows of the war so far. The centrepiece of the Verdun fortifications was the Fort of Douaumont. Five acres of reinforced concrete, Douaumont stood on one of the highest points of the sector, pointing menacingly into the German-occupied lost provinces. Equipped to be the impregnable heart of the defensive system, it was set up to house over 1,000 men, able to fire the fort's medium artillery housed in steel mushroom-shaped cupolas that lay flush with the fort's concrete and thick earthen roof. In addition they had lighter artillery and machine guns to defend themselves and the infantry in trenches and smaller forts and strongpoints all around. Unfortunately this ideal picture concealed the reality that the fort had been stripped of most of its fortification, and that as the battle unfolded it had become nothing more than a refuge for an elderly sergeant major and about fifty unfit and untrained reservists. On the afternoon of 25 February, on the fourth day of the battle, German Pioneer Sergeant Kunze was one of a working party sent to clear obstacles in the Douaumont area in preparation for a further advance. Curious about the lack of fire from the fort, he advanced with two of his soldiers, climbed into the dry moat that formed part of the outer defences of the fort, found an undefended point where he could climb in, and set off to explore. For the next several minutes a strange hide-and-seek was played out, as both French and Germans encountered each other in the dark underground corridors. At one moment, with battle raging all around outside the fort, Kunze opened a door into a dining hall and found most of the garrison sitting on benches attending to a mandatory training lecture about hygiene discipline. Quickly retiring from the room, Kunze locked the door and resumed his explorations. Eventually, after further adventures with the crew of one of the fort's remaining artillery pieces, Kunze found an officer's dining room, with a meal laid and ready to eat. He sat down to take advantage of the unexpected feast, and left the fort to take care of itself. Kunze's entry into Douaumont had been observed, and shortly after his own completion of taking the fort, three German officers arrived separately, each with reinforcements, and very soon the fort was in the hands of the tiny German force. Hardly a shot had been fired.

The Germans announced that 'a principal pillar of the permanent fortifications of the Verdun fortress system' had fallen. In Germany the church bells were rung and a public holiday was declared. The Kaiser came to review troops at a safe distance behind the fighting line, and the flags and band instruments were brought even closer to the front; the parades in Verdun itself could not long be delayed.

Two German captains who had followed Sergeant Kunze into the fortress were awarded *Pour le Mérite*, the highest gallantry award of the German nation. After the war, Sergeant Kunze complained to his former commanding officer about the injustice of these awards and received one himself, more appropriate to his military non-officer rank; he was promoted from constable, his job before joining the army, to assistant police inspector.

The French released a low-key communication. An 'advance element in the former Verdun fort system' had fallen after a heroic battle that had involved several unsuccessful German attacks and great loss of German life. The French communiqué included the further news that the counter-attack had actually reached and passed the fort, implying that it had been recaptured. It had not been, and apart from a single day's French partial occupation three months later, would not be for another eight months, to the day. On this same day as Douaumont fell, Joffre made another of his frequent changes in command. General Herr, the man who had been ignored when asking for resources to defend Verdun, was replaced. Joffre preferred to see what a new man could do.

General Henri Philippe Pétain was not immediately available when the call came. Withdrawn from immediate active command, he was preparing his army for its role in the coming Anglo-French offensive in the north. Having taken time off from his command, he was not to be found until a staff officer recalled some light gossip, took a car to Paris and there found, outside a bedroom door in a station hotel, a pair of general officer's riding boots alongside a pair of pink slippers. The new commander of Verdun had been tracked down.

One of Pétain's first actions was to address the issue of communication. The one road offering safe access to Verdun was suffering from the weight of traffic, occasional direct hits by shells and lack of organisation. He delegated extraordinary authority and responsibility to Major Richard, who was the head of motor transport for the region. Richard scoured France and commandeered every available motor lorry in the country. The French Army's supply of 140 lorries at the beginning of the war was now a huge fleet of over 3,500 in the Verdun sector alone, of all sorts and in all states of repair and reliability. The single decent road, from Bar le Duc to Verdun, was divided into six 'blocks' and managed as though it was a railway line. Within each block were workshops and depots. All along the road units of pioneers and over-age reservists were stationed with all the stone, equipment and tools needed to repair any break in the road's surface, caused by shell-fire, wear and tear, or weather as the dreadful winter dragged on. Things got even worse when the frozen ground thawed at the end of February and the whole road threatened to collapse under the weight of traffic. Any lorry that broke down or was stranded was immediately manhandled off the road and abandoned for collection by the workshop troops, there was simply not time to spare for any actions that might cause delays. Every eighteen seconds, night and day, for the rest of the battle's long months to come, another lorry passed the checkpoints. This long never-ending stream of vehicles passed along the road itself, and on either side marched troops, some heading north for the battle and others south to rest and await their next turn in the eye of the storm. A journalist and politician, Maurice Barres, saw this sight, lit at night by the lights of the stream of lorries, and coined the name *La Voie Sacrée,* by which the road has been known ever since.

Before the war, the French military authorities in Verdun had successfully opposed attempts by higher authority to build a defensible railway line into Verdun, and Pétain now had to rectify that situation. A full division, twelve battalions, was set to labouring on building a new full-gauge line running alongside the Voie Sacrée, and in time this would take much strain off the road itself.

After the fall of Douaumont, intense fighting continued incessantly in every part of the salient. Von Falkenhayn realised within days that the Crown Prince had been right in stressing the impossibility of pressing the attack only on one bank of the river and had expanded the offensive to cover both banks. His plan was now to actually capture Verdun, not just threaten to do so. The battle now stretched across a salient about 10 miles wide and 8 miles deep, covered with the anchoring forts and with each fort protecting its local area of trenches and earthworks. Within the salient a new world came into existence, where men ceased to have any effect as individuals, where artillery was the prime weapon of attack and defence, and where fear of the random destruction of the human body by an artillery explosion was added to the everyday horrors of battle.

> In all armies the idea of destruction of the body by artillery fire was more fearsome than the everyday fear of death and wounding by rifle or machine gun.

Of all the battlefields of the war this is perhaps the most intense, in terms of the physical experience, the sheer degree of destruction and the sheer terribleness of the ordeal faced by each soldier who passed through it. More than thirty years later, French veterans would sum up the whole experience in one sentence '*J'y étais*' – I was there. Nobody needed to ask where 'there' was. Soldiers would not try to explain the experience of Verdun even to other soldiers; if they had been at Verdun, they knew; if they had not, they could not begin to understand. An impenetrable veil concealed Verdun from the eye and imagining of all who had not seen it. People came to know and recognise this division between those who had and those who had not. One officer described how, on leave from Verdun, he went in his uniform to a restaurant near his home. He described how the restaurant fell quiet as he entered the room, and stayed quiet; the diners knew he had 'been there'.

Pétain faced serious difficulties as this battle moved into a second and third month. The strain on soldiers was such that he had to introduce 'Noria', the concept of rotation of units, a novel idea in French military circles at the time. In the Noria principle every soldier should bear the same burden as every other, and as a result almost three-quarters of the manpower of the French Army fought at Verdun for at least one period, although some returned three times or more. This rotation ensured that soldiers from every town and village in France went to Verdun, and fought alongside fellow citizens from every other village and town. It was thus to become a truly 'national' battle, with nobody failing to be involved at some personal level. Pétain used a simple rallying cry as his statement of intent: *'On les auras'* – 'We'll have 'em'. The soldiers could understand those simple statements of strategy and reacted to bring them about.

In May, long after the Germans had expected to be housing their headquarters in the safety of the tunnels under Verdun citadel, a second crisis arose for the French defenders. Fort Vaux was one of the other main forts in the eastern side of the salient, close to Douaumont and part of the same inter-linking chain of mutually defensive points. It became clear that a German attack was determined to take the fort, and the French took the unusual step of asking for a volunteer officer to command its defence. Commandant Raynal, already wounded three times and much-decorated, stepped forward. A company of men of the 142nd Infantry Regiment but including men from a number of other regiments and units were not given the option to volunteer, and during the night of 30 May Raynal led them into the fort to hold out against the coming onslaught. They had ample supplies and expected to hold out until stronger forces could be prepared and sent to relieve them. Almost immediately, the Germans succeeded in occupying the roof of the fort, and tried every possible means, including gas, to dislodge the occupiers. After four days the garrison discovered that the water in the cistern of the fort was almost exhausted; the container was far shallower than anyone had realised. Raynal prepared to send out a party of the weaker men, the wounded and others suffering from shell shock as a result of the constant German attempts to break in. After they had gone he and the few remaining men prepared to defy the siege for as long as they could hold out. Four carrier pigeons had been carried into the fort by Raynal's men, and were let out at intervals, asking for relief and reinforcement. The last message was sent out by this means as the party of weaker men were leaving on 4 June. By that evening water was desperately scarce and two days later the last drop was gone, the garrison reduced to licking the walls to take in the condensation and water seepage that gathered on them. The German assaults ceased overnight, and on the morning of 7 June Raynal and his few survivors marched out of the fort into captivity. The Crown Prince had Raynal brought to his headquarters and personally handed back to him the sword that he had been wearing at the moment of capture. Almost at the same moment the French government was announcing the immediate award of the *Legion d'Honneur* to Raynal in recognition of his heroic leadership. The last pigeon, named *Le Valliant* was awarded the *Croix de Guerre*, posthumously, having died at the end of its journey from the fort.

The terrible intensity of the battle went on unabated. Soldiers ceased to think in conventional terms; they were *'Ceux de Verdun'* – the Verdun people, a race apart, condemned to defend the spirit and style of France, but with no spirit or style of their own. On the Voie Sacrée a never-ceasing stream of traffic passed in both directions. Troops approaching the city for the first time would set out up the road in good heart, singing regimental marching songs, marching easily. As they moved up the road they would see the smaller groups of men coming the other way, the survivors of a turn in the salient. Filthy and unshaven, gaunt and with expressions of stark horror on their faces, these survivors inhabited a different world. Among the survivors were the ambulances carrying the wounded; shot, gassed, burnt, hit by fragments of artillery shells or maimed and losing limbs through the effect of being near a shell's explosion. The two lines passed each other by. Few going up dared ask of those going back what it was like; the gulf between those who knew and those who did not was too great. One soldier did ask, and described how a man, even more terrible than those around him, simply stood up and with a slow gesture of his extended arm swept the horizon behind his back, saying nothing and seeing nothing. His questioner later wrote that he then began to understand the meaning of *Le Minceur*, the Mincing Machine, which was grinding France and her soldiers into nothingness. The Press and their readers spoke of *Le Moulin sur la Meuse,* the Mill on the Meuse, but the soldiers used the shorter description, with its overtones of butchery.

Meanwhile Pétain could offer little more than tenacity and the ability to last longer than the Germans. He was acutely aware that initiating an offensive strategy in the Verdun Salient would be every bit as costly as every preceding offensive elsewhere had been; France needed time to recover before being ready to resume the attack. But a new general was offering more, and Joffre listened to him. Robert Nivelle and his associate Charles Mangin had a plan to recover the lost ground and turn back the Germans from their threatening positions. Pétain could not be dismissed, but could be promoted to command the whole stretch of the front, leaving Nivelle to take over day-to-day command of the continuing struggle. Pétain had lasted a few weeks in command of the eight-month battle with which he would be associated for the next thirty years. As Pétain's successor, Nivelle's fitness for high command was based on his repeated claim '*J'ais le Secret*', but if he had the secret it was one that would lead the French armies to near-ruin over the coming months, as 1916 would turn into 1917.

New objectives must be set and victories recorded. Douaumont and Vaux must be recaptured, and the Germans driven back. At one moment in early July, German patrols had indeed penetrated so close to Verdun that German soldiers would stand on the roof of Fort Souville, the last fort that barred to way into the city. From there, they claimed, they had seen the sun glinting on the River Meuse as it flowed through the city centre of Verdun itself. The moment inspired Nivelle to an Order of the Day that reflected the desperation of the moment, ending with the cry '*Ils ne passeront pas*' – 'They will not pass.' The French were not to know it yet, but this momentary occupation of the roof of Souville was the last gasp of German offensive action on the front at Verdun. On 24 June von Falkenhayn had issued orders that reflected his increasing concern about the scale of the build-up of forces in the Somme area. A great bombardment had started in that sector the day before, and was clearly the precursor to the great Allied offensive. From now on, very little artillery ammunition was to be sent to Verdun, and no new large formations of troops. General von Knobelsdorf, the Crown Prince's military tutor before the war, and his chief of staff since its beginning, still believed that Verdun could be captured. By mid-summer he was almost alone in this delusion. However, despite several requests to his father the Kaiser, the Crown Prince had been unable to dislodge his mentor and right hand. Eventually the Kaiser, although increasingly isolated at Potsdam from the realities of the war, recognised that the offensive had failed, and that von Knobelsdorf's determination had destroyed too many lives for him to be supported. In the autumn General von Knobelsdorf was sent to the Eastern Front to command an army corps there. Almost his last instruction was to order that the regimental colours and bands that had been awaiting their triumphal entry into Verdun should be sent back to Germany; they would not be needed.

Nivelle and Mangin now set about their tasks, making good use of the increasing availability of decent artillery and taking advantage of the diminished

German commitment. At the end of October, Douaumont was recaptured, after a series of actions that were later calculated to have cost 100,000 casualties. Vaux was less expensive. By now both sides were utterly weary and, on 15 December, almost by mutual agreement fighting died down, with the line around Verdun itself about halfway between the original positions and the furthest point of German advance. Verdun had not fallen, but the true German plan, to kill more Frenchmen than Germans, had succeeded. It had been a close call; it was true that the French had suffered about 380,000 casualties, but that toll had cost the Germans 320,000. Of the French casualties, about one quarter were dead, one quarter captured and prisoners, and one half wounded. The combination of ineffectual medical services, the effects of gas and artillery, and contamination of wounds ensured that a very high proportion of the wounded would not recover to fight again. One ardent French officer, who had so admired Pétain's teaching before the war that he had asked to be commissioned into Pétain's own 33rd Regiment, was severely wounded and given up for dead by his comrades. Taken prisoner by the Germans, he was to spend the rest of the war in German hospitals. Charles de Gaulle would never forget the humiliation of being unable to fight when his country needed him. His path and Pétain's would cross again in unhappy circumstances.

As the battle came to its end, Joffre was relieved of any active command. Promoted Marshal of France he undertook a number of ceremonial duties until in 1918 he succeeded as French representative of the Supreme War Council, the body set up at the end of 1917 to oversee the increasing political and logistical complexity of fighting the Allied war as separate French, British Italian and American armies. Foch would take over as Commander-in-Chief.

Verdun in the Air

The fluctuating struggle on the ground at Verdun was matched by another in the air; the first true use of air power for more than relatively small-scale observation and reconnaissance with occasional gladiatorial duels between like-minded individuals. Neither France nor Germany could maintain dominance for any prolonged period; new machines were in constant development and the tactics of air warfare were equally changing almost weekly. However, both sides were able at different times to exploit air superiority, keeping enemy reconnaissance patrols away from their own areas, recording enemy dispositions, and observing the shell-fall of their own artillery fire and sending back instructions to correct aim as necessary. Air superiority frequently led to advantage on the ground as well, and local parts of the battle field did change hands because of domination of the air above them.

France's young aircraft industry developed many different types of plane, each factory and designer independent of the others, leading to a degree of waste in both research and manufacture. Germany, more methodically, tended to concentrate on fewer initiatives, which led to great temporary superiority when new machines did become available. From the outset the cult of the 'Ace' was popularised by both sides. France had René Fonck and Paul Guynemer as their particular figures; Germany had Manfred von Richthofen, The Red Baron, as theirs. Episodes of courtesy from an earlier age were not rare. When the German ace von Boelcke was killed in aerial combat, pilots from a number of French squadrons flew over his squadron airfield and dropped wreaths. At this early stage of air combat both enemy and friend alike recognised and respected the courage and danger, and near-certainty of death that accompanied the air war.

Verdun also saw the debut of the American Squadron as a precursor to the country's entry into the war. The *Escadrille Lafayette* was made up of a number of rich young Americans bringing their own planes to war, joined by assorted professional stunt pilots who had previously made their precarious living by giving flying exhibitions in towns and villages that were still coming to terms with having first seen motor cars only a few years before. Resolutely declining to be absorbed into the French air arm, the squadron was to provide invaluable support to France, especially at moments when the Germans were enjoying one of their periods of technical or tactical superiority. This squadron caught the American imagination, and ensured plentiful sympathetic coverage of Verdun in American newspapers. It may be argued that this squadron was largely responsible, perhaps almost as responsible as *Lusitania* and the U-boat campaign, for creating the climate of opinion that would bring America into the war in 1917.

In the months of the battle alone, aircraft speeds multiplied from scarcely 50 miles per hour to three times that. Heights that were unimaginable became routine, not least because added speed meant that aircraft could climb much faster than hitherto, and reach several thousand feet before needing to return to base to refuel. Even at these heights, aircraft were often rocked by air turbulence as huge shells, weighing half a ton or more, reached the high points of trajectory before their plunging descent on the fortresses and works beneath.

However, the most important development was in armament, when a Dutch engineer called Anthony Fokker who had emigrated to Germany before the war invented the 'interrupter mechanism' that enabled a machine gun to be mounted on the cockpit of a plane and fired through the arc of the propeller. The firing sequence synchronised with the propeller rotation to ensure that the bullets would not shred the propeller blades. Not only did this permit heavier weaponry to be mounted, it meant that a daring pilot, willing to stand up in his seat and fly the plane with his knees, could re-arm the weapon if it ran out of ammunition or jammed. This gave overwhelming superiority to the Germans for a while, until the Allies captured a plane with this mechanism fitted and were able to copy it.

Specialist aircraft began to be developed. Reconnaissance planes with rudimentary radio and Morse signalling lamps, protective fighters, planes armed with incendiary rockets to shoot down observation balloons and zeppelins, and elementary bombers whose payloads developed from steel darts to explosive bombs. Verdun marked the end of the belief, expressed by Haig before the war, that aircraft were interesting as leisure machines but would never have a place on the battlefield.

Jutland – A Winning Defeat

As Commandant Raynal was leading his company into Vaux, the war's only major battle between the British Grand Fleet and the German *High Seas Fleet* was in its preliminary stages. Off the Jutland coast, the latter fleet was emerging from its main North Sea anchorage and harbour at Bremerhaven to challenge the Grand Fleet's control of the North Sea, break the blockade of Germany and strangle the BEF's supply lines across the English Channel. Various intelligence sources gave ample warning of this movement, and Admiral Sir John Jellicoe took the Grand Fleet to meet the threat. In the subsequent battle that took place over the next two days, 31 May-1 June, the greatest naval battle of the modern era took place. Admiral Reinhard Scheer, the *High Seas Fleet* commander, commanded ninety-nine warships, but certainly had not anticipated finding that the entire Grand Fleet of 151 Royal Navy ships was moving to confront him.

Actual numbers of ships at Jutland are of little importance. A new battleship, HMS *Dreadnought*, had been commissioned into the Royal Navy in 1906, and at a stroke had rendered obsolete every other capital – major – warship in the world. *Dreadnought* was the fastest capital ship in the world, and was the first to carry only one calibre of heavy guns. Hitherto, capital ships had a few large guns for fighting other capital ships and many smaller ones for fighting smaller torpedo-carrying craft such as destroyers. With five gun-turrets, each mounting two 12-inch guns, *Dreadnought* would be able to out-fight any ship, at ranges that would make torpedoes obsolete in fleet warfare. What would matter in any future war would be the number of dreadnought battleships on either side. At Jutland, Sir John Jellicoe had command of twenty-eight dreadnought battleships, whilst Scheer had sixteen at his call. In addition to the dreadnoughts, a relatively recent class of capital ships had appeared. The battlecruisers were similar in size to the new dreadnoughts, but gave up defensive strength and some firepower in return for even greater speed. Thus,

3,000 tons less weight and two fewer guns of the same calibre as carried by the dreadnoughts gave a top speed of up to 30 knots, against the 21 of dreadnoughts. The battlecruiser squadrons saw themselves as the fast, glamorous and hard-hitting élite of the Royal Navy. They existed to rush in, hit hard and make their exit quickly. Sir David Beattie commanded the three squadrons totalling nine ships and was second-in-command of the Grand Fleet as a whole. He was a dashing and glamorous figure himself who epitomised all that the battlecruiser squadrons thought about their role in the Royal Navy. The German battlecruiser squadron was smaller, with five ships, and was commanded by Scheer's second-in-command, Franz Hipper.

> There had been ten ships in the Grand Fleet's battlecruiser squadrons, but HMAS *Australia* had recently come off worst in a collision with HMS *New Zealand* and was in dock for repairs when the Battle of Jutland took place.

The British battlecruisers were found wanting in their dashing role – as a third one blew up in an explosion caused by a design fault that left a battlecruiser's main ammunition magazine vulnerable, Sir David Beatty gave his opinion to the captain of his flagship, HMS *Lion*: 'There's something wrong with our bloody ships today, Chatfield.'

Throughout the two days of the battle itself, the main bodies of the two fleets never came firmly to grips with each other. Opportunities arose for the Grand Fleet to block the *High Seas Fleet's* route back to its anchorage at Bremerhaven. On the evening of 31 May Jellicoe had achieved the upper hand, placing his fleet across this German line of withdrawal. This also gave him the advantage of seeing the Germans back-lit by the setting sun, whilst the German fleet looked into the darker eastern skies. However, poor communications procedures enabled the *High Seas Fleet* to pass behind the Grand Fleet and escape to run for its home port. Jellico was reluctant to follow. He was mindful that the German navy had mined the approaches to their base, and he was aware that so close to the main fleet base the submarine threat had to be potent. The Germans returned with little further trouble from the Grand Fleet.

At first glance Jutland was an indecisive battle, and certainly not obviously a victory for the Royal Navy. The Royal Navy lost fourteen ships against eleven. British tonnage lost was over 110,000 tons against 62,000. Casualties were almost 6,800 against a few over 3,000. Both sides claimed the victory of the engagement, but there was no doubt about the real strategic winner in the context of the war as a whole; the German *High Seas Fleet* returned to harbour and did not put to sea again during the war.

> The *High Seas Fleet* sailed to Scapa Flow in the Orkneys in 1919, to be interned as part of the de-militarisation of Germany. Here, in the end, the German crews sank their own ships, preferring this to the humiliating detention of the former pride of Germany.

The Brusilov Offensive and the Isonzo

As with Gallipoli in 1915, we have to look briefly beyond the Western Front to gain a rounded picture of 1916. French pleas for help in early 1916 led to the failed Russian offensive at Lake Naroch, on the Eastern Front in what today is Lithuania. Here about 350,000 Russians, parts of two army groups, attacked the smaller German *Tenth Army*. Russian casualties were about 100,000, German about 20,000. Nonetheless, the Russians launched another offensive in June, again in response to Joffre's pleas, this time attacking the Austro-Hungarians. On a front of 200 miles, stretching from the northern end of the Carpathian Mountains almost to Warsaw, about 630,000 Russians attacked about 470,000 Austrians, who had a cadre of Germans in one of their armies. The offensive was stunningly successful from its first day on 4 June. By mid-June von Falkenhayn was already withdrawing support from his attack on Verdun to deal with the threat on the Somme, and very soon was having to send some of these resources to help his allies in the east. The German Army came to recognise the awful truth spoken by one of its generals – 'We are fighting chained to a corpse.' Alliance with Austria-Hungary was dragging Germany to defeat.

The offensive gained ground everywhere, up to 70 miles in places. The Russians did not count casualties as carefully as did other nations, but the accepted total is that about 500,000 were killed or wounded, from the original attacking force or later reinforcements. The Austrians suffered a little short of one million casualties including about 400,000 prisoners, soon to suffer the suffering and mortality rates associated with being a prisoner in wartime Russia. Austria-Hungary was scarcely able to fight effectively again during this war after this shattering reverse. Thereafter, the Germans were obliged to divert increasing resources to help the Austrians in their struggles against the Italians, whilst the Russians had to support Romania, a late entrant to the war in 1915 on the Allied side following Brusilov's success.

A secondary effect of Brusilov's victory was von Falkenhayn's downfall. He was to be replaced by the commanders of earlier successes in the east, Hindenburg and Ludendorff. Hindenburg was to be First Chief of Staff, and Ludendorff Second Chief of Staff. However, he refused to accept a secondary title and was appointed First Quartermaster General instead. Whatever titles they chose, these two were to command the German Army effort until the end of the war.

The Italians had come relatively late into the war in 1915, joining the Entente powers and not the German/Austria-Hungarian Central Powers as pre-war planners had expected. They too now came to assist in relieving the pressure on France. To do so, they launched no less than five separate assaults, the Fifth to the Ninth battles in the twelve separate Battles of The Isonzo River. These were attempts to cross the river as a necessary precursor to driving the Austrians off the Dolomite Mountains and out of northern Italy. They enjoyed little success, but the Italian army suffered about 100,000 casualties as they sought too contribute to the relief of Verdun. In total the fighting on the Isonzo over three years cost about 300,000 casualties.

The Somme

As we have seen, the planners' conference at the end of 1915 had agreed that the main British and French activity of the coming year would be a joint effort, based on the axis of the River Somme, the junction point of the BEF and adjoining French. However, as the battle at Verdun threatened to destroy the French armies, Joffre's habitual suspicion of his allies gradually hardened into the thought that the British actually had a plan of their own; to let France and Germany destroy each other and enable the British to profit at the expense of both. He still insisted on going ahead with the summer offensive, but began to change the terms of the agreement bit by bit.

Haig wrote a note to his staff on 22 May. He wanted views on when the army would be ready for the proposed Somme Offensive. He noted four possibilities, 1 July, 15 July, 1 August or some other later date to be given by his staff. Haig was due to meet Joffre later that week and needed to know what he could commit to. At the meeting four days later Joffre demanded that the attack date in mid-summer would have to be brought forward to 1 July at the very latest; France could not hold out alone for any longer time without this offensive to relieve the pressure on Verdun. The French would still commit about twenty divisions to their effort in the battle. However, on 6 June, less than three weeks before his last possible date for starting the assault, Joffre changed the plan again. The British would have to provide most of the forces to fight the battle; France was already in her own vital struggle. France's commitment would be no more than Emile Fayolle's Sixth Army, of thirteen divisions, soon to be twelve. They would act, Joffre confirmed, 'in support of the British.' The battle must, at all costs, force Germany to commit enormous numbers of men to fighting it; without that diversion of effort, Germany would win the war by destroying the armies of France at Verdun. The French demands, pleas and orders took different forms, but were delivered with utmost urgency, and had a strong effect on Haig. He undertook to do all he could do to relieve pressure on France at the first possible moment. On 1 June he wrote to London to confirm his intention to fight the battle at the time and place of French choosing. He would fight, he wrote 'with the object of relieving Verdun.' No other objective or plan was mentioned, but Haig went on to note that 'one ought to foresee the case in which the British Army must alone undertake the offensive.' Even as he wrote he feared that the French might not contribute at all on the Somme and he entertained the idea of moving the proposed attack from there to the north, where targets with genuine strategic importance could be captured by the British breakthrough. All Joffre's suspicions of British motives were rekindled at once, and Haig backed down. Thus, by stages, he was manoeuvred into agreeing to launch a battle at a time, in a place, with objectives, that were none of his choosing. Above all it was a battle to be fought by troops who were largely inexperienced in any sort of warfare, and against experienced veterans who had taken almost eighteen months to prepare some of the strongest defensive positions in the world. Haig was very aware of the French difficulties at Verdun and he saw that without the BEF's intervention on a massive scale the French would soon be out of the war, which would be lost as a result. On 15 June, Haig issued an instruction to his army commanders, re-stating that relief of pressure on Verdun was a key objective, but adding a new second objective: 'inflicting loss on the enemy.' He met Joffre the following day. Joffre spoke of the advance beyond Bapaume, 10 miles from the British starting point. Haig was more temperate, and in his diary that night wrote of limited advances, 'if all goes well and we reach Bapaume.' Bit by bit, the objective of the proposed battle was becoming nothing more than attrition, the battle to cause more casualties than you suffer yourself.

However, having committed himself to the battle, Haig typically now began to look optimistically beyond the immediate objective to relieve German pressure on Verdun and to see this offensive as an opportunity to break the stalemate in France, perhaps even to win the war. Brigadier General John Charteris, his Chief Intelligence Officer, would always see a silver lining in any cloud, and Haig was a general who liked his staff to offer assessments that reinforced his own wishes. As a result the staff at General Headquarters (GHQ) delivered the most optimistic assessments of recent German casualties and the most optimistic analysis of the effects of artillery bombardment of the German front line. As news of Brusilov's success in the east began to arrive, hopes developed for something comparable in the west.

Meanwhile, what of the Germans? Given the quietness of the sector and the advantages of holding the high ground along its entire length, they had used the last year productively. Nine villages lie along the ridge: Gommecourt, Serre and Beaumont Hamel north of the Ancre, with Thiepval, Ovillers, La Boiselle, Fricourt, Mametz and Montauban to its south. These villages lie slightly ahead of the main ridge, on small outlying ridges. The valleys between them run up to the main ridge. The whole German defensive line was anchored on these villages. However, that was not the whole story. The Germans had no need to carry their invasion further into France; they already controlled the iron and coal mines of the Northern French Plain, and would have indeed have achieved satisfactory territorial gains if the war ended with them able to keep what they now occupied. The onus lay on the French to drive the Germans back to their own borders and recover the lost lands. Thus while the French and BEF thought in terms of attack and movement, the Germans were able to think in terms of building their fortifications as the static points of their new frontier. Using the village as anchors they built a series of fortified redoubts all along their defensive line. Each redoubt was a fortification in itself, and each could provide protective machine-gun fire across the front of its neighbours. On the dry higher ground, the Germans did not suffer the problems of digging trenches and dugouts that filled with water from the high water table. Having started with existing cellars under the village houses, they developed a large system of underground shelters, built to house their soldiers in some comfort. As much as 40 feet below the surface, these shelters provided dry safety, with electricity as a normal feature and often with piped running water on tap. Each shelter had a number of entrances and exits, to ensure that the German defenders could take cover easily in the event of bombardment and man their trenches quickly in the event of an infantry attack.

A typical defence line of trenches consisted of three lines of trenches. The forward line was the thinly-manned firing line, where sentries could be posted and into which troops held further back could be rushed into line to repel an advance. The main trench was some little distance behind this and constituted the main defensive bulwark, where the main body of troops and the local area defence weapons like machine guns and mortars were sited. The reserve line was built to provide an extra defensive point to cover the lines in front and give troops the ability to achieve defence in depth in the event that an attack might gain a foothold on the front two lines. Wide and dense lines of barbed wire obstacles were laid out in front of the firing trench, and lesser obstacles lay between all three lines. As we have seen, the whole was anchored on the fortified villages and redoubts that lie along the ridge above the plain of the Rivers Ancre and Somme.

The Germans had space, time and resources to build such a system to its maximum efficacy, but they had time to do more; they were able to replicate the whole defensive system of trenches and shelters a second time, usually some few hundred yards or so behind the first. In the key places there was some work done on a third or even a fourth series of trenches. This meant that to achieve the longed-for breakthrough, attackers would have to cross a forward system of three trenches with redoubts and fortifications then a further three, six or nine trench lines before reaching the German rear areas where static warfare could be replaced by the cavalry war of movement.

General Sir Henry Rawlinson was fully aware of the size of the task that faced him. He had been a Divisional Commander at the outbreak of the war, and commanded an army corps in 1915. His regular questioning of his superiors' plans and orders had caused his removal from command on the Western Front in time to be sent to Gallipoli and there he had contributed to Monro's management of the evacuation. His brilliant achievement there brought him back again to an army command on the Western Front in late 1915. Success in the forthcoming battle would require all his planning and management skills. Unfortunately, he immediately ran into his first great obstacle; all the BEF's armies lacked senior officers proven as commanders in battle and they were especially short of the large numbers of trained and experienced staff officers needed to manage a battle of the planned size. Even at battalion level, shortage of experienced officers was a constant problem. Any New Army battalion with more than one or two pre-war officers was a rarity, and the same applied to the warrant officers, serjeants and corporals, so many of whom had been lost in the first blood-letting of the original BEF. This shortage of experienced officers and men of all ranks made problems for any plan that depended on local battle management. Rawlinson was also very aware of the other great problem, battlefield communication. Once the infantry climbed out of their trenches, the battle would largely pass from his immediate control and his future planning would be based on imperfect knowledge, transmitted uncertainly from the battalion commanders upwards via brigade, division and corps commanders. Any orders from him had to travel the same route in reverse. The battle plan was therefore, necessarily, based on a huge timetable. The clock would control all actions, from the start of the bombardment, during the assault by the infantry and later as the cavalry moved up to exploit the breakthrough into the 'soft' areas behind the German front line. Everyone depended on someone else fulfilling his allotted task successfully and on time.

This appreciation of his army's limitations led Rawlinson to plan a less ambitious battle than Haig now wanted, but more like the battle to which the latter had committed the BEF in his letter of 1 June. Haig demanded more ambitious plans from Rawlinson, and although relieving the French crisis at Verdun was paramount Haig now believed that a breakthrough battle could be fought and subsequently exploited. Only a week before the opening bombardment Haig and Rawlinson were debating the purpose of the battle and its territorial objectives. Rawlinson still wanted to limit his ambitions to what he knew he could expect to achieve with inexperienced troops and diminishing commitment of support from the French on his right, but Haig was again thinking of a bigger picture. Thus the territorial objectives went beyond Rawlinson's limited expectations. The first phase would capture German defences on the ridge from Serre and Thiepval, on through Pozieres Ridge and to Montauban. Then, assuming success thus far, the ridge running north to south behind these first objectives would come into the picture, followed by '…our cavalry to push through into the open country behind the enemy's line of defence.' Haig did give himself a get-out-of-jail card when he said 'After gaining our first objective we may find that a further advance eastward is not advisable,' a card that might permit him to abandon the Somme Offensive and go back to his preferred campaign around Ypres in Flanders.

Apart from the main attack, a diversion was planned. The village of Gommecourt lies a little to the north of the main battlefield. Like the villages along the rest of the Somme sector, it formed a strong point in the German front line, jutting forward to overlook the BEF trench lines below it. The village was strongly fortified of course and provided Haig with an ideal diversionary target, well worth capturing in its own right and close enough to distract the Germans from the main attack being launched simultaneously only a couple of miles further to the south.

Behind the BEF's attack area, new roads were built from rear areas right up to within German artillery range. Two full gauge railways were built to service the battlefield and were connected to seventeen railheads, of which two were reserved for use by the medical services. A network of prefabricated light 'Decauville' railways was also laid down to service more local needs. Water pipelines were laid right into forward areas, and ingenious steel rings were devised to 'bandage' pipes fractured by shellfire. Huts were built to house 400,000 men, infantry, artillery, cavalry, pioneer troops, labour battalions and all the others. In any hut a soldier's allotted sleeping space was 24 inches wide, so perhaps fewer huts were needed than might be expected. Preparation included building ammunition dumps to hold over two million shells and other ordnance stores, forage stores for tens of thousands of horses, equipment stores and cages to hold prisoners of war. Rawlinson paid considerable attention to the needs of the many dead and wounded that he knew must follow the attack. He was student enough to know that fighting an undefeated German Army in mainland Europe has always been a bloody business. From the Regimental Aid Posts in the front lines, to the Dressing Stations, back to the Casualty Clearing Stations, on to the Base Hospitals and so back to England, the medical chain must be ready for the test of its resources. He demanded, and went on demanding until he got them, special trains that would be used solely to ferry casualties back from the two dedicated forward area railheads. He wanted ambulance trains for the seriously wounded and more conventional passenger trains for the walking and lightly wounded. He had special frames built to hold stretchers on the canal barges that were used to bring supplies from the ports into the BEF's sector of the battlefield. On a more macabre note, he ordered that large mass graves be dug at many points behind the lines.

Miners had been at work for many weeks digging tunnels from behind the British trench lines, deep under no-man's-land and on under particularly well-defended German positions. At the end of each tunnel they would create an underground magazine, to be filled with high explosive and detonated as the infantry were setting off to assault the German positions.

The overture to the battle was the bombardment of the German lines and artillery. Starting on 24 June, artillery fired non-stop, working to a plan that envisaged this continuing day and night for five days. However, the weather was unkind and on 26 June Rawlinson postponed the attack two days before it was due, leaving the artillery to conserve ammunition, to spread the last two days' firing over four. Nonetheless, despite this hold-up, 1,500 artillery pieces managed to fire about 1.7 million shells during the seven days of bombardment, about eleven shells per day for every yard of the whole 12-mile front to be attacked. Despite the delay, there was a general feeling of confidence about the final hours before the infantry were to assault. On the night before the attack, Rawlinson himself took time to attend a dinner of Old-Etonian officers in his Fourth Army. Despite the imminence of the attack, 167 officers found time to attend. Haig visited some headquarters of formations that were to take part on the attack, and recorded his impressions in his diary.

'Preparations were never so thorough, nor troops better-trained. Wire very well cut and ammunition adequate... .

'With God's help, I feel hopeful for tomorrow. The men are in splendid spirits: several have said that they have never before been so instructed and informed of the nature of the operation before them. The wire has never been so well cut, nor the artillery preparations more thorough.'

Haig was perhaps unaware that low cloud had severely hampered the work of artillery observers flying with the Royal Flying Corps to direct artillery work. At the start of the preliminary bombardment on 24 June, only forty of the 117 German positions selected for destruction had been registered, the process of firing to establish accurately the co-ordinates required to deliver effective artillery fire onto a target. Continued bad weather meant that subsequent attempts to catch up with the timetable were always behindhand.

Day One

At 0720 on Saturday 1 July a single huge mine exploded under the German front line at Hawthorn Redoubt, a key German strongpoint built in front of the village of Beaumont Hamel. The official war photographer filmed the explosion and created one of the best-known photographs of the whole war, as the huge mine containing 18 tons of ammonal high explosive erupted, blasting earth, bodies and weapons three-quarters of a mile into the sky. The Germans already knew the place and date of the attack, and now knew the exact start time. Eight minutes later, sixteen more mines exploded, under strongpoints along the 14-mile front. One of them, the Lochnagar mine at La Boiselle beside the road from Albert to Bapaume that formed the axis of the planned advance, contained 26 tons of ammonal high explosive and was the largest mine of the war so far. As the debris settled, leaving vast craters, the largest being 55 feet deep and 220 feet across, the guns of the artillery fired their last barrage onto the German front line trenches before lengthening their range to engage their next targets, deeper into the German trench systems.

At exactly 0730, 2,000 officers blew their whistles and the largest and most dramatic foot race in human history began. Along the 12-mile front, 65,000 men of the BEF, the assault parties of eighty-four battalions, climbed up out of the trenches and started the infantry assault of the Battle of The Somme. Within about an hour 30,000 of them were casualties, about 10,000 dead and the rest wounded. Within minutes of its starting something had gone catastrophically wrong with the best-planned, best-prepared and most confident battle in British history. Ninety years later, with the passing of the very last of the survivors who fought in the battle, the arguments still rage about what went wrong, why, and above all who was to blame.

Before we follow the rest of the day, with another 90,000 British launched into attack and another 30,000 to become casualties, let us review the first twenty minutes and the reason for such a complete mismatch between expectation and result.

There seem to have been principal reasons for the disaster that befell Britain and the Empire that morning:

1. The German's preferred to site their trenches with the advantage of good ground rather than simply as far forward as they could be. This meant that almost every British soldier in the advance was faced with an uphill

rush, in some sectors only a matter of dozens of yards, but in others a full half-mile and more of open uphill country had to be crossed, in full view of anyone who might be watching.

2. The Germans had developed their defences to degrees that were unknown to the BEF.

3. In many places the attackers also had to cope with advancing on foot through the clinging chalk and clay soil still wet after the rain of the previous week and churned up by the artillery preparation.

4. Before the war, artillery was expected to break up enemy attacks and to kill defenders in primitive shelters at ground level. Shrapnel was the artillery shell for that purpose and it was in plentiful supply. Nobody had imagined the need to cut barbed wire and destroy entanglements of it, often 50 or even 100 yards wide, and nobody had foreseen the need to be able to destroy shelters deep underground. Shrapnel was useless for either purpose, and so the problems of dealing with barbed wire and deep underground shelters tended to be overlooked in any practical way; it was just assumed that shrapnel would do the job. The scandal over shells, both quantity and quality, had brought down the Asquith government in 1915, but there had been little enough time for the situation to have been overhauled sufficiently to provide for a battle like this one.

5. Liaison between British artillery and infantry was primitive, and failed when needed most. Flexible firing plans were to come later, but at this stage of the war the artillery had neither means of knowing what infantry might need as the battle developed nor the weapons or skills that would have enabled them to act if they had known. The inability of the RFC to fly effectively in the days before the battle had added to the problem in that too many German defensive positions had come through the preliminary bombardment unscathed.

6. Very few officers in the BEF realised that they were planning a foot race. We already know that Sir Douglas Haig's thoughts were of a well-prepared attack after a devastating bombardment. Sir Henry Rawlinson had told his subordinate commanders that '*nothing could exist at the conclusion of the bombardment in the area covered by it.*' As result, few officers in more junior positions saw the need to think differently.

7. Planning gave no urgency to getting across no-man's-land and into the German trenches, but much thought had gone into deciding what would be needed for defending the captured trenches against the inevitable strong German counter-attacks. As a result, some of the attacking infantry, even those who would be the first to arrive in the German trenches and capture them, were heavily laden with the tools and supplies

needed to defend the captured trenches from the expected counter-attacks, in addition to their own weapons, rations and equipment. It is commonly alleged that the average load carried by an infantryman as he assaulted the German lines was about 60 pounds in weight, something between 25 and 30 kilograms. Thus many infantrymen, generally smaller and slighter than their modern equivalents, were expected to advance whilst carrying one third or more of their own body weight in equipment. Whilst there were instances when soldiers went over the top grossly over-laden, the majority of evidence is that they were actually exceptions, not the rule.

8. Finally, few of the soldiers actually taking part in the assault knew what they were doing in the context of the overall scheme. Lacking training and experience, they were not expected to think for themselves and all were tied to the inflexible timetable.

Thus the British competitors in the foot race were mostly unaware that they were in such a race, and fewer still realised that the race included some unknown entrants, the German machine gunners sheltering underground but still able to emerge into their own trenches when need arose. In due course the actual race would have its own name, 'The Race for the Parapet'. If the British infantry could get to the parapet before the Germans, they would win this heat of the race, preventing the Germans from manning the trenches and so taking control of them. If the Germans could get to the parapets first, they could set up their machine guns, and the rest would be obvious.

These factors came together to reveal the fatal flaw in the battle plan. All the plans had presumed on German counter-attacks, after their trenches had fallen to the assault, but always presumed the success of the assault beforehand. There was no contingency plan for the possibility of not reaching the German trenches, let alone for deciding what to do if the attack might succeed in some places but not others.

Let us return to 0730 and the events after the whistles were blown. There can be no short way of describing the experiences of 60,000 men as they climb out of their trenches and discover the reality of uncut wire and undestroyed machine guns. It is more practical to focus on a few individual events and places, selected only for the reason that all the sites can be visited and the events visualised by the visitor. They run from north to south. They are Serre, Beaumont Hamel, Thiepval, the Schwaben Redoubt, La Boiselle and Mametz.

Serre

The fortified village of Serre lies at the very north of the main attack front, and therefore a mile or two south of the diversion at Gommecourt. Thirty-first Division was to take the village, hold it and form a guard on the flank of the divisions further south who would be attacking deeper into the German lines. After success further south the division would form the fulcrum around which the attack could develop as Lieutenant General Sir Hubert Gough's Reserve Army swept through the gap and rolled up the German armies northwards.

The story of 31st Division and its part in the Battle of The Somme is perhaps as tragic as any single paragraph in any chapter of the history of Britain's armies in the war. To understand the tragedy we need to list the battalions who made up the Division, with their names in common use at the time:

Fourth Army – General Sir Henry Rawlinson, Bt.
VIII Corps – Lieutenant General Sir Aylmer Hunter-Weston, promoted since Gallipoli
31st Division – Major General Robert Wanless O'Gowan

92 Brigade
Hull Commercials, 10th (Service) Battalion East Yorkshire Regiment
Hull Tradesmen, 11th (Service) Battalion East Yorkshire Regiment
Hull Sportsmen, 12th (Service) Battalion East Yorkshire Regiment
Hull T'Others, 13th (Service) Battalion East Yorkshire Regiment

93 Brigade
Leeds Pals, 15th (Service) Battalion West Yorkshire Regiment
1st Bradford Pals, 16th (Service) Battalion West Yorkshire Regiment
2nd Bradford Pals, 18th (Service) Battalion West Yorkshire Regiment
Durham Pals, 18th (Service) Battalion, Durham Light Infantry

94 Brigade
Accrington Pals, 11th (Service) Battalion, East Lancashire Regiment
Sheffield City Battalion, 12th (Service) Battalion, Yorkshire & Lancashire Regiment
1st Barnsley Pals, 13th (Service) Battalion, Yorkshire & Lancashire Regiment
2nd Barnsley Pals, 14th (Service) Battalion, Yorkshire & Lancashire Regiment

Divisional Pioneers
Halifax Pals, 12th (Service) Battalion, King's Own Yorkshire Light Infantry.

The thirteen infantry battalions of this division amounted to about 13,000 volunteers, from the early days of the war, almost all drawn either from a small area of about 40 miles wide and 25 miles deep north-east of Manchester, or from the town of Hull to the east of there. The men of these battalions had joined up together and had been promised that they would serve together too. They were not totally inexperienced; the division had recently returned from a short posting in Egypt, defending the Suez Canal against any attempts to capture it or prevent its use by the British. The troops had acquired some experience of front-line conditions, albeit under such different conditions that the experience might be considered irrelevant.

The planned attack at Serre allowed twenty minutes to capture four lines of trenches, twenty minutes to consolidate and re-group, twenty minutes to take the village itself and a final ten minutes to capture the orchards and wood on the far edge of the village. Ninety-four Brigade was tasked to capture the village itself. Brigadier-General Hubert Rees had only been appointed to command the brigade two weeks before the battle, and thus had little time to know the ground or his men, but he did know what could and could not be done. He argued fiercely, one of the few officers of any rank prepared to do so, with his Corps Commander that such a timetable was utterly impractical. Furthermore, as the northernmost brigade was next to the sector between Serre and Gommecourt that was not being attacked, the assault forces were even more than usually vulnerable to be fired at from their left, northern side, by German forces under no sort of bombardment or attack.

It was Rees's misfortune that his Corps Commander, Hunter-Weston, was known throughout the army's officer ranks as 'Hunter-Bunter', but to the soldier ranks he was 'The Butcher of Helles'. He fits in every detail the common perception of the ignorant, stupid and stubborn general of the First World War; even his tall, upright stance and enormous moustache fitted the picture.

A short idea of Hunter-Weston's impact is given in Appendix I.

Hunter-Weston reluctantly allowed a compromise, an extra ten minutes, for the capture of the orchard at the extreme end of the brigade's objectives. Thus Rees and his men were to overrun four lines of trenches, capture a fortified village 800 yards deep, and capture a wood and some orchards 300 yards beyond, all in the space of eighty minutes. No thought appears to have been given to the German menace from the left.

When the officers' whistles blew at 0730 that morning, reality hit instantly. The Germans were not slow to use their advantage of higher ground and carefully prepared defences. Machine guns, away to the British left, between the Gommecourt diversion and the main assault, and under no risk of any kind, fired relentlessly into the mass of men moving up the muddy hill towards the trenches and village of Serre. Seven hundred and twenty men of the Accrington Pals had set off in the first wave of the assault, leaving, as usual, men to guard the vacated trenches, move forward after the attack with extra supplies, act as stretcher-bearers and form a core around which any battalion that was severely mauled could re-build. The distance of the advance to the first trenches was narrow at this point, a matter of perhaps 50-75 yards. A small handful was seen to reach the first German trench, along with some pioneers of the Halifax Pals. They were never seen alive again. Of the 720 men of the Accrington Pals in the advance, records show that 584, 80 per cent, were killed, wounded or missing.

A similar fate was to befall almost every one of the other seven assaulting battalions of 93 and 94 Brigades and the Halifax Pals. This last had been holding the line in the days preceding the assault, whilst the assaulting battalions were out of the line and preparing for their part in the attack. At a late moment many of the Halifax pioneers were moved into the assaulting battalions, where numbers were too low because of earlier casualties. Casualties in this small stretch of the front, on this first day of the battle, exceeded 3,600, about 450 men per battalion, 45 per cent of the nominal strength but nearer 60 per cent of the numbers actually engaged in the assault. With the exception of the few already mentioned, not one of the number had achieved an advance of more than about 50 yards.

The news from the Somme struck hard everywhere, and in Accrington the effect was typically terrible. Local papers published lists of the casualties, with photographs whenever possible. In every street in the town blinds were drawn down in mourning. This was a small town, where families worked together in the mills, inter-married, played their sports together and prayed in the same non-conformist churches and chapels. Every person in the town knew at least one person lost on this day. Most people knew many. There were many such tales of the fates of the Pals battalions, but as an illustration of many of the widest-held perceptions of the war, this story perhaps tells the most about what they meant in practice.

The village of Serre, of all the first day objectives the closest of any to the BEF trenches, remained in German hands until 24 February 1917. On that day the Germans abandoned their positions in the area as part of their withdrawal to the newly built Hindenburg Line a few miles back. Soldiers of the Manchester Regiment occupied the village on the following day unopposed. In the ruins of the village they found, unburied, fragments of bodies, clothing and equipment that showed the furthest extent of the failed assault by the Accrington and Halifax Pals eight months previously.

Beaumont Hamel

The German positions at Beaumont Hamel were based on two natural features, a small promontory in front of the village itself and a narrow ravine to the south. The former was one of the anchor strongpoints of the German front line, and the latter a superb natural position for tunnels, *Stollen,* that would be totally impervious to all British shelling and thus able to produce large numbers of reinforcements for the trenches in the area.

We have already heard that the mine under the Hawthorn Redoubt had been blown at 0720 rather than 0728. Here, more than anywhere else, the Germans had time to emerge from deep underground and man the trenches in time to repel the attacks that must follow such an explosion. British artillery fire onto the trenches between the redoubt and the ravine had ceased at 0720; the reason may have been a simple administrative error arising from arguments about when the mine was to be fired, the exact timing had been in doubt until the last days of the bombardment.

Hunter-Weston had given the task of taking this key segment of the front to the division he himself had commanded in Gallipoli, 29th Division; 'The Incomparable'. Major-General Henry Beauvoir de Lisle had taken command after Hunter-Weston had been invalided home from Gallipoli in circumstances that have never been explained. The division had been formed in 1915 of battalions drawn from British garrisons in the Dominions and Colonies around the world. Almost all regular army units, they were still partly made up of men of the pre-war army, although the division's months under Hunter-Weston's command in Gallipoli had diluted the ranks considerably.

On the right of the divisional front directly facing Y-Ravine stood four battalions of 87 Brigade, one from each of the four home counties. Two battalions would go forward in the first wave and two in the second. Three battalions of 88 Brigade – the 1st Battalion of the Essex Regiment, 2nd Battalion of the Hampshire Regiment and the 1st Battalion of the Newfoundland Regiment – were behind them, ready to go in as third and fourth waves later in the morning.

The Hawthorn Redoubt had been blown up, but deep in Y-Ravine a few dozen yards away the main numbers of Germans had huddled for a week, sleepless no doubt and fully aware of the dangers ahead, but unharmed and well-armed. As soon as the redoubt exploded, the Germans rushed from the ravine and took up their places in the trenches ahead of it. Across the open ground in front of them they could see the advancing South Wales Borderers and Royal

Inniskilling Fusiliers. As these battalions advanced, a machine gun post on their right, on the lip of Y-Ravine, opened fire. The South Wales Borderers were destroyed as a fighting force in moments. Advancing in smaller groups rather than extended line, the Fusiliers actually made their way into the ravine, to be met by the unharmed Germans in numbers.

Spasms of fighting continued in the trenches until 0805. Now the second wave began their advance, the Border Regiment and King's Own Scottish Borderers side by side. All order in the advance broke down at once, in the confusion of the remnants of the advance that had gone before. No troops of these battalions reached the German front line.

Back at divisional headquarters lack of information naturally led Beauvoir de Lisle to believe that all was going to plan, and he ordered 88 Brigade to advance in their turn. The right hand battalion, the Essex, simply could not move until the piles of dead and wounded had been removed from the trenches and gaps in the wire ahead of them. That left the Newfoundland Regiment to take up the running. They had reached their positions in the rearward trenches during the previous day and were due to move up to the front line, using communication trenches, immediately after 0730, ready to advance into no-man's-land at 0900.

By this time, nothing was moving anywhere in no-man's-land in front of the ravine. The Newfoundlanders knew that the battalions ahead had been checked and urgently needed help. They were blocked in the communication trenches by the effects of German counter-attacking artillery fire, by the stream of wounded already being carried back and by the sheer chaos of trying to move at speed in a ruined landscape. Impressed by the urgent needs of their comrades, a few, then more, and eventually all of the Newfoundlanders left the safety of the communication trenches and began to move more quickly across the open ground between the lines of British trenches. They were the only figures now moving above ground. Within moments a torrent of machine-gun fire was addressing them from the sides and front. As a unit the Newfoundland Regiment would not even reach its own start point for the assault. Numbers will be disputed forever, but one credible account recalls that 700 men had started the advance to assault, and that the evening roll call that day gave sixty-eight answers of 'Present'. The dead or missing accounted for 246, 386 were wounded. Every single officer was dead or wounded.

Y-Ravine fell to the British on 13 November 1916. Five days later General Haig closed down the Battle of The Somme. In the north progress had been slower than expected; Beaumont Hamel was a target for the first wave on the first day, not for four and a half months later.

The Newfoundland Regiment had insisted on being included in the British Army. They were not Canadians but subjects of the separate Crown Colony, and wanted to maintain their non-Canadian identity.

The Newfoundland Regiment re-formed and fought on. In 1917 it became only the third regiment ever to be renamed as a Royal Regiment during war, the first and only regiment of the Empire to be so honoured. Newfoundland remained a Crown Colony until 1949, when it became a province of Canada. Throughout Canada 1 July is celebrated as Canada Day, commemorating the creation of modern Canada by the British North America Act in 1867. In Newfoundland it remains Memorial Day during the morning of that day, in recognition of the events of 1 July 1916.

The Schwaben Redoubt

Thiepval Ridge rises from the River Ancre south of Beaumont Hamel and leads southward through the village of Thiepval and beyond. It is a particularly strong natural defensive position, and the Germans had improved its natural advantages by creating a large and complex defensive fortress on the crest of a spur running out of the ridge towards the British trenches and just behind their own forward defensive lines. The task of capturing this formidable obstacle fell to 36 (Ulster) Division. The division retained the name Ulster in its official title for good reason. Loyalist Ulster politicians had raised the paramilitary Ulster Volunteer Force – the UVF – before the war, to be ready to resist any attempt by Westminster to impose Home Rule from Dublin on the Ulster provinces. Westminster gave assurance to the Loyalist politician Sir Edward Carson that Home Rule would not be imposed on Ulster whilst the war was in progress, and Sir Edward accepted that assurance. In a considerable act of patriotism the entire UVF had volunteered for war service and the whole 36 (Ulster) Division was formed of men, already with unofficial military training, from the Force.

The early stage of the attack at 0730 was successful, and troops of the Royal Irish Rifles and Royal Inniskilling Fusiliers broke through the forward German trenches. As the Germans rallied their defence around the redoubt, opposition stiffened and casualties began to increase in numbers. The brigade in the second wave made good progress but in isolation from those on either side of the redoubt. The Ulstermen also caught up with their own artillery support and lost many men under that fire. Large numbers of German reinforcements began to arrive whilst fresh British reinforcements could not get past the now-intense German defensive fire from artillery as well as machine guns in strongpoints set behind the redoubt itself. The advances of the divisions on either side had failed to make progress, and at the end of the day the Ulstermen were ordered to fall back, unable to consolidate their own successes and unsupported on either side.

Casualties here, as in so many other parts of the assaulted front, were extremely heavy. Of the 13,000 infantrymen of the division, over 5,000 were casualties. These casualties were about 50 per cent of those who took part in the attack.

Thiepval

Thiepval village stands on another spur, further along the Thiepval Ridge. It is another natural defensive point and has been the site of human settlement since history began. In 1914 a village and chateau stood on the spur. There had been actions here since the start of the war, and the ruins of the buildings, and their cellars, provided ideal foundations for fortification of the area. Any possibility of a general advance towards the ridges to the north-east depended on taking this strongpoint.

> **More Pals battalions were to be found here. Three battalions of Salford Pals of The Lancashire Fusiliers, The Glasgow Tramways, Glasgow Boys Brigade and Glasgow Commercials Battalions of The Highland Light Infantry, and The Newcastle Commercials and Newcastle Railway Pals of The Northumberland Fusiliers were amongst them.**

Not only was the spur and village well-defended on the ground; strongpoints ahead and on both sides added to the overall strength of the position. The Schwaben Redoubt was only a few hundred yards to the north and well sited to provide machine-gun cover over the ground in front of Thiepval. The Leipzig Salient stood a short distance to the south, another heavily fortified position on a spur jutting right into the British trench line. The front line curved round the Thiepval spur in a horseshoe. The attack plan was simple; a frontal assault on Thiepval itself, coupled with a two-pronged attack from either side of the Leipzig Salient.

Inevitably, in general the attacks on this part of the front failed. To add to the failure, a few advancing BEF troops were seen to enter Thiepval village during the early stages of the day's work, and British artillery fire was therefore directed away from that strongpoint for the rest of the day. This allowed the Germans, who had not been dislodged, to deliver unhindered defensive fire from the Thiepval strongpoint for the rest of the day. Despite this general failure, the Leipzig Salient was taken and was held. The success was Pyrrhic; the success could not be exploited whilst Thiepval village remained in enemy hands.

That evening the Divisional Commander, Major-General Rycroft, wrote in his daily summary that the 19th Battalion of the Lancashire Fusiliers, the Third Salford Pals, had not left their trenches during the assault on the Leipzig Salient. They must be roused out and sent to work the following day. That order would not be obeyed; over three-quarters of the Third Salford Pals were casualties in the Leipzig Salient and few of that number had lived. Total casualties in the division on this day amounted to 3,949.

Thiepval itself was a key not just to this ridge but to the whole of the Somme battlefield. It would not fall until 26 September, almost three months after it had been set as an objective to be overrun in the first hour of the battle. The Glasgow Boys' Brigade Battalion, much reduced in numbers and several times reinforced with fresh drafts of men, fought in this area from the first day of the Somme battle until late November, after the battle had been 'closed down', in the jargon of the time.

La Boiselle

The D929 is a dead-straight old Roman road that runs almost exactly north-east from the town of Albert in the Somme *département*. The road was a particular feature in the Somme planners' minds; it lies in the middle of the BEF's sector where the battle would be fought. Its route lies exactly in the direction of the general line of advance, ending in the village of Bapaume, about 3 miles away from the BEF front line and at the crest of the ridge where lay the last lines of German defence in the area. To reach Bapaume one must pass the village of La Boiselle and then take the ridge of Pozieres lying at right angles to the road in front of and parallel to the main ridge at Bapaume itself. La Boiselle, Pozieres Ridge and Bapaume Ridge form three conveniently placed objectives, on a map, for the first assault, second wave of morning attacks and afternoon follow-up on the first day of the infantry part of the battle. Once past Bapaume, open country beckoned and the cavalry could be let loose on the unprotected German depots and lines of communication.

At the centre of the front of the BEF's assault, the trench lines crossed the road a mile or two from Albert where the village of La Boiselle lies just to the south side of the road. As usual, the Germans had used the land and resources effectively, fortifying the hillock that lies beside La Boiselle, and of course making the best possible use of the village buildings and cellars. The village and hillock lie between two valleys that lie parallel to the road. Sausage Valley lies to the south of the road and village, named by the BEF because of the sausage-shaped German observation balloon that occasionally flew over the German lines at the head of the valley. With obvious logic, the valley to the north of the road was named Mash Valley. Because the German lines followed the contours, the fortified area of village and hillock jut forward from the main north-south German line in a rectangular area about 400 yards by 300 yards. The area of the fortified village so dominates the ground in front of it that no-man's-land was exceptionally wide here, in places hundreds of yards of open land between the forward positions of each army. However, just by the village and road itself there is some ground not directly overlooked by the German defences, and here the old French trench system ran up to the limits of this 'dead ground'. No-man's-land was only about 50 yards wide here. This point of close proximity to the Germans was an area of constant sniping, mortar attacks and other activity, where casualties tended to run high even at times when no specific large-scale action was taking place. The trenches earned the ironic name 'The Glory Hole', in recognition of the opportunities for death or glory to be found easily there.

The strongpoint of La Boiselle would have to be eliminated for progress to be made in this sector. Mining was the answer, and in the months before the battle two tunnels were dug, from some distance behind the BEF lines to avoid German observation of activity round the tunnel entrances. One the north side of the road Y Sap mine contained 18 tonnes of Ammonal high explosive. To the south of the road under the fortified hillock, the Lochnagar mine was a complex affair with a single tunnel leading to two chambers. One chamber was packed with 15 tonnes of ammonal, the other with 11 tonnes.

> **Ammonal is a mixture of TNT, ammonium nitrate and aluminium powder. It is almost as powerful as pure TNT, trinitrotoluene, which formed the basis of most explosive mixtures in the twentieth century before the general use of 'plastic' explosives. Gelignite was the first plastic explosive, invented in 1875, but it was not much used in the Great War.**

The assault on this vital strongpoint was entrusted to the New Army 34th Division. The four battalions of Tyneside Scottish (102 Brigade) and four more of Tyneside Irish (103 Brigade) were in this division. These were all battalions of the Northumberland Fusiliers. The third brigade of the division, 101, was made up of a mix of battalions: two from Edinburgh, 'The Cambridge Battalion' from Suffolk, and The Grimsby Chums. The Division's pioneer battalion, being used as a fighting battalion for this assault, was another battalion of the Northumberland Fusiliers.

The plan was simple. The Tyneside Scottish and two battalions of Tyneside

Irish would lead the assault on the village and hillock, on either side of the main road. The remainder would by-pass the fortified area and advance across no-man's-land in Sausage Valley and capture the redoubt at the head of it. This was an advance across a full half-mile from one front line to the other. At the same time the remaining Tyneside Irish would leave their trenches, almost a mile behind the front line. Advancing through the first wave of assault troops they would press on towards Pozieres Ridge and take that in preparation for the afternoon assault on Bapaume itself. Major-General Edward Ingouville-Williams – 'Inky Bill' – decided that his 34th Division would achieve its objectives by a single all-out assault. No reserves would be held back and he was prepared for heavy casualties.

It was thought that when the mines were blown it would take two minutes for the thousands of tonnes of earth to fall back to earth, so the two mines at Y Sap and Lochnagar were blown at 0728 along with the others all along the line of assault. Two minutes after the mines were fired, officers blew their whistles and the division set off, nearly 10,000 men in this one sector of the front. Patrols and raids had confirmed that the German wire was inadequately cut, but there were gaps. Ingouville-Williams' Divisional Staff Officers were confident that there were enough gaps for the assault to succeed. As the infantry set off, the artillery barrage that had lasted the whole week moved on, from the German front line to the next lines.

The assault was a disaster. Despite the bombardment and despite the mines, enough Germans had survived in the shelters under the village and hillock to drag their machine guns up to the parapets. The debris from the mines had long settled before the BEF men were even moving out of their trenches and where German trenches had disappeared, the high lips thrown up around the mine craters by the settling debris formed raised vantage points on which to mount the machine guns. From here the Germans saw the whole of 34 Division spread out in the fields in front of them, some very close, some a mile or more away. A handful of the Newcastle men did fight their way into the German trenches. A few actually got as far as Contalmaison, the village behind La Boiselle on Pozieres Ridge. The majority got nowhere. The thirteen attacking battalions lost an average of 500 men each, out of about 700-800 from each battalion who actually went into the assault. Ingouville-Williams had been ready to accept high casualty rates in pursuit of success, and had told his brigade commanders so. The end truth was that his division suffered the highest casualty rate of the whole Somme first day and utterly failed in its mission. Over 10 per cent of all the casualties of the first day fell in this one of eighteen divisions taking part, almost all within one hour of the battle's beginning.

British troops eventually entered Bapaume, an objective for Day One, in

February 1917. The village had been abandoned, like Serre and the rest of the Somme battlefield, in the German retirement to the Hindenburg Line. It would fall again into German hands in early 1918 before finally passing into Allied hands for the last time.

> The Lochnagar crater at La Boiselle has been preserved, the last highly visible evidence here of the underground warfare that was the only answer to the problems of breaking down strongpoints and creating breaches in the line.

Mametz

This is one of two villages lying at a pivotal point in the line. To the left the line runs north, but to the right it turns at a right angle and runs east. Mametz itself lies at the tip of a pronounced spur with a valley running like a crescent moon around it. It would be impossible to advance up the valleys, on either side, without first securing Mametz. Unfortunately, the general principle of attacking all along the front simultaneously dictated that the advance up the valleys would begin simultaneously with the assault on the village strongpoint.

Almost opposite Fricourt and Mametz villages, 7th Division were to move through the villages and on the adjacent village of Fricourt and the woods behind. The 9th Devonshires were almost at the very point where the BEF line turned from east to west and started north. They had been here for some time, and knew the view from their trenches. Captain D. Martin, the Regimental Bombing Officer, had made a particular study of the German defensive layout. It was his task to ensure that his bombers would know exactly where to go and what defensive positions they were to destroy with their hand-thrown bombs. The more he studied the ground, the more certain Martin became that a German machine gun sited under the concrete foundations of a large cross in the Mametz village cemetery would cause great damage to his battalion during this early part of their planned advance. He took maps home when he went on leave and made a Plasticine model of the ground and the main features. Looking at the model from every angle simply confirmed his certainty.

In the Devonshires' trench, as all along the line, the officers blew their whistles at 0730 and the attacking troops rose up from their trenches to advance. The German machine gun under the cross was already in position, and many Devonshires fell back into the trench that they just vacated, dead. At the end of that day burial parties were hard at work, and as there were so many Devonshire dead already in the trench the burial party simply placed more from the area into it as well, and filled in the trench as a makeshift mass grave. Tradition has it that a surviving member of the battalion placed a hand-written placard above the mound: 'The Devonshires held the trench, The Devonshires hold it still.' It is one of the most poignant moments in any trip to the Somme battlefield to stand in that cemetery, a double row of graves on the side of the hill, to visualise the moments of carnage as the whistles died away and the troops climbed up to their deaths. It is easy to walk from that trench across the valley in front of it to the crucifix in the cemetery and understand how it was impossible for anybody to take the same path in front of that machine gun. However, the machine-gun nest was taken by other troops during the morning, and the 8th Devonshires, with the Gordon Highlanders on their right, were able to advance again and join the operation to clear the fortified village of its defenders. On this part of the front the day was also ultimately a success.

The traditional tale of the sign above the line of burials in the trench is more emotive than the prosaic diary entry of the chaplain of the battalion, Ernest Crosse, who wrote: 'All together we collected 163 Devons and covered them up in Mansell Copse. A colossal thunderstorm at about two pm delayed us sorely. At six pm, in the presence of the General, Fosse, Milne and about 60 men, I read the funeral service and "Thanksgiving for Victory". The working party was deadbeat and the task of filling in the trench was awfully slow. I got the pioneer serjeant to paint a board with red lead borrowed from the Royal Engineers to mark the cemetery. I put up the board – Cemetery of 163 Devons Killed July 1st 1916 – I placed 12 crosses in two rows, and after wiring in the area I rode back.'

Eighteenth Division occupied the next part of the line beyond Mametz for some months, and the commander of that division, Major-General Ivor Maxse was as unlike the stereotyped 'donkey' general as any in the war. He had realised by March that the major offensive of 1916 must involve the sector occupied by his division and had diligently used the time to prepare for the offensive. He ordered constant patrolling in no-man's-land to gain every possible piece of information about the German defences. As the picture built up he had the layout of the front lines replicated in the country behind his divisional frontage. He planned every aspect of the coming attack on the principle that the Germans would not be destroyed by the preliminary bombardment, and he planned his own use of artillery rather differently. He wanted his troops trained to advance in small groups, some rushing forward whilst others offered covering fire, the roles of each group alternating to maintain momentum, and ensuring that the effectiveness of the covering fire increased as the covering groups got closer and closer to the German defences. This method had been developed in the various colonial wars after Waterloo, and perfected in the South African wars of the 1890s and first years of the new century, but Maxse was one of the few generals who believed that the new volunteer army could be taught it in time for the 1916 offensive.

Maxse's other insight was to recognise the need to get his troops as close to the German lines as possible before they came under fire. To achieve this he started the building of Russian Saps, another system that had fallen into disuse elsewhere. A Russian Sap is a tunnel dug towards the enemy lines so close to the surface that when the attack is launched the attackers can collapse the tunnel roof, advance troops into what has now become a trench far closer to the defenders than the latter have expected, and advance from there with less distance to move under fire. In addition to the fortifications of Mametz village, Maxse's Division faced two well-known strong points on the spur of the hill on which Mametz lies. Tunnelling companies placed small but effective mines under both. They both achieved their aims, neutralising these key defensive points at the moment of the actual assault.

Recent suggestions by the BBC TV Timewatch programmes give credit for success at Mametz to the Livens Large Gallery Flame Projector, a giant flame-thrower deployed in the assault. In reality this fearsome machine could only dominate about 75 yards of front. There was undoubted small and local tactical advantage, but nothing more.

Apart from believing in preparation and using imaginative tactics, Maxse was confident in the ability of his command to learn to fight according to circumstances rather than to a rigid timetable. Further to the right, 30th Division and the left-hand side of the French assault, under the redoubtable Fayolle, also succeeded. The advance was limited only by the local Corps Commander's recognition of the dangers of trying to do too much, and by the failure of the attacks to his left.

Sir Ivor Maxse was acknowledged as having created the best fighting division of the BEF in 1916. He commanded a corps during 1917 including Third Ypres and ended the war as Director General of Training. He was convinced that the Armistice in 1918 would achieve nothing but buy time for Germany to re-arm and try again for world conquest.

The End of Day One

Planning for the start of the battle seemed to have assumed a neat one-day affair, taking as many as nine lines of German trenches and followed by sweeping cavalry charges across the disordered German rear areas and bases. There was no plan for dealing with the actual outcome, achievement on the right and total failure everywhere else. Haig himself had mixed feelings from the outset of planning for the battle. On the one hand he was acutely aware that the Allies could only win the war together, and that campaigning on the Western Front needed cooperation with the French. After all, that was the reason why he had agreed to fight the battle at a time and place not of his choosing. But he was not blind to the probable cost of this battle, and indeed he was fully aware of Rawlinson's own preparation for the evacuation of the high numbers of expected casualties. However Haig's misgivings did resurface and he stated that he would abandon the battle if the first stages were not successful. That begs the question: what measure enabled him to think that the first day was anything but a disaster? Sixty-thousand casualties, little tangible gain of ground, and no major inconvenience to the Germans along most of the front scarcely constituted success. The truth was that Haig did not know, could not know, just what had happened that day until later. So what had gone wrong with the essential business of gathering information on that day? The answer falls into three categories, gathering information, interpreting it and delivering it.

Gathering Information

At 0730 on 1 July the conduct of the battle passed from the hands of the generals and planners into those of the lieutenant-colonels and battalion officers, who were to become proportionately the most likely to be casualties as they led from the front. Most of them were fully occupied in fulfilling their immediate tasks in the assault, and the flow of information back from the front was slow and in places almost impossible to maintain. 'Runners', the message carriers of the infantry battalion, were the only practical way for getting information back from the advance, and the casualty rate among the runners was inordinately high. The advance, where it had achieved any progress, had taken the assaulting troops into the ground over which rain had fallen for the early days of the preliminary bombardment and which had then been ploughed and re-ploughed by the bombardment itself. The Germans were still in command along most of the front, and crossing the open ground between the opposing front lines to get information back was an invitation to any alert machine gunner. Under these circumstances, it is no surprise that there was much speculation at brigade and divisional headquarters about what was happening. However, in many places almost no hard information came back from the attacking battalions to the commanders behind them.

Interpreting Information

The generals had set out their expectations and had issued their orders. Haig himself was satisfied that he had done his best and the result was now for God to settle. Rawlinson had written that the German front lines could not survive the week-long storm of shell-fire, and at lower levels of command there had been Orders of the Day stressing the overwhelming certainty of success. He was a brave man who dared throw the stone of truth into this pool of calm certainty. Intelligence officers were ordinarily human and few wanted to face the wrath of the commanders who had promised a victory. As a result the general tendency was for the intelligence assessments of the first day to seek the positives and play down the unpalatable. Casualty numbers were placed at the lower end of any suggested range and successes in taking German positions were played up.

The intelligence officer's analytical process is meant to provide clear, rigorous analysis; misinterpretation or distortion of intelligence information should have been anathema to the officers of the intelligence branch. But another insidious factor of human nature was at work. Where enough reports were coming through to permit analysis based on fact rather than hope, and the true picture could have been pieced together, the truth still did not come out. The concept of cognitive dissonance may have been known but it was not named or understood. The hierarchical training and way of life of the conformist officer of the late Victorian era placed store by confident certainty and top-to-bottom command structures. Perhaps we should not be surprised that these intelligence officers could simply deny evidence that cast doubt on their superiors' pre-formed decisions. Delivery of contradictory evidence reflected on the messenger and so debased the quality of the message. Thus the intelligence reports were simply inadequate as the basis for any decisions about the future of the battle.

Delivering Information

When the daily intelligence gathering was done and its analysis completed, it ultimately fell to Charteris, Haig's Chief Intelligence Officer, to deliver the whole truth to Haig himself. Rawlinson may have been the army commander fighting the battle but the ultimate decision and responsibility always remained Haig's own. Indeed history has criticised Haig for his over-interference in Rawlinson's battle. Charteris had been with Haig since before the war, as Assistant Military

Secretary during Haig's term at Aldershot Command and thereafter as a key member of the staff in intelligence positions. He was known behind his back as 'The Principal Boy', the theatrical support for Haig as the leading man. In his later writings about Haig, which became his principal source of income in later life, Charteris confirmed that he saw part of his role as Chief Intelligence Officer as being to manage Haig's information sources and avoid distressing him with upsetting news. We cannot know how Charteris presented what was known of the casualties and wreckage of 1 July when giving his report that evening, but in the event the battle was not called off, and indeed it would continue, in its twelve separate sub-battles for a further 140 days.

2 July and Onwards

It is easy to see the Battle of The Somme as an isolated incident, a single day on the middle day of the middle year of the war. We have already placed it alongside Verdun, the Brusilov Offensive and the Isonzo Offensives of the same year, and that certainly implies that this was no one-day affair. At its end, the first day was not seen as the disaster that we recognise today; nonetheless the lack of success was not denied. However, it was too soon for Haig to abandon the battle, as he had planned to do if unsuccessful. In any event, that was not a real option given the French Army's plight. Fortunately, generals could learn quickly when faced with the reality of events as they unfolded so tragically. Rawlinson, in particular, was able to plan and mount successfully a major night attack within a fortnight, starting from the ground in the south won at such cost only thirteen days earlier. A night attack is a singularly difficult battle to stage and manage, and the success on 14 July suggests that the BEF were quicker learners than its leaders had thought possible before 1 July. The second-line village of Longueval was taken in this attack, and the BEF had a foothold along the southern edge of the important Delville Wood, near Montauban at the southern end of the battle.

Fromelles

Recently attention has turned to an engagement that was originally intended to divert German attention from the Somme before the battle, but which eventually became an attempt to force the Germans to move some reserves from behind the Somme front after the battle had started. The small village of Fromelles stands 40 miles north of the Somme on a pronounced spur projecting from the German defensive line and dominating all the lower ground surrounding it on three sides. The Germans had prepared this small area thoroughly, and turned it into a miniature fortress. An intense but short bombardment preceded an attack in broad daylight at 1800 on 19 July. The British 61st Division and the 5th Australian Division, who had arrived in France less than two weeks before, were inexperienced troops, facing their first action of any note. Both divisions were wrecked, the Australians suffering 5,533 casualties and the 61st Division about 1,500. This was the most costly single day in Australian military history. On the following day British GHQ issued a press communiqué, noting that 'Yesterday evening, south of Armentieres we carried out some important raids on a front of two miles in which Australian troops took part. About 140 German prisoners were captured.' In his own report, the local Corps Commander, Sir Richard Haking, noted that: 'The attack, though it failed, has done both divisions a great deal of good.'

Official British reaction to the attack on Fromelles caused very deep and lasting resentment among the Australian forces and at home in Australia. After the war the Battle Nomenclature Committee did not consider Fromelles important enough to be given the title of Battle. After this action the Australians referred to 'Butcher Haking'. At least one author has tried to give this a positive slant, suggesting that to the Australians this might almost be a term of affection. This interpretation is not generally accepted, especially in Australia.

After the battle, the Germans buried the Allied dead in three mass graves, which were uncovered, with the bodies re-buried in nearby cemeteries in the 1920s. Almost ninety years after the action an Australian amateur historian, Lambis Englezos, provided enough evidence for a detailed investigation of a site where he believed that one mass grave had been missed by the Imperial War Graves Commission.

In 2010 the Commonwealth War Graves Commission created the first new war cemetery since the Falklands War, when the Prince of Wales and the Governor-General of Australia attended the dedication of the Fromelles (Pheasant Wood) Military Cemetery. It contains the bodies taken from the re-discovered mass grave, of which 203 have been identified as Australian. All of the first seventy-five bodies for which DNA testing has been completed have been identified, and the process of matching names to bodies will continue.

Delville Wood

'Devil's Wood' lies behind the village of Montauban at the south-eastern end of the ridge that formed the main German defensive line. As with villages, the German defenders used the dense woods of the area as anchor points for their defences, and Delville Wood's commanding position made it an obvious strongpoint. The night attack on 13 July gave the slightest of footholds along the southern edge of the wood.

One South African Infantry Brigade had arrived in France in November 1915, and after training had arrived in the Somme sector on 2 July to take part in the actions in the area at the south-eastern end of the BEF line. The brigade took part in actions in the notorious Bernafay Wood and Trones Wood in this area. They suffered 537 casualties.

Following the success of the night attack on 13 July, the most immediate local objective was to capture the main part of Delville Wood, still in German hands. At its greatest dimensions the wood stretched about 500 yards in width and little more than that in depth. Given its size, the wood scarcely warranted a full brigade's attack. The South African brigade was set the objective of clearing the wood and on the morning of 15 July, 3,153 men of the brigade launched their attack from the modest area already held.

For seven days the South Africans held on in the wood. German artillery counter-attacks destroyed almost every tree, and smashed their trunks into pieces that made movement around the wood almost impossible. The bombardment also made it impossible for reinforcements or supplies to reach the South Africans. Food and water ran low and ammunition was entirely gone. The only way of holding the wood was to wait until German infiltrators got close enough to where the South Africans were taking cover in shell holes and behind trees, and then attack with bayonets.

On the eighth day fresh troops could at last relieve the South Africans, who withdrew. One hundred and forty-two men of the brigade came out of the wood. After assembling brigade troops not taking part inside the wood, the 1 South African Brigade could count 780 men remaining of the 5,628 officers and men who had landed in France six months before.

> **Three VCs were awarded for actions during the five-day engagement, and a fourth for actions in the wood a week later. In all the South Africans received sixty-three gallantry medals for their part in the action at Delville Wood.**

Pozieres Ridge

This ridge lies astride the Albert to Bapaume road, almost at a right angle. It is a pronounced height above the German first lines of defence, and formed a natural second line behind them. The usual German plan to anchor the defences on fortified villages worked as well here as in the front lines that this second line overlooked. Any plan to take ground in the region demands that the ridge be captured. Whilst it remains in enemy hands no significant progress can be expected on either side. A breakthrough here could indeed lead to great results, because the third line of German defences was little more than a plan at this time. It had been a part of Rawlinson's plans to take the ridge on 1 July.

By mid-July, Rawlinson's Fourth Army was in little state to assault, take and hold the ridge. Gough's Reserve Army took over the responsibility. On 23 July, after some very hurried planning and preparation, and just two days after their arrival on the Somme front, 1 ANZAC Corps assaulted the village of Pozieres, 200 yards from their own trenches. The village fell quickly, in less than two hours. Getting up onto the ridge took a further four days, and by this time the BEF casualties, largely Australian, reached about 3,500. Two weeks after the first assault the ridge was in Australian hands. However, as so often, mere possession was insufficient. German positions, at Mouquet Farm behind the immediate slope of the ridge and at Thiepval, had to be subdued if the ridge was to be held. Gough instructed the Australians to press on. Success simply created a pocket where the Australians had penetrated further than other BEF formations were able to do on either flank. Seeking to develop this foothold absorbed attention for another three weeks, whilst the number of Australian casualties rose inexorably. In five weeks, Australia suffered 23,000 casualties, but Mouquet Farm and Thiepval remained in German hands.

The area around Pozieres, centred on the local windmill, saw more bloodshed than any other piece of ground in the whole Somme sector. The Cemetery beside the Albert Bapaume road has a memorial wall that marks the names of 14,600 men who died here and whose bodies were either not found or not identified. The cemetery, often passed as one visits the Somme battlefields, also contains 2,758 burials, including 1,380 graves of unidentified bodies. The ground around Pozieres contains a great many unfound bodies.

Flers-Courcelette

The battle ground through its third month, but in the north objectives set for Day One had not yet been achieved. To help break the deadlock a new weapon was about to take to the field. By mid-September the BEF could boast slightly fewer than fifty tanks ready to take part, and all were sent to the area behind Pozieres to support a new attack. On the morning of 15 September, the attacking infantry of twelve divisions went over the top, with about 100,000 men in the advance. One third of the tanks due to take part did not get to the start line, and another third failed to get past it. Only fifteen tanks actually proved reliable enough to take part in the advance. The effect was tremendous. German resistance broke in many places, and a famous report by a reconnaissance pilot of the Royal Flying Corps noted that 'A Tank is walking up the High Street of Flers with the British Army cheering behind'.

Closing Down The Somme

As the summer went on a series of further battles were fought, each intended to take ground that originally had been fleetingly mentioned as places through which the attacks would pass on the first morning of the infantry assault. The first battle, starting on 1 July itself, was actually the Battle of Albert. What we know as the Battle of The Somme actually covers this whole campaign of a dozen separately identified battles.

The last battle of the campaign was the Battle of The Ancre, starting on 1 October. It was one last attempt to capture Thiepval and other heights overlooking the River Ancre. As with some of the other later battles in the campaign, Gough's Reserve Army was selected for the task. Careful planning and by now skilled execution achieved the desired result, a victory for Haig to take to the Allied planning conference due to start at the end of the month. Haig neglected to order the end of the offensive after these successes, so Gough pressed on again, and the result was that the battle over the last four days of the Somme campaign was another failure, a lot less costly than that first day of hope in July, but a failure nonetheless.

October had turned into November, winter set in and the ground broke down into that singular clinging combination of clay and chalk that made all off-road movement almost impossible. Haig had something he could call success to take to the conference at Versailles; and so on 18 November, 140 days after that first calamitous day of assault, the battle formally ended.

The French on The Somme

It is rarely mentioned in short histories that the French did indeed take part in the Somme campaign during the summer and autumn of 1916. They were to the east of the BEF, astride the Somme River, and had set the town of Péronne as the central objective of their line of advance. The initial French contribution was an attack by only five divisions on a relatively short front. However, the greater fighting experience of the troops involved and the much better equipped and trained artillery presence gave the initial French assaults an impetus that their highly skilled commander, Marie-Emile Fayolle, never let flag. With smaller numbers, Fayolle's Sixth Army attacked on an 8-mile front, compared with the 12 miles of the BEF's front in the campaign. By the close of the campaign the French gains in territory were broadly the same as the BEF's. Even this parity of achievement in territorial terms reflects the French need to hold back their advance in order to maintain contact with the BEF on their left.

> **It is rightly argued that the strongest German defences were situated opposite the BEF front, and that the French faced little to compare with the fortress villages that formed the heart of the German front line north of the River Somme. Nonetheless, the French achievement during what was for them the secondary campaign of 1916 was one of the few bright achievements for France after three years of the war.**

Verdict on The Somme

Arguments continue to this day about whether the Battle of The Somme was a success. However, it has never been disputed that during the opening moments of the assault, which are generally called the first morning of the battle, the British Army suffered its greatest-ever one-day disaster. The day's official final casualty toll, 57,540 or some number close to that, can more easily be remembered as 20,000 dead and 40,000 wounded; 40 per cent of those who climbed out of their trenches on that day. A further 360,000 casualties would be the toll of the continuation of the battle.

The Germans lost almost the same overall numbers during the whole battle over five months, 437,000 against 420,000 of the BEF, but when the French casualties, 200,000, are counted as well it must be admitted that if the principal plan was to kill Germans it backfired horribly. The simple casualty figures conceal another truth. Whilst the French casualties were about 200,000, the German casualties on the French front were similar. This suggests that the BEF's 420,000 casualties must be weighed against the Germans' loss of about 220,000 on the BEF front. If the plan was to relieve pressure on Verdun, which was undoubtedly the prime reason for Haig's committing to the campaign, the plan succeeded as soon as von Falkenhayn ceased all reinforcement on the Verdun front. If the plan was to break through as a preliminary to driving the Germans out of France, it has to be called a failure. However, the counter-argument is that in 1916 the twin battles of Verdun and The Somme laid the seeds of the collapse of the German Army in 1918, and on those grounds the Battle of The Somme may be called a great Allied victory. Or not.

Noel Chavasse VC, MC

The Liverpool Scottish came out of the line to re-form after their losses at Ypres in 1915. In August 1916 they were back in action, in the very eastern, right-hand, end of the Somme front. Chavasse was, as always, much in evidence, believing that the soldiers were encouraged by seeing him, 'a practical civilian', as he described himself, sharing their hardships. A tooth abscess led to a visit to the dentist, known to Chavasse through their peacetime work. The dentist extracted half the tooth but broke it during the extraction and left the other half in place. A couple of shell splinters in Chavasse's back were also painful.

The battalion was part of 55th Division, which was to mount an offensive on 9 August against the woods and strongpoints east of Mametz and below the overhanging mass of Delville Wood, by now almost universally known by its anglicised name 'Devil's Wood'. The Liverpool Scottish medical officer was at his usual post in the very front lines. A chapter of errors and setbacks preceded the attack, and despite the battalion's rallying four times and making four charges on their particular objective of the village of Guillemont, the attack was wrecked in the fields on uncut barbed wire, with seventeen of the twenty officers and ninety-six other ranks killed or missing and 167 wounded.

That night Chavasse was seen in no-man's-land, torch in hand, searching for wounded, collecting identification tags from corpses and marshalling stretcher-bearers to take the wounded back into the battalion's trenches. He was again slightly wounded, this time in the thigh by another shell splinter, but was only away from the battalion for a month. In October the Under-Secretary of State for War, Lord Derby, wrote to his old friend the Bishop of Liverpool; the bishop's son Noel was to be awarded the Victoria Cross. His constant willingness to expose himself to mortal risk if that would enable him to do his job better, as he saw it, had been acknowledged.

Walter Tull

Less than a mile away to the north another of the war's extraordinary men was taking part in the same attack. The story of Walter Tull is remarkable, even among many others. He was the grandson of a Barbadian slave, but an orphan from nine years old, raised in Bethnal Green Methodist Orphanage. A keen footballer he had been signed by Tottenham Hotspur, playing for them in their first ever game in the old first division. He was transferred to Northampton Town, which at that time was one of England's leading clubs, for whom he made over 100 first team appearances. He was the second black professional player in English football history. As soon as the war started he joined up as a volunteer in a new battalion, the 17th 'Sportsmen's' Battalion of the Middlesex Regiment. He had been promoted from Private to Lance Corporal, to Corporal and then again to Serjeant within a year. Tull was to survive the Somme, and service in Italy in 1917, before returning to serve again on the Somme front in 1918. He fought in six major battles including the Somme in 1916, Second Somme in

1918 and Passchendaele in 1917. None of this is as remarkable as one last fact. He was commissioned in 1917, the first, and for another thirty or so years, the only black officer in the British Army.

> For many years it was believed that King's Regulations specifically prohibited granting the King's Commission to 'Negroes and men of coloured blood'. This theory was set aside in a letter to *The Times*, 12 November 2010, pointing out that there was no such regulation as applied to a natural-born British subject such as Tull.

Feelers for Peace

Across the Atlantic, the peace-minded President Wilson was again seeking to act as the honest broker of agreement to end the war. The Austrians had a new Emperor Karl, who had already offered peace with France. Both initiatives had failed. America's motives were mistrusted, especially in Germany, where growing American industry and financial power were considered to favour the British far more than was right for a declared neutral power. Austria made no friends at all: the offer of territory to France in return for armistice was discovered to involve German lands, and they could neither show the French how they would deliver on their promise nor persuade Germany that they had not been making those promises.

5

1917 – The Year of Waiting

1916 was the year of Britain's trial on the Somme and France's ordeal at Verdun. 1917 was to produce the place-names of other battles that ring perhaps even more loudly across the years to the Canadian and ANZAC nations: Vimy Ridge and Passchendaele. However the year was to begin with events on the French front, at the Chemin des Dames, and end with the arrival of the Americans.

The Chemin des Dames

In the hilly and wooded country north-west of Reims and scarcely 80 miles from the city centre of Paris lies a long level ridge along which King Louis XVth made a ride for his daughters, Le Chemin des Dames. This formidable natural defensive position is perhaps the strongest on the whole Western Front. The Germans had been on the ridge since the trench stalemate had begun in late 1914, using their time to develop a complex of strongpoints, trenches and shelters dug into the hills. From here they looked down over the broken ground that lay between their lines and the River Aisne.

Following his success at Verdun, General Nivelle was promoted again, on the last day of 1916, and was now Commander-in-Chief, a stunning achievement for a man who had been a regimental colonel approaching retirement less than three years before. But, as he had claimed at Verdun, he had the secret.

The precise reasons for choosing to attack the Germans on the Chemin des Dames remain unclear. It had not been the point of attack agreed upon at the Allied planning conference in December 1916. However, Joffre had been Commander-in-Chief at that meeting and Nivelle felt no need to stick to that agreement. After all, Joffre had failed and Nivelle himself might reasonably think that he had been promoted for his better ideas. The best reason for attacking here was that here the lines were at the end of a huge German salient, whose northern end was at Arras, north of the Somme battlefield. Nivelle wanted the BEF to drive into the northern side of the mouth of this sack whilst he drove into the southern. The two armies would join up behind the Germans and capture everything and everybody in the salient. Pétain, who had been appointed Nivelle's deputy, and Haig both opposed this ambitious proposal. Paul Painlevé, the new Minister of War in the French government, also had doubts about the Nivelle plan. However, Nivelle countered political and military opposition easily, by threatening to resign. He knew that the government did not feel secure enough in public opinion to accept his threat. The Nivelle method by now seems familiar; a brisk artillery bombardment by 7,000 pieces of artillery, to be followed by an overwhelming assault involving over one million men in various ways, including the first line of assault units. The attack was so certain of success that Nivelle undertook to halt it after forty-eight hours if the breakthrough was not clearly being achieved. By the time he was ready to launch his attack, the Second Battle of The Aisne, Germany too knew his secret, not least because Nivelle was famously indiscreet in his conversations with politicians and newspapermen. It did not help that a French officer carrying a copy of the complete planning memorandum was killed on a reconnaissance patrol during the build-up, and the plans arrived safely in German higher command headquarters and were accepted as genuine. The Germans were as ready to receive the assault as any defender could possibly have wished.

The first day, 16 April, ended in disaster. Records were difficult to reconcile, but it is accepted that about 97,000 French were killed, missing or wounded at the end of the first day of this battle, about 60 per cent more than the BEF had lost on the first day of the Somme. For the next five days French casualties ran at about 6,000 a day, and on 3 May the French Army decided it had had enough. Troops began to demonstrate discord. One battalion marching towards the front passed a reviewing general with every man in the ranks bleating like sheep. Others were willing to stand in defence but make no further attacks. Unpopular officers were in danger of their lives. The government and military leadership feared that the French Army would simply leave their posts and go home, leaving France to a fate even more humiliating than the Franco-Prussian War. Nivelle's attack to win the war in 1917 was abruptly halted on 9 May. Nivelle was sacked and sent home.

> Nivelle's period as Commander-in-Chief had lasted less than five months. His periods of command at Verdun and on the Aisne, under the Chemin, had cost France more lives in less than two years than Napoleon cost her in nearly twenty.

Pétain, grumbling that 'They only ever send for me in an emergency', was hastily appointed Commander-in-Chief and set about addressing the crisis. He forced through much needed reforms in matters of leave, welfare and discipline, and undertook that he would launch no attacks on the Germans until his army would be ready to fight again. He also used the stick effectively; courts martial handed down numerous sentences of death, although the official records state that only fifty-five sentences were actually carried out. It is more likely that most regiments dealt with mutiny privately, and that the actual count of executions was rather higher.

> Folk history persists in recording that whole battalions where mutiny had been strongest were posted to quiet sectors where they could be cut to pieces by their own artillery. Rather stronger evidence than folk history indicates that a Russian division, fighting in France and aware of the collapse of both the Russian army and the Romanov Dynasty, joined the mutiny and was destroyed by French artillery units that had not mutinied.

For the rest of the year, Pétain was occupied in restoring the ability and will of the French Army. There could be no question of attack, and the contest must await the arrival of America before the next phases could begin.

Arras

In the meantime, as part of the Nivelle plan, the BEF had been fighting in the Arras region since early April. Preliminary bombardment had started on 20 March, and on 9 April the first attacks took place exactly one week before the Nivelle assault on the Chemin des Dames. The BEF were fulfilling their side of the agreement, despite Haig's and others' misgivings. The north of the campaign area brought immediate but patchy success. New German defensive tactics had been badly interpreted by the commanders on the ground and failed in places. The First Battle of The Scarpe, one of nine defined battles in the Arras campaign, ended to the BEF's advantage.

Vimy Ridge

To make any advance that could threaten the point where the German salient bulged out into the BEF's and French lines, Vimy Ridge, north of Arras, had to be captured. The French had been below the ridge ever since failing to take it in 1915. There had been the usual uncountable casualties in a number of attacks on it, about 150,000 in 1915 alone. However the BEF had taken over this part of the line to free French units to fight at Verdun. Nivelle's plan to attack the great German salient only needed an attack to penetrate south of this vital natural feature, but Haig insisted that capture of the ridge itself was essential for the protection of his Third Army's left flank as they conformed to Nivelle's plan. The task of capturing Vimy fell to the Canadian Corps, which for good reason the Germans viewed as the leading edge of BEF capability. As a rule the Canadians resisted all attempts to dilute their national force with any outsiders. Unusually, the Canadian Corps was reinforced by an English division for the attack on Vimy Ridge.

> **Sir Julian Byng had recently taken over command of the Canadian Corps. He was a descendant of the famous Admiral Byng, shot '*pour encourager les autres*', as Voltaire described his execution, for his performance at the Battle of Minorca in 1757, during the Seven Years' War. The admiral had been Commodore-General of Newfoundland before then, and his descendant, Sir Julian, was intensely proud of his family's renewed connection with the colony and the rest of Canada.**

For this attack, preparation was to be everything. Prefabricated light railways were built according to the Decauville model invented some years before the war. These brought supplies, especially of ammunition, water and food, right into the areas immediately behind the front lines. Twelve tunnels were dug from entry points well behind the BEF lines and out of German view. These tunnels ran right up to the front line, and were at different levels to allow troop movements, transport of stores and ammunition, laying water pipes, electricity cables and so on. Large shelters were built at the sides of the tunnels to give shelter to 24,000 troops who were right up close to the front line but in complete safety. A small hospital capable of full-scale surgery was built, together with headquarters and communications centres, all underground. In addition to the tunnels, mines had been dug under the German trenches at the top of the ridge some months before; General Horne in command of the First Army had long been aware that Vimy would have to be taken at some stage.

As the preparations for the assault developed, intensive training went ahead. A replica of the whole area to be attacked was laid out on ground with similar topography behind the army's front, and every man rehearsed his part in the assault. All knew exactly what they faced and what they were asked to achieve. The idea of the half-trained infantry advancing in lines to its slaughter was long out-dated. Artillery techniques were refined, and cooperation with infantry was taken to high levels of mutual confidence. When the advance took place the infantry would know that the shell-fall of the artillery's creeping barrage, was advancing across the ground at the same pace as their own advance on foot. It would be just in front of them and keeping the Germans below ground until they would be too late to emerge from shelter to resist the assault. Training included teaching troops a particular walking gait that ensured advancing at the predictable rate of 100 yards every three minutes. This was known as 'The Vimy Glide'.

A large force of Royal Flying Corps squadrons came into the sector. A force of twenty-five squadrons, with 365 aircraft, provided reconnaissance, artillery spotting and interdiction of airspace to German fliers. Casualties were heavy; the force lost over 130 machines in the week before the actual assault and another 150 or more as the month progressed. Manfred von Richthofen, The Red Baron, commanded *Jasta 11,* whose pilots claimed eighty-nine of the 298 RFC aircraft shot down in the battle. To the RFC this became known as 'Bloody April'. Despite this, the Germans did not establish control of the airspace, and were unable to obtain adequate intelligence about the build-up for the attack on the ridge.

The preliminary bombardment lasted over a week. Over 150,000 shells were fired each day, concentrated on specific targets within an area of about seven square miles. In total the shelled area was not significantly larger than Richmond Park. Over 700 light and medium guns and howitzers dealt with wire-cutting and preventing use of roads, whilst a further 250 large-calibre guns and howitzers delivered counter-battery fire and destroyed local strongpoints.

The infantry attack took place on the morning of Easter Monday, 9 April, the Canadians advancing out of their shelters, straight into their front lines, over the top and up the slope of the ridge. It took just two hours for the Canadians to take the majority of the ridge into their hands, and by nightfall most of the remaining pockets of resistance at the northern end had been taken. The last objective, the highest point on the ridge, fell on 12 April. A force of 100,000 soldiers had taken part in the assault. Casualties were under 10,000, and the ridge was in Allied hands, to remain so until the end of the war, despite events that would unfold to the south. As a set-piece assault on a strongpoint it was a classic success, delivering exactly what was promised, on time and below budget.

South of Vimy

With the ridge secured, the Third Army, under the vile-tempered Sir Edmund Allenby, could press ahead south of Arras and during the next six weeks the front line moved east for distances up to 5 or 6 miles on a front of 20 miles. One brigade of the 9th Division advanced 1.5 miles in a morning, behind a creeping barrage, hidden by smoke shells, and achieved all their objectives. This brigade suffered fewer than 250 casualties in return for capturing 2,100 prisoners and several machine guns. Other divisions passed through the stop-line of the

9th Division's attack. Twelve Brigade, made up of four English county regiments, typical of any infantry brigade at this stage of the war, took the fortified village of Fampoux at the cost of 147 casualties. They also captured 230 German guns. To their right, 11 Brigade achieved a record for any advance in the war so far, advancing over 3 miles against positions that the Germans had been fortifying for three years, and losing 302 men, killed wounded or missing, in the process. Clearly, it seemed that either the Germans had suffered the collapse in fighting ability so long prophesied by Haig and promised to London, or the British armies had thoroughly mastered the difficult business of attacking a heavily defended position. In due course it would appear that in fact the Germans had not tried too hard to defend these positions and had only been providing a screen of defence against too easy discovery of what was actually happening in this region.

First news of the French mutinies reached Haig's headquarters at the height of the Arras campaign. This desperate news could not be allowed to leak out, and the French effectively went into quarantine. The BEF must now bear the entire brunt of responsibility for engaging the Germans in 1917, and Arras must be continued, almost regardless of cost, until the French would be ready to take their share of the offensive again.

Arras was considered a success overall, but nothing could conceal the fact that after the early gains, particularly at Vimy Ridge, there had been little achievement of tactical or strategic importance.

The Hindenburg Line

Meanwhile what of the Germans sitting in the sack of their great salient? The Germans had known for months of the coming Nivelle Offensive, and without knowing the precise details of the BEF's contribution at the northern end, 60 miles away, had plenty of information to deduce that the forthcoming dual offensive was designed to pinch out this huge intrusion into France north-east of Paris. Rather than sit in the salient waiting to be evicted, the Germans built a new fortress line, the *Siegfried Stellung* – called the Hindenburg Line by the BEF – and its subsidiaries. This was a line across the mouth of the salient, running from east of Arras, behind the old Somme battlefield and on more or less south, past St Quentin, La Fere and on to Soissons, a distance of about 70 miles. They withdrew into the new shorter line in February and so released large numbers of troops from defence of the salient. They had systematically destroyed every road, bridge, building and well in the salient as they left, and had done everything possible to make the land unusable by enemy forces moving into the vacated area. Even the woods had been felled and burned. Crown Prince Rupprecht of Bavaria, already prominent in the battles in the area in 1916, was moved to protest at highest levels about this destruction. He believed it would haunt the German peoples in years to come, regardless of the war's outcome. He was over-ruled, and where there had been a salient the armies were now separated by miles of desolation, where even to move from place to place was a dangerous struggle. The battlefield was covered with unexploded artillery shells, the remains of barbed wire entanglements, deep shell holes and old trenches full of water, much of it within range of the German artillery behind the new lines. A final touch was applied by booby-trapping buildings and objects that might tempt a British soldier to pick up a discarded helmet or other souvenir.

A classically educated German planner gave the whole project, the building of the new line and withdrawal into it, the name *Operation Albericht*, after the malignant and deceitful dwarf of the legends of the Nibelungen.

Not only had the withdrawal shortened the German front line by 30 miles or so, it had taken them closer to the railheads and depots on which their long supply lines ultimately rested. In contrast, the Anglo-French advance up to the new front lines took them into a bleak and devastated land that would tax their ingenuity in logistics management for months to come.

Thus, in mid-1917, military honours so far for the year were not all to one side. The Germans had bloodily repulsed the French on the Aisne and the latter would be unable to play any more than a defensive role for some time. The BEF's Canadians had pushed the Germans off Vimy Ridge, and the Third Army had pushed the German line back east of Arras for about 5 miles. However, the Germans had improved their strategic position at the expense of the tactical withdrawal to the Hindenburg Line. In the east the Russians were collapsing into revolution and civil war, whilst the Austrians were making heavy weather of their struggles with Italy. On balance the outlook for the rest of the year seemed to favour Germany.

The Yanks are Coming

On 7 April, far-sighted German officers and politicians recognised that the war had been lost, with the US declaration of war the previous day. From now on there would be limitless supplies of matériel of all kinds, and effectively limitless supplies of troops available to take up where the Anglo-French effort might be hoped to have run its course.

The first US troops arrived in June, under their commander Major-General John Pershing. He had been a successful commander of cavalry recruited from the black US population, earning the nickname 'Black Jack'. He was stubborn, determined that his troops would not simply fall into any Anglo-French mincing machine, and utterly untrained for the scale of the task ahead of him. At the declaration of war the whole US Army owned fifty-five aircraft, and could ship fewer than 25,000 men to France. Pershing determined that he would husband his resources and await the build-up of men, matériel and experience before he allowed his army to take the field in any decisive way. He did not have to wait too long for the men or matériel; by the end of June he had about 175,000 men either in France or on their way. By the end of the war, just seventeen months after the US had joined it, Pershing had almost two million men under command in France, and an air force that boasted 17,000 aircraft. In 1917, the Allied question was how best to employ this war-winning recruit. The German question was how to win the war before the Americans could usefully intervene.

Third Ypres and Passchendaele

At the political level the French demanded renewed aggressive actions to divert German attention from their fragile army. In London, attention turned again to the Belgian coast and the U-boat menace. Shipping losses were mounting, and the supply of supplies across the Atlantic was threatened. The Royal Navy was not confident in their ability to counter the menace, and insisted that capturing the German bases was essential. Clearing the Belgian coast remained an objective of highest importance, and Haig was given his chance to undertake it.

The Ypres Salient was still Plumer's command, and that far-sighted man had long foreseen the need eventually to clear the Germans from the semicircle of hills to the south and east overlooking the salient's plain. By June 1916, the ground under the ridge contained 24 of the largest mines ever placed by the BEF. They were ready a year before Plumer would have the opportunity to use them. Mining could actually be conducted on a grand scale despite the low-lying marshes and streams. The trick was to start by digging downwards, a steeply inclined tunnel lined with waterproof membranes behind a concrete reinforcement. These main tunnels, about twenty in all, would go down over ninety feet, through the marshy top layer, through the heavy and dangerous blue clay that lay beneath and into deep chalk. They would be started well behind the front lines, and the telltale blue clay would be taken far from the tunnel entrances before being dumped. Boring machines, used in building the London Underground network were shipped across the Channel, but could not operate in the heavy blue clay. Yet again the ranks of the BEF were combed for men with mining experience, and the undertaking reverted to a system of manual tunnelling.

> Tunnelling took on an existence of its own. The Germans knew of the tunnelling and their counter-tunnelling was vigorous and aggressive. To protect their own deep mines, BEF miners responded to the German measures. Occasionally, one side's tunnel would break into another's, whereupon hand-to-hand fighting, in pitch darkness or by the light of small lanterns, would break out. When the presence of a major enemy work was detected, a small charge of explosive, a camouflet, would be laid and fired, sufficient to destroy other tunnels close by but not to destroy trenches and ground above.

The Prime Minister, David Lloyd George, had not yét endorsed any decision to fight north-eastward out of Ypres to clear the coast. He distrusted Haig and his repeated promises of successful offensives and reducing casualty rates. Indeed he had gone so far as to send South African general Jan Smuts, a former Boer commander but now a member of the War Committee, to France to review the possibility of finding a Commander-in-Chief to replace Haig. Smut's failure to produce a better choice had not changed Lloyd George's opinion, nor had he given up on his plan to place the British armies under direct command of a French Commander-in-Chief. At the time of this proposal General Nivelle was French Commander-in-Chief. However, he was sacked after the disaster of the Chemin des Dames before the transfer of command was implemented. Then Lloyd George's mercurial temperament was buoyed by the successes at Arras and the triumph at Vimy Ridge, so he authorised planning for Third Ypres to go ahead. He was not willing to authorise the battle's taking place, but recognised the need to plan for it.

Messines Ridge

Before any serious breakout could be launched out of Ypres the southern end of the long low ridge south of Ypres had to be cleared, to provide a secure flank protecting the axis of the greater breakout to follow. Lloyd George had now reached the stage of overtly controlling the conduct of military operations. His approval was needed before any plan could be turned into action. On this occasion he allowed the attack to go ahead. He understood its limited scale and objectives and was confident that this attack had none of the potential for the over-ambitious grand offensives that he associated with Haig's leadership.

Now Plumer had his chance to show what he had been doing for the last several months. The Germans had had plenty of time to create formidable defences. They had learned about the cost of heavily manned front line trenches and had refined the concept of defence in depth. At the southern end of Messines Ridge the defences were at their best, with a belt of barbed wire and mutually supportive strongpoints stretching in places a mile and a half in front of the main defences and artillery positions.

On the morning of 21 May Plumer played his first card. Artillery in plentiful supply, 750 heavy artillery pieces and 1,500 lighter ones, set to work to destroy the German defences. The principal aims were to destroy the German barbed wire and outlying strongpoints whilst engaging and neutralising the Germans' own artillery counter-efforts. The guns fired day and night, batteries only pausing to allow gun crews to rest and guns to cool down, and continued to do so for ten days.

At 0310 on 7 June Plumer played his ace of trumps. The mines were detonated. Two had been lost to German counter-mining, another three were not due to be fired until the second stage of the assault, but the remaining seventeen were fired simultaneously and had their effect exactly as Plumer had wished. A total of one million pounds of high explosive, about 420 tons, re-configured the whole landscape of Messiness Ridge. About 10,000 German soldiers were killed instantly. In Lille, 20 miles away, citizens ran from their beds into the street, believing that the city was suffering an earthquake. In London, over 100 miles away, the noise woke sleeping civilians. Messines Ridge was free for the taking.

As the earth, bodies and impedimenta of war fell back to earth the infantry assault set off. No straight lines, no hold-ups at strongpoints, the assault troops simply passed them by and left them for following specialist troops to eliminate. By midday all nine miles of Messines Ridge planned to be taken by the assaulting troops were firmly in British hands, with 80,000 troops at last on one end of the higher ground surrounding the Ypres Salient. The assault had been so swift and successful that the three remaining mines would not be blown and could later be dismantled.

Nineteen mines should have been detonated but only seventeen actually exploded. The remaining two were unaccounted for. One announced its whereabouts in 1955, thirty-eight years later, by exploding during a thunderstorm. A solitary cow was the last victim of Messines Ridge. The last mine remains, out there somewhere, perhaps affected by the wet and no longer able to inflict harm, but perhaps not.

The mines gave rise to one of the few memorable witticisms to survive the war. As Plumer dined with his senior officers on the evening of 6 June he proposed a toast: 'We may not change history tomorrow, but we shall certainly change geography.'

The Breakout

Messines Ridge was a significant tactical victory, but only a preliminary one to make possible greater ones to come. However, it gave Haig the argument he needed to press for the next step, the breakout itself. The Belgian coast beckoned in the distance, and indeed the obvious plan was to launch a joint offensive by land and sea. A breakout from Ypres would take place as a sea-borne assault landed on the Belgian coast. The forces would meet south of Antwerp and roll up the German coastal defences northwards. If this plan might be too ambitious, the railway junction at Roulers, under a dozen miles north-east of Ypres was closer. Without the railways through Roulers, Germany could not maintain itself on the coast and would have to withdraw. Once they started to withdraw, where might they end? At a planning conference in London, in early July, as the debate about the breakout phase continued, Haig used a large-scale map to illustrate how the Germans could be harried back through Belgium from Ypres and the coast together. His hand swept back and forth across the map, and, as a commentator noted, it came to rest near the Belgian-German border, with his little finger resting in German territory. Lloyd George refused to approve that the battle could be fought but agreed that planning for it should begin. In later years it was said that 'Lloyd George never forgave that little finger'. At this meeting, Haig was hampered by his inability to express verbally his reasons for wanting to go ahead with a second attack on the line of ridges surrounding Ypres to the south-east, east and north-east. Lloyd George wavered in his decision, but was undone in his resistance when the new First Sea Lord, Sir John Jellicoe, announced that unless the army would have cleared the Belgian coast by the end of the year the Royal Navy would be unable to cope with the submarine menace that came from the North Sea coastal ports.

Lloyd George agreed on 21 July that the next phase of the Ypres Offensive could go ahead. Six weeks had passed since the capture of Messines Ridge. The campaigning season, always short in Flanders, was half gone already.

Then Lloyd George had another change of heart, and on 25 July he proposed that instead of fighting at Ypres the British should send several divisions and supporting heavy artillery to Italy. He thought that Italy might knock Austria out of the war and cause Germany to collapse as well. This was a complete reversal of all strategic wisdom, which avers that you knock out the strongest enemy first and the rest will follow, whereas knocking out the supporting players does not affect the main drama. At last the War Policy Committee asserted itself, and Lloyd George backed down to the extent of greatly reducing the scale of the transfer. Sir William Robertson may be given the credit for leading the pressure that gave Haig the freedom to fight one of the most controversial battles of the war, perhaps of all British history. Lloyd George had approved the plan to fight a way of the Salient, but he could not accept the logical next step: in order to fight the battle Haig needed troops; troops available in England and troops in France who should not be sent to Italy. Lloyd George believed that the generals, led by Haig, were wasteful of life, so he had been reluctant to provide reinforcements in the numbers that Haig and others knew were necessary if the breakout could succeed. The issue of supply of reinforcements was to be a constant cause of argument and distrust for the rest of the war.

It was extremely unfortunate that the two soldiers responsible for the Army, Haig in France and Robertson in London, were as inarticulate as each other and both deeply suspicious of the lawyer Lloyd George's oratory. Indeed they had reason to be; the latter was as happy to lie to his War Committee colleagues as to tell the truth, just depending on what suited his purpose at the time.

Given the approval to fight this, the major BEF campaign of 1917, how did Haig propose to proceed? To begin with he made a terrible blunder. In 1916 Rawlinson, an infantry soldier, had watered down Haig's own plan that the Somme should be a breakthrough battle to finish the war. Only months later Plumer, another infantry soldier, had showed little ambition to do more than capture Messines Ridge and had spent too long consolidating his position thereafter. For this breakthrough Haig wanted a different sort of man, a 'thruster' in the hunting parlance of the cavalry world. One was to hand. Sir Hubert Gough was an Irish cavalryman, an old friend of Haig. He was excitable, hot-headed and above all a relentless believer in the attack, a quality that Haig saw as admirable in a general in command of an attack and breakout. However, Gough had a deserved reputation as a less than careful general, too willing to sacrifice lives in pursuit of his objectives, and unable to create the sort of headquarters where debate and cooperation could flourish. It is to his credit that on this occasion even Gough himself could see that he was not the man to take over the breakout from the Ypres Salient. He had not fought there, and he recognised the importance to success of familiarity with the particular characteristics of the Ypres ground. Nonetheless, Haig had his man and Gough and his recently re-named Fifth Army staff moved to Ypres to take over the primary role in the next phase. Plumer, conveniently, was therefore able to take command of the reduced and ill-fated Italian expedition.

Gough set about his planning. Haig had told him to use the Second Army's foothold on the southern, Messines, end of the ridge surrounding Ypres, and press east and north-east along it. This axis of advance had multiple advantages; it would clear the threat to Ypres, then bring Roulers within easy artillery range of the new front line, and finally threaten the Belgian coast. Above all it would free Gough's cavalry instincts to sweep into central Belgium, destroy the German rear areas and force Germany to retire from the coast. Once the demoralised German armies were on the move the British cavalry would at last have the chance, denied them since 1914, to drive the retreat into a rout. Unfortunately, Haig was famously unable to express his intentions in words, and Gough was already almost equally famous as a general unable to direct the fortunes of a formation as large as an army. As the planning progressed it became clear that Gough had largely failed to understand the purpose of the break-out. He was more interested in a different plan of his own making. This would clear the Salient more thoroughly and enable his army to drive on a more northerly rather than north-easterly axis. He acknowledged that Roulers would be missed in the drive north, but intended to deal with the Germans on the coast anyway.

In the build-up to what would be Third Ypres we see Haig's glaring weakness, his reluctance to control his subordinate commanders when their plans did not conform to his own strategic vision. He commented on Gough's plan, noted that it seemed to miss the point of his own larger vision, and then did nothing. So, after slight further delays, the next phases of the eleven separate battles that are called Third Ypres were launched.

The weather in Flanders is never wholly reliable. During the six weeks delay after Messines Ridge, from mid-July until late August, whilst Haig debated his plans with Lloyd George in London and planning was going ahead with the latter's limited approval, it had been so hot and dry that horses went lame in numbers that began to have an effect on the army's ability to move. Dust hung everywhere in the air as men and horses moved around the rear areas, and every shell explosion added to the prevailing dust clouds. However, as the first assaults were launched on 31 July, it began to rain, and rain, and rain. After only twenty-four hours the low land was a marsh in the better areas, a huge lake of mud in all the others. Flanders lies largely at or below sea level, and the centuries-old system of ditches that drained the natural marshland had long since been destroyed by the artillery war that raged incessantly around the Salient. The early attacks were largely successful, but the pattern of all other attacks in wet weather was gradually emerging. It became ever harder for the infantry to advance, difficult to move even the least bulky supplies forward to the infantry, and almost impossible to move artillery at all. Tanks were used in large numbers and lost in equal ones. The rain affected the Royal Flying Corps' effectiveness, as support for ground troops, as artillery spotters and as reconnaissance observers. And still it rained.

The only way to move around was on the roadways of duckboards laid on trestles above the mud. Any man, horse or mule that slipped off the roadways would fall into the deep, soft mud on either side. It was impossible to free oneself and all too often impossible for others to do anything to help. There are accounts of men gradually slipping further into the mire, certain of their slowly coming death, pleading with comrades for the shot that would end their lives quickly rather than in the earth's slow embrace. There are also accounts from soldiers who found it kinder to shoot their own close comrades than to leave them to that fate. To carry a single wounded man on a stretcher needed as many as sixteen men to provide the necessary regular changes of carrier that the effort of getting through the mud demanded. And out in the open could be heard the cries of the wounded, often only ending as their struggles served only to sink them further into the drowning mud.

Getting supplies to the troops in the fighting line across the mud was as desperately dangerous, backbreaking work as getting the casualties back. During the day, from their positions atop the ridge, the German machine guns could beat the whole area for a mile or more behind the BEF's front-line troops with barrages. At night those same machine guns would be set to cover any small landmarks that might enable troops to navigate their way around the swamp. From further back, German artillery fire continued incessantly, sometimes at low levels of intensity, sometimes with great force, depending on their need to support German advanced strong points. Gas shells were always a part of these German firing patterns and BEF troops had to wear gas masks for long periods. The air that arrived in a man's lungs had been laboriously drawn through chemical filters, tasted of those chemicals and was always totally de-humidified. No soldier could work at better than half pace, and even that effectiveness diminished as time passed. The slightest area of exposed skin was at once found by the gas, and became a mass of agonising blisters and sores. To make matters worse, as the BEF's artillery pounded at the German lines and artillery positions, gun barrels began to wear, causing shells to fall short onto their own infantry. The idea of 'friendly fire' was not a concept only identified in later wars – soldiers resented this risk of death more than any other, and to call it 'friendly' was certainly not in their minds.

Rats abounded, as they had since the beginning of trench warfare. Now they were huge, fat and totally unconcerned by any efforts to drive them away. If a man found a tiny shelter from the incessant rain and cold, he could be sure that rats had found it as well. A man awakening

would find rats swarming near him to take advantage of his body warmth. Occasionally a particularly fierce period of artillery bombardment would panic the rats, which would fight their way past sheltering soldiers, biting and fighting to get away from the gas and shelling. As the rats scrabbled for food and shelter they would uncover decaying and broken bodies, and would feed on them with complete indifference to the attempts of soldiers not yet hardened to the sight to drive them away.

Lice were equally a completely unavoidable part of the front-line experience. Soldiers might, if they were lucky, get occasional clean clothes, and would usually go through a de-lousing station on leaving the line, but the lice were never deterred for any time. As two soldiers sat together, each picking lice out of the other's hair and clothing, they would talk, and the talk came to be so associated with the activity that lice-clearance became known as 'chatting'.

The attacks went on. The end of the campaigning season was approaching, and there stood the ruins of Passchendaele village, only a few hundred yards ahead on the crest of the low ridge across which lay Roulers. Gough could see that his army was effectively wrecked by its efforts. Plumer, back from Italy and effectively in command at the southern end of the Salient, wanted to call a halt to the campaign. Lloyd George was in agonies of worry about having allowed yet another campaign to promise much and deliver nothing. Haig stood alone. If the ridge would not be taken this season it would be impossible to stay in the marsh and the BEF would have to fall back to its starting points, with the whole campaign to fight again in 1918. With a last throw of the dice the ridge at least might be taken and something held to show fruit of the campaign. The BEF had suffered 300,000 casualties this summer and Haig felt that there had to be some tangible achievement from that expenditure. By now, Plumer was again placed in overall command in the Salient. The attacks went on as September became October and the season turned colder, with winter weather arriving unseasonably early.

Haig sent for the Canadians to save the day as the season drew towards its close. Lieutenant General Sir Arthur Currie had been appointed to command the Canadian Corps after Byng's recent promotion, and he laid down a number of requirements. The Canadian Corps had served on the Somme under Sir Hubert Gough's command and had unofficially let it be known through their government that they would not welcome a repetition of the experience. Currie now made it specifically clear; the Canadians would not fight under Gough: Haig transferred them to Plumer's Second Army. The Canadians would not fight without the quantities of artillery that Currie required: Haig undertook to provide guns in plenty. The Canadians would not fight until Currie had the wood he needed to build roadways across the mud: Haig could not provide that, so Currie called for lumberjacks in the Canadians ranks, of whom there were many. They felled whole forests, commandeered a sawmill and Currie had his timber. Roadways and tracks were laid across the bog in which the BEF lay, east of Ypres. Then Currie began to question the whole point of the final attempt to force a foothold on the ridge around the ruins of Passchendaele. Haig and Currie liked and respected each other, and perhaps this mutual bond enabled Haig to talk more clearly than usual about the need to make the final advance to the ridge. Currie told Haig It would cost 16,000 Canadian casualties, and he needed reassurance that Canada would not give those lives in vain. Haig went to speak to the Canadian officers himself. He explained that the ridge had to be taken, asked for their confidence in his saying so, explained that their commander had freely expressed his worries, and that he had tried honestly to assuage them. He then asked the Canadians to undertake the task. Canadian officers who heard the speech recalled it in later years as a masterpiece of oratory; Haig had found his voice when it was most needed. Haig may have lost his nerve at Le Cateau in 1914, but now he displayed moral courage in meeting face to face the men whom he asked to give their lives for the attack.

The final assault on Passchendaele took two weeks, and at the end the Canadians were atop the ridge, at a cost of 15,633 casualties, almost exactly what Currie had forecast. The Third Battle of Ypres could now be halted. Plumer's assessment of what could be achieved had proved correct. The ridges around the Salient had been taken, except for the northernmost tip of them. German pressure on Ypres was relieved and the armies in Belgium had a springboard from which to launch their offensive operations in the coming year. However, there had never been the slightest chance of Haig's longed-for break-out during this year.

Haig's many critics have always used the decision to fight on at Ypres in the autumn of 1917 as their final proof of his unfitness for command and lack of care for the lives of soldiers entrusted to him. Others have asked what other choices were open to him. The Admiralty had said they could not defeat the U-boat menace without the army's clearing the Belgian coast, the French insisted on constant attacks on the Germans, and Ypres was the only place where Haig could meet both needs. Lloyd George, addressing his own needs, was entirely aware of all these conflicting pulls on the Commander-in-Chief's freedom to act. However, he could reconcile his own doubts by allowing the battles to be fought whilst ensuring that the men needed to fight them were kept out of harm's way, in England where Haig could not use them.

German casualties were as heavy as the British and Empire ones. One stretcher-bearer, serving in the German Army despite being Austrian by birth, was based in the crypt of the parish church at Passchendaele. He had been awarded the Iron Cross for his courage in rescuing wounded under fire, and would survive the war. Adolf Hitler would re-visit the scene of these, his, actions in later years.

Noel Chavasse VC and Bar, MC

The Liverpool Scottish had moved back to Ypres after the Somme battle had closed down, at the end of 1916. They were almost entirely newly-officered and with the ranks full of new recruits as well. They were to take part in the first wave of attacks of the break-out. Chavasse was back with them.

Throughout July the Liverpool Scottish, like every other unit detailed to take part in the assault, was hard at work, training, preparing and rehearsing their part in the coming battle. Three full-scale dress rehearsals involved all the infantry units, artillery, tanks and aircraft that would be taking part. During a short spell in the line there were more casualties than usual when a German artillery bombardment included mustard gas shells for the first time. Mustard gas affected exposed skin, causing agonising open sores and blistering. The Liverpool Scottish men were still wearing the kilt. In total the battalion suffered casualties of four officers and 141 men in this quiet period before the offensive actually began. After these earlier actions the battalion was now reduced to exactly 500 souls, twenty-five officers and 475 other ranks. These 500 men were about to set out to achieve objectives set for a full battalion, 1,000 men.

On 29 July the much-reduced battalion marched to the front, each man carrying his rations, ammunition and other necessary stores. Most carried extra ammunition for the Lewis guns, or grenades for the bombing sections. The march lasted five hours and as it began, so it began to rain. Every man was wet through and exhausted, with no prospect of getting dry before the morrow. They were able to take shelter overnight in deep dugouts at Weltje, where there was room for 'several hundred' men. They rested here until late afternoon on 30 July and then moved out into their starting positions for the actual assault at 0350, first light, on the morning of 31 July.

The assault went well and Liverpool Scottish carried their objective, crossing the German front line and carrying on for a further half-mile to the second. Halfway between the two lines they captured two small German bunkers. Chavasse took one for his Regimental Aid Post (RAP) whilst Battalion HQ took the larger. Chavasse should have stayed at Weltje behind the original starting point and have wounded men brought to him there, but he knew the importance of prompt attention to wounds before they could become infected, and had come as far forward as possible. Being a German bunker the entrance had been sited to face rearwards, from the German perspective, but in fact forwards as it appeared to its new occupants. The door faced the Germans and the firing slits faced the old British lines. During the morning Chavasse emerged from time to time to stand at the entrance where he could wave to his stretcher-bearers to indicate his station's whereabouts. Inevitably, he was hit, by a shell splinter in the skull. He walked back to the shelters at Weltje, where his wound was dressed and he was told to await evacuation with the other wounded. However, Chavasse was well aware that he was the only medical officer available to man his RAP and decided to return to it.

For the rest of that day, and into the evening, Chavasse worked on the constant stream of wounded being brought to his small RAP. The next day brought the same demands. Fortunately a German doctor had been captured and he started to assist in the cramped space of the improvised medical centre. Outside, the rain continued to fall and intense shelling covered the area as the Germans prepared for their counter-attack. That evening, as night fell, Chavasse took a party of stretcher-bearers out into the rain and shellfire. Wounded men lay around the scene, some had been there during four days of heavy fighting and he wanted them rescued. Working by torchlight he gave what little immediate treatment was possible before sending the wounded back with his stretcher-bearers.

During the following day, with a lull in the stream of wounded men needing attention, Chavasse went back into his bunker and stretched out in a chair to catch a few moments of sleep. As he slept, another German shell flew through the entrance that faced the wrong way, and exploded. Chavasse suffered five wounds, including a cut that opened his abdomen. Every other man in the place died instantly or was rendered unconscious. Aware of the need for haste, Chavasse walked, holding his wound closed with his hands, towards Ypres, the nearest place where help might be found. From here he was taken quickly to a special hospital for abdominal wounds just behind Ypres.

The Commanding Officer of this special abdominal wounds hospital at Brandhoek behind Ypres was Lieutenant Colonel Martin-Leake, Royal Army Medical Corps, at this time the only person ever to have won the VC twice. His first award had been for actions during the South African War in 1902 and his second for actions close to his present station, in the Salient, during the First Battle of Ypres.

Abdominal wounds were always serious, especially in the days before penicillin, and Chavasse's was to prove fatal. He died two days later, on the third anniversary of the outbreak of war and four days before the first anniversary of the actions that had led to his first VC.

At the end of the month it was announced Noel Chavasse had been awarded a second VC, joining Colonel Martin-Leake in the remarkable group of only two people thus far ever to receive the award for a second time.

Cambrai and the Tank Corps

Whilst Third Ypres' subsidiary battles ground on, one group of officers was demanding that their contribution to it be halted. The new Royal Tank Corps could see no reason for tanks to be involved in a landscape that promised only breakdown, loss of machines and occasional drowning of whole tank crews as they sank into the marsh. Only a few miles south the ground was firm, not yet fought over, and beyond it lay a tempting target, the Hindenburg Line. The corps could not promise a battle to win the war, a breakthrough into the German rear areas, or even a bite-and-hold of part of the German line. The Tank Corps offered a huge raid in strength, involving hundreds of the latest models of tanks. It would be a surprise attack to take part of the line, execute great damage to it, and then retire to the start point, all within one day. Preliminary bombardment would be minimal; tanks would perform best on unbroken ground. The whole thesis was that, properly executed, the raid would force the Germans to spread reinforcements along the whole length of the front, to cover the possibility that the next raid might turn out to be the real breakthrough battle.

Haig was not interested; Ypres was taking all his attention. However, as Third Ypres began to show all the usual signs of stalling, he looked at the plan again, became enthusiastic and then convinced. This would be more than a huge raid with limited aims; it could be the breakthrough battle that he needed. It would keep Lloyd George at bay and win the war before the Americans could steal the credit. Charteris, his long-serving Intelligence Chief, duly fed him the figures that proved that the battles on the Chemin des Dames, at Arras and Ypres had reduced the German armies to demoralised second-rate groups, who would only fight for long enough to find someone to whom to surrender. The Cavalry Corps would at last have the chance, the first since 1914, given that all other expectations had failed, to break through and reap the whirlwind amongst a broken enemy.

The Tank Corps and infantry were to attack together, the tanks to overcome local strongpoints and machine-gun posts, the latter to deal with infantry and anti-tank units. The Cavalry Corps would be held in reserve, ready to sweep through the gap that would be punched in the German lines and drive on, into the undefended areas and railway systems of the German rear areas.

The assault on the strong fortified town of Cambrai began with a limited artillery bombardment of German strongpoints and artillery positions. No indiscriminate shelling of the whole area would be allowed to break up the ground ahead of the assault. However, 1,003 guns were able to achieve the objective of keeping German heads down and limit German artillery response to the attack. The first wave of attackers 'went over the top' on 20 November. Two hundred and sixteen tanks, each with its attendant infantry of up to 200 men, advanced across the relatively unbroken ground, swept round the early obstacles and achieved their objectives. For the loss of about 5,000 men, the assault on the right achieved more in a morning than had been achieved at Ypres in months. The success was remarkable. To achieve all their objectives two battalions of The Durham Light Infantry lost, between them, four men killed and seven injured.

In the centre things did not go well. Major-General Harper commanding the Highland Division believed that tanks would only draw German artillery fire upon themselves, and his divisional plan of attack therefore kept the tanks well ahead of the advancing Jocks, instead of the two arms being mutually supportive as elsewhere in the attack. The Highlanders were doubly unfortunate in their opponents. The German front was mainly manned by reservists and territorial troops, but opposite Harper was General von Walter, one of the few Germans who had troubled to think about using artillery to attack tanks. His reservist troops, dismissed by BEF Intelligence as 'fourth rate', were perhaps the most dangerous formation for advancing isolated tanks to face. Walter's divisional artillery had trained to attack moving targets even before the German Army had a single tank of their own. As the tanks breasted the ridge at Flesquieres the Germans took a terrible toll. Sergeant Kurt Kruger, the last member of his gun crew left alive after the artillery bombardment, accounted for five tanks on his own, as each in turn presented its thinly armoured belly as it tipped over the crest of the ridge. Without the tanks to keep the infantry down, the Highlanders were left to advance alone against German positions that had not been shelled with any real intensity in the days before the battle.

Harper's plan was another example of a weakness that Haig had showed since his over-management of the Somme; the belief that the general who would fight the battle should be allowed to plan it his way, even if his way flew in the face of doctrine issued from Haig's headquarters. The Highland Division was cut to pieces by the Germans as a result and the attack failed here.

To the north, on the left, the attack went well, and most objectives were reached. The extremely strong German position in Bourlon Wood would be taken on the morrow, by fresh troops passing through the ranks of the first day attackers. In the meantime the tanks had delivered on their promise and broken through the Hindenburg Line, the strongest defences that the Germans could offer.

In the air the Royal Flying Corps also excelled themselves. A force of only nineteen squadrons kept the air free of German fighter and reconnaissance aircraft, and contributed to the day's success with new ground attack tactics, as well as artillery spotting and aerial reconnaissance.

After this first day church bells were rung throughout the British Isles. Despatches went back from GHQ and the government were persuaded that Haig's great breakthrough had begun.

On the second day the impetus began to fade. As on other occasions, Kavanagh's Cavalry Corps headquarters were too far back for him to be able to handle his cavalry effectively, but he insisted that all orders for employing his two divisions must come from himself. This was scarcely a wise insistence, given that any message back from the attacking front would have to come back by runner, and that his troops would then have to move forward some miles before coming into action. As a result, the cavalry were too far back, too slowly ordered forward, and hindered by the inevitable press of men and supplies moving forward and injured being brought back. Thus they were unable to get into action in time to maintain the momentum of the first day. Indeed, they had not even begun to move until late in the first afternoon. Of the tanks, over 175 had been destroyed, ditched or lost in other ways; about one third of these were the tanks left unsupported by Harper's planners. Fresh troops and tanks were brought up as planned to take Bourlon Wood. After several days fighting the wood was taken and the exhausted BEF soldiers found themselves in a tiny salient, less than 1 mile wide, surrounded on three sides by Germans.

After about a week the continuing advance had created a pocket, about 10 miles wide and 5 miles deep. Cambrai was still a couple of miles beyond the depth of the advance and Byng, the local army commander, called for a pause. Commanders would come back from the front line for a short rest before the assault would be resumed. Meanwhile Crown Prince Rupprecht of Bavaria, still the German commander in this sector, had used the flexibility of resources that came from the shortening of the German line earlier in the year. On the tenth day he launched his counter-attack.

In the air the leading German air ace, the 'Red' Baron von Richthofen, had arrived to see what his Flying Circus could do to counter the RFC's superiority in the air battle. His fresher fliers with advanced machines were able to neutralise much of the RFC's numerical advantage, and make Byng's task rather greater than it had been until this point. On the ground Crown Prince Rupprecht had gathered a counter-attack force of twenty divisions. These troops were not tired and recovering from Ypres, as many of the BEF troops in their assault had been, but fresh and battle-hardened. The BEF gave way at every point, giving up half their gains in the north, and actually losing several miles of their own front line in the south.

> If we judge by expectations, Cambrai must be considered a failure. The Germans had captured as much of the British front line as the British had captured German. Casualties were about even, about 40,000 on each side in the two-week battle, and whilst the British had captured 145 German guns they had lost 158. The ringing of the church bells had certainly been premature.

The Russian Revolution

In the east the Russians were effectively out of the war by late 1917. The Tsar abdicated in March and was killed, along with his family, in July. The October revolution had brought the Bolsheviks to power, and they would sign the Treaty of Brest-Litovsk early in the New Year, but the Germans were already moving troops from east to west in recognition that Russia's bolt was shot. From now on Russia was effectively non-combatant and willing to surrender large parts of her western empire just to be left alone. She renounced all claim to Finland, the Baltic countries and parts of the Ottoman Empire captured in earlier wars. The treaty lasted just two months before being violated by the Turks, and only until the end of the war before being repudiated by everyone else.

A Bad Year for All

There was no hiding the fact that this had been a bad year all round for the Allies.

The French had suffered the disastrous offensive on the Chemin des Dames, and there had been a distinct lack of ardour to press on with the war until November, when Georges Clemenceau had become Prime Minister, officially President of the Chamber of Deputies, and appointed himself as Minister of War. His political philosophy was clear, and re-stated in every speech and address to his parliamentary colleagues – 'I make war'. It was simple, and with this support the French armies were beginning to recover their poise, but it had been a bad year nonetheless. Despite all French and BEF efforts the Germans had given up little territory in France except that which they chose to evacuate. The recovery of that small area around Ypres that was achieved in Belgium, and the area recovered between Arras and Reims as the Germans retired behind the

Hindenburg Line may have been important tactically, but was insignificant when one looked at a map and saw how much of Belgium and France was still in German hands.

The Russians were defeated and out of the war. The Ottoman Empire was collapsing, its military capability ebbing away under the hammer blows delivered by Allenby, himself no great success as an army commander in France but an inspired choice to command the forces in the Middle East who would capture Baghdad, Jerusalem and other regional centres.

The Italians had suffered yet more grievously in their never-ending battles to clear northern Italy. The ring of mountains around the area, the Dolomites and Maritime Alps, effectively dictated that any Italian offensive against the Austrians must seek to break out east, around the coastal plain and into Slovenia. There had already been nine previous attempts, every one expensive but indecisive, and the tenth battle, early in 1917, had been similar. After some success in the Eleventh Battle of The Isonzo in August of this year the Italians were comprehensively routed by the Austrians, stiffened by German divisions freed for this action by the collapse of Russia. The Twelfth Battle of The Isonzo, the last of the series, was in every respect a dreadful way in which to end 1917. Casualties over the series of battles were not as high as had become commonplace on the Western Front, but in the context of the short front over which these battles were fought, casualties exceeding 300,000 were enormous.

The British Empire had endured a battle that has been a by-word ever since as a statement of the horror and futility of the war as a whole – Passchendaele has a sombre sound to it, one needs no Flemish to know that it translates as Passion Valley. The successes at Arras and Vimy Ridge were over-shadowed by this end to the year, and Cambrai had done nothing but lift hopes only cruelly to dash them down again.

For British Prime Minister Lloyd George it had been a bad year. He had looked for, and failed to find, a general who could replace Haig. Failing in that resolution, he had tried to limit the BEF's limitless capacity to accept casualties in return for promised results that never transpired. He had done this by holding back all except the absolute minimum flow of reinforcements sent to France. This was a dangerous and weak policy. He lacked the courage to change the military leadership of a nation at war, had tried to interfere in the military conduct of the war, and now sought to impose his will by holding back the forces that the nation's armies needed if they were to be able to fulfil the will of their political masters. He had not persuaded the Army and his political colleagues that the answer lay in helping Italy to defeat Austria, and leave Germany with no allies. It was now clear that defeating Germany meant defeating the German Army in the field; nothing else would do the trick.

Lloyd George was not simply minding his own political wellbeing, although he was always aware of the risk of becoming associated with the ever-lengthening casualty lists. He also believed that accepting the status quo – the generals' theory that one last, admittedly costly, push would lead to the collapse of Germany – was simply wrong. He had seen that theory tried too often, and failing each time, to give it any further credence. As Prime Minister he was trustee for the lives of the nation, and he had a moral obligation to seek other options for fighting the war, ones that might achieve more than the paltry results of the Western Front but without the cost. Naturally, his qualms reached their climax as Third Ypres ground to an end, and the Empire counted the cost, well over 300,000 casualties to take a piece of land that a man could walk from end to end in a comfortable morning's stroll. He was deeply concerned about these results of trusteeship as 1917 ran into 1918, with no end in sight.

Mutual trust was all but gone, and mutual dislike added to the problems. Haig, the dour, inarticulate Scot, had weathered the first year of the war having little in common with the excitable and sometimes unbalanced Irishman Sir John French. He was now tied to the volatile, voluble, scheming and distrusted Welshman, Lloyd George. The differences in character were proving a handicap to the business of fighting the war, at all levels.

For the United States it was by no means a good year either. President Wilson had tried in vain to act as the honest intermediary in trying to set up peace proposals. Despite the provocation of German submarine warfare that sank several US ships, and caused loss of American life in 1915 when the *Lusitania* was sunk, he had reminded America that there was no shame in being '*Too proud to fight*'. Domestic pressure had forced him to bring the US into the war, but he felt a deep sense of failure and regretted his inability to achieve an end to the war without being drawn into it first.

For Germany 1917 was the turning point. The Royal Navy's North Sea blockade was slowly but inexorably destroying Germany at home. Food was short and the armies at the front needed most of the essential materials, like shoe-leather, food beyond a bare subsistence diet, and fuel. All manufacture was directed by war needs and suffering at home was increasing. In the armies, food and supplies were a little better, but the constant drain of loss of men and matériel was itself affecting the conduct of the war. The withdrawal to the Hindenburg Line in the early part of the year had itself been a pointer to the difficulties of manpower and equipment management that now formed a major part of German strategic and tactical planning.

6

1918 – The End in Sight

Nobody faced the beginning of the year with confidence. No army had the solution to the problem of creating a breakthrough, and nobody knew how to exploit one if they achieved it. Governments needed to address the issues of the long years of shortages and loss of life, and the increasing rise of what were nervously referred to as socialist tendencies. The idea was taking hold that perhaps this war might go on forever, taking on an existence of its own and destroying one generation after another. Nowhere were these matters more pressing than in Germany, but no country had more stamina to suffer them.

Submarine Menace

The value of submarines had been recognised during the American War of Independence, and both sides had built them during the American Ciivil War. Although the modern vessels were far more advanced than these early models, they were of limited value in the early years of the war. They could travel totally submerged for only limited periods, although a simple snorkel meant that travel over long distances was possible whilst offering only the smallest of visual targets. They could influence the conduct of great battles, as they did at Jutland by threatening an oncoming fleet. They could sink any ship with a single torpedo. They could attack shipping bringing materials and men into Britain. They could force the Royal Navy's blockade to operate further from German-occupied shores and increase the possibility that merchant supplies might slip through. However, they could not bring any supplies into Germany and they could not significantly threaten the dense traffic flows between the British south coast ports and France.

Even by 1914 U-boats could circumnavigate the British Isles and the voyage of *U-20* that culminated with the sinking of *Lusitania* was comparable in terms of distance. Most, of course, emerged into open seas by the route north of Scotland, avoiding the defended English Channel, and returned the same way. U-boat design continued to improve and by the end of 1917 the British merchant marine was at risk from these larger, faster and more powerful U-boats throughout the northern Atlantic. In these open waters the German vessels could prey more or less undisturbed on the unescorted shipping that brought men, food and material from around the world into British ports.

Third Ypres had failed utterly to clear the Belgian coast of German refuges from which some of the U-boat fleet operated. The scale of shipping losses in the Atlantic had shaken the confidence of naval leadership on both sides of the Atlantic. In fact, the crisis of shipping losses would pass in mid-1918, after Lloyd George arbitrarily over-ruled the Admiralty's objections to any system of shipping convoys. Under the convoy system, shipping losses fell by over 90 per cent, and in some months losses were scarcely more than 1 per cent of previous regular losses. However, the nervous damage had been done and the U-boat threat was taken more seriously than it warranted with the new arrangements in place. Something had to be done about the Belgian coast.

The Zeebrugge and Ostend Raids

Zeebrugge is the point where the canal from Bruges, 6 miles inland, enters the North Sea. By 1917 it was an important German U-boat base, safe from sea-borne attack and sited ideally to threaten both North Sea and Atlantic shipping. Jellicoe's insistence on the need to clear the coast and deny the port to Germany had been a key factor in Lloyd George's acceptance of the rationale behind Third Ypres in 1917. With no prospect of a new campaign in Flanders in 1918, the Royal Navy set out to deny Bruges to Germany by other means. A plan was hatched to sink three old cruisers in the channel leading from the inner port to the open sea, thereby blocking it and preventing German U-boats from entering or leaving port.

The port and access channel were sheltered by a mile-long wall, the Mole, curving out from the shore and providing shelter from both weather and silting of the channel into the port. The Mole was itself heavily fortified with artillery batteries that made any sea-borne assault perilous.

The raid took place on 23 April 1918, St George's Day. It was clearly going to be a high-risk venture. Unusually, it was decided to be an all-volunteer affair. Over seventy ships took part. For the Zeebrugge operation there were the three old cruisers, fully laden with concrete. They were to be sunk and would block the narrow channel that joined the seaward navigation channel to the port itself. Three small submarines were laden with high explosives. The crews were to position them under the road and rail viaduct that joined the Mole to the shore, set fuses and abandon them. The Mole would thus be cut off from the mainland. Another three transport vessels were to land troops on the Mole and cover the evacuation of the crews of the block-ships and submarines. The remaining ships were either undertaking a similar but less ambitious operation against the locks at Ostend or were in support, creating mine-cleared approaches to the ports, laying smoke barrages, and neutralising German defences.

The first effects of the raid seemed to justify the 200 dead and 300 wounded of the 1,700 who took part. Eight VCs testify to the gallantry displayed. Two of the three block-ships were sunk across the narrow channel as planned, the viaduct was cut and Zeebrugge was neutralised as a U-boat base, but for just three days. By the end of that time the Germans had cut a new channel that by-passed the two sunk cruisers, and submarines could pass in and out of the port, inconvenienced a little by the shallow channel that restricted passage to when the tide was high, but no more than that.

A second raid, The Second Ostend Raid, was mounted three weeks later. The results were even less effective, with that port not out of effective operation for even a single day.

Ludendorff's Gamble

Hindenburg and Ludendorff could now foresee the end of the war and defeat for Germany. As an ally the Ottoman Empire was now totally worthless, and Austria-Hungary was fast becoming so. Blockade was effectively starving Germany of food and resources, and social unrest was growing. The two leaders of German war policy decided to gamble that one last great battle could force the British to the peace table, whilst the French remained ineffectual and before the Americans achieved sufficient skill to take their place in the battle line.

> **The overall name for this series of battles was to be *Kaiserschlacht,* The Kaiser's Battle. Even doubters could be relied upon to support a concept so important that it was worthy of the Kaiser's own name.**

The gamble was to launch a series of offensives at different points of the Western Front. Starting at the junction of the French and British sectors, a drive south-west would split the allies. Then, in the north, the BEF would be driven back to the Channel and forced either to leave France or to re-deploy so far south that they would leave the western flank of the Paris region undefended. Then, further east, a great attack would be launched towards Paris. Fresh troops, deployed from Russia, would be available. Lessons learned at Cambrai about the effective deployment of infantry in the counter-attack would be applied on an incomparably greater scale. In addition, the great German artillery expert Georg Bruchmuller had been given control of the artillery fire-plan. Although only a colonel, Bruchmuller was accorded a respect and authority that reflected very fully German high command's appreciation of his mastery of firepower. For a battle worthy of the Kaiser's own name, the gunnery expert refined his new tactics, the *Feuerwalze*, the Fire Waltz. First, the enemy's communications would be broken and their artillery eliminated. Then the front line strongpoints would be neutralised. All this would be done in a few hours before the assaulting troops attacked. Gas shells would saturate the rear areas, high explosive fall into the gun lines, and then more gas and high explosive flood the trenches.

The offensives were gigantic in concept, reflecting both the numbers of fresh troops available – about sixty divisions, totalling about one million men – and the desperation of Germany's overall position. There would be four major offensives and numerous minor ones. The most important offensives, *Michael* and *George* were named after Germany's patron saints. One of the major supporting attacks, *Blucher/Yorck*, was named after the key Prussian generals of the Napoleonic wars. The campaign was designed to shock the Entente powers into armistice before the end of the year, after which Germany would probably be unable to keep the war going.

There was no disguising the scale of the blows about to fall. In the face of this overwhelming threat both French and British sought to protect themselves as best they could. The French needed to shorten their front; the war was biting deep into her reserves of manpower. Also, after the mutinies the government was not totally confident of the staying power of the forces at their command. Haig was naturally concerned about the threat to the Channel ports and wanted to concentrate more forces in Belgium and northern France, where he foresaw the attack that must fall on his front. A compromise was reached; the French would shorten their line, and General Gough's Fifth Army would move into the sector south of Bapaume and Péronne that had been in French hands for most of the previous three years. The two headquarters exchanged notes of intent to provide troops for a joint Anglo-French general reserve force. It was unfortunate that neither Haig nor the French could actually commit troops to the reserve, each being overwhelmed by the need to strengthen his own front.

Gough took over French positions that were poorly constructed and worse maintained. The French doctrine of attack had little time for defence measures, and in many French sectors the preparation for defence was negligible. In places there was little serious attempt even to be safe and relatively less uncomfortable. Doctrine dictated that all resources and efforts were to be directed to the attack. Thus Gough was forced to prepare for the blow to come, simultaneously trying to create some defence in depth whilst addressing the weakness of the single ill-prepared line of defence that he had inherited. There was too little time and too much to do; Gough would have to do what he could where he stood and then fight a retreating action, falling back as far and fast as the German advance would force him, until eventually the advance would lose momentum and offer the chance of counter-attack.

Michael

The first offensive began on 21 March, on a broad front from Arras to Fere, about the length of the Hindenburg Line. Much of the German plan, even the start date, was already known to the Intelligence Section, and from Haig downwards the generals and their staffs could all calculate the weight of the attack about to be launched upon them. Conventional wisdom dictated that defensive reserves should be held back until the first attacks would have lost their momentum in the tangle of barbed wire and defensive artillery zones. The reserves could then be thrown into counter-attacks that would first hold the attackers and then drive them backwards again. However, in applying conventional wisdom, largely based on the BEF's experience of assaults on unbroken trench systems, nobody had foreseen the effect of the Fire Waltz and the new German infantry tactics. Within an hour or so of the start of the bombardment, commanders of BEF formations had lost all contact with units under their command, and the combination of low cloud, smoke discharges and German fighter patrols rendered most aerial reconnaissance impotent. On the ground British units faced small groups of Germans, who seemed to have no interest in stopping to fight but swerved around strongpoints and occupied areas, seeming to be more interested in getting past than in eliminating them. The truth was that the new tactics had been successful beyond even the German commanders' best hopes. Equally, even before the attacks Gough had been unable to create any coherent defensive position out of the muddle and lack of preparation that had greeted his army as it took over this previously 'quiet' sector from the French. Within two days he had been driven out of his positions and the Fifth Army was falling back everywhere, in pell-mell retreat according to some contemporary opinions, but actually conducting a skilled fighting withdrawal with tired and out-numbered troops under desperate conditions.

Second Lieutenant Walter Tull, commissioned in 1917, now serving with the 23rd Battalion of his regiment, was killed at Bapaume. He was back on the Somme front about 5 miles south of the site of his failed attack in 1916. Whilst leading a counter-attack on a position from which his battalion had been forced shortly earlier, Tull was hit by a bullet out in no-man's-land. Several of his men risked their lives seeking to bring him back to safety, but his body was lost and never recovered.

His Commanding Officer wrote to Tull's brother: 'Personally, I have lost a friend.' By any standard of the time, that tribute paid by an old-school English colonel to the black grandson of a colonial slave, offers a profound assessment of a remarkable man, one of the outstanding men of his time and place.

Bapaume and Péronne fell, and even the town of Albert itself came under pressure and fell. The latter had been a key town behind the Somme battlefield, never falling throughout the long battles just to its east in the previous three years. However, the Germans were about to learn for themselves the lessons learned at such cost by the BEF during their assaults in the three previous years. As the advance progressed its very speed meant that the infantry outran their own artillery support. Just as the BEF had always found that advance without artillery was a costly and dangerous venture, so did the Germans. To get artillery, ammunition, food and other supplies forward, and casualties back, across the wasteland of the old Somme battlefield was an almost impossible task. In addition, as the Germans advanced and reached the BEF rear areas and the huge stores and dumps that supplied the five British armies, discipline began to break down. The best efforts of the British to destroy that which they could not remove had not been enough. German troops who for a year had seen minimum rations, ersatz tobacco and coffee, almost no rations of spirits or beer and only limited fresh clothing and equipment, did not pass these stores without stopping. For two or three precious days the German Army would not or could not move further on this front. Glimpsed through smoke by day and lit by burning piles of stores by night, the Germans looted and destroyed.

A German observer in Albert on 28 March wrote: 'Men were driving cows before them, carrying a hen under one arm, a box of note-paper under another. Men carried a bottle of wine in one hand, an open bottle in the other. Men were dressed in comic disguise, with top hats on their heads. Men were staggering, some could hardly walk.'

That description would have been familiar to any observer of the aftermath of the great battles and sieges of the Napoleonic wars, right down to the disguises and looting of useless articles.

Aveluy Wood

Every group that visits the Western Front passes this wood on the quiet road north from Albert to Thiepval. It had been behind the front line ever since the line of trenches from the Channel to Switzerland had become a reality at the end of 1914. A large storage area alongside the road, the Lancashire Dump, had been a major supply point for the troops assembling for the Battle of The Somme in 1916. The front had moved slowly away from the neighbourhood of Albert, as far as the Hindenburg Line by 1917, and the entire area for some miles around the town became a large military city. There were many headquarters here, training schools, hospitals, workshops, rest camps, stores and depots of all kinds, bakeries, butcheries, and even prisons and prisoner of war camps. Apart from the road system, some of it dating back to Roman times, and the railways, there was the Canal de la Somme, a major transport artery that ran eastwards from the coast, to the south of Albert and beyond. Traffic ran non-stop along the canal; a barge that could carry 50 tons was a valuable asset at a time when railways were running at full stretch. At points along the canal there were transhipment yards, where loads brought from the coast on the barges could be transferred to one of light railway systems that criss-crossed the whole area.

> **Just one of the light railways survives to this day, at Bray-sur-Somme, a preserved relic of a forgotten part of the services that were built to service the front.**

As the *Michael* Offensive erupted on 21 March, beyond Bapaume and a good 20 miles away, this area around Albert was unprepared for fighting any battle, let alone like the one about to engulf it. German attacks were simply not expected to reach this area. With two exceptions, no BEF assault had ever taken significant ground even after months of continuous attack, and even the two successes, at Arras and Cambrai, had been the results of specific factors. Yet now the Germans were pressing ahead everywhere from Arras to Reims in a matter of hours. Advances were not being measured in yards along fronts of a mile, but in advances of miles across fronts of tens of miles. Gough's Fifth Army was bundled backwards, fighting hard all the while. The Germans came out from the Hindenburg Line and swept forward across the land that they themselves had devastated in the retreat to the Line. Having crossed that, they worked their way across the old 1916 Somme battlefield, after Verdun the most shelled land of the whole war. Suddenly they were near Albert, amongst the stores and depots of the BEF.

Meanwhile, scrambling backwards and parallel to the German advance, units of the BEF were hastily summoned. They came from rest, from training and preparation for Haig's own planned attack due to start later in the year. They came from stores, depots and offices. Long days of desperate marching were the lot of many troops; luckier units were transported by lorry or train. One such unit was the 7th Battalion of The Royal Sussex Regiment. They had come out of the front line near Ypres on the morning of 21 March, and marched to their familiar rest area in the Nieppe Forest south-west of Ypres. They were looking forward to the usual few days of rest that enabled a unit to 'catch its breath' after a turn in the front line. The battalion expected to spend its rest days in providing fatigue parties to work at an airfield nearby. However, the German offensive put paid to the programme. Instead the battalion was bundled into lorries and set off, on country roads congested with traffic heading south on the same mission. Additional traffic flowed in every other direction, part of the usual mêlée of activity behind the lines. Over the next two nights the battalion travelled south, regularly stopped by German aircraft carrying out bombing raids on villages and crossroads to slow down the flow of BEF reinforcements. Four days after being relieved at Ypres, and after many men, including one whole company, had been separated from the battalion in the traffic en route, the battalion re-assembled a little way out of Albert at Bray. They and the other units arriving piece-meal were too late to form any line of resistance east of Albert, and after further local manoeuvring the Sussex arrived in Aveluy Wood, north of Albert, at 0630 on 27 March. They were there to prevent progress by any German troops who might be able to cross the River Ancre.

Gradually during the day other battalions of the 12th (Eastern) Division arrived and formed a defensive line from Albert towards Thiepval, facing east along the line of the road overlooking the river. This was an improvised defensive position, the best that could be done when there were no spades for digging, no wire for entanglements and almost none of the other essentials of modern warfare. However, the marshy course of the River Ancre lay in front of it. The river could be relied upon to slow down the already exhausted Germans as they came upon the meagre defences.

As the day progressed, the situation deteriorated from its already low point. To the right, Albert fell to the advancing Germans and Aveluy Wood was at risk of being over-run. The Royal Sussex Commanding Officer controlled the existing defences facing the river, whilst Major George Osborne, Second in Command, hastily set up new lines of meagre trenches. The Germans might be expected from the east across the river, or from the south, where they had already harried the British out of Albert, about 2 miles to the south. In fact the Germans came from the north, down from the heights at Authuille, near Thiepval and only a mile away, sweeping towards the rear of the wood. The wood was in danger of being surrounded, but by good fortune the area behind it was occupied by Anson Battalion of the Royal Naval Division. These sailors had been fighting as infantry throughout the war and were battle-hardened troops. As the German attack approached the sailors, the evening rum ration had just been distributed and the sailors were 'doubtless in good fettle', as the Royal Sussex war historian described them. The Germans were bundled back and the line had time to take some rather more substantial form. It was to be needed; there were two bridges over the Ancre at this point and there had been neither time nor wherewithal for their destruction. The Germans crossed the river in numbers several times over the next few days, and on 28 March penetrated beyond the Sussex's second trench line, set back in the wood.

Fortunately Lieutenant Colonel Impey, in command, had foreseen the possibility and had ordered Osborne to form a reserve defensive position, centred on an old quarry pit in the wood. This last line of defence under Osborne's command held, and shortly afterwards the bodies of a number of Germans were found surrounding battalion headquarters at the line of this reserve position. The German offensive had reached its furthest point and the northern part of the *Michael* advance was over.

> The Royal Sussex received thirteen gallantry medals after their action at Aveluy, and the Belgian government awarded their *Croix de Guerre* to one of the serjeants – history does not record his reaction to the embrace and kiss on the cheek that was the traditional greeting when any general in the Belgian or French armies was decorating a soldier.

Doullens and Unified Command

At the very moment when the last Germans were dying in the wood at Aveluy, and along this part of the front the German gamble was beginning to fail, a conference was taking place at Doullens, a dozen miles away to the north-west. Haig was there with most of his army commanders, although Gough had more urgent matters to deal with and was absent. After conferring with his generals, Haig walked across the square to the town hall to a second conference. Here was Lord Milner, a member of Lloyd George's war cabinet, and with him that ardent believer in France and all things French, Sir Henry Wilson, now successor to Robertson as Chief of The Imperial General Staff and legally the adviser to the British government on all military matters. They were meeting Foch, recalled from having been sidelined to make way for Nivelle and now French Chief of Staff. Pétain, who had been the Commander-in-Chief since the months of Nivelle's command, and other senior French commanders accompanied him. The politicians and military leaders of the two leading nations of the Allies had one matter to consider; using the resources available to them to stop the German advance.

Haig offered his opinion that he could hold the vital road rail and canal junction at Amiens, and noted that he had already agreed that his forces south of the River Somme should come under French command for the time being. Pétain pointed out that the forces south of the river, most of Gough's Fifth Army, were not much to rely on at that time and that Amiens was by no means secure. Foch made an emotional appeal that Amiens must be held and that further retreat was out of the question. At this, Haig made his historic offer: 'If the general is prepared to give me advice I shall be happy to follow it.' Having been deeply and rightly offended when Lloyd George had subordinated his command to Nivelle in 1917, Haig could now see that Foch, having committed himself to the security of Amiens, would have to provide the reserves that would make the place defensible. Unity of command under Foch was a price worth paying to get that outcome.

In fact, the issue of reserves had become the major bone of contention between the two nations. Both Haig and Pétain as the national commanders on the ground agreed on the need for a central reserve, and both had committed to provide divisions in the sorts of numbers that would make such a multi-national reserve a valid resource. However, in the event neither could actually spare any divisions to make the reserve a reality. Facing this lack of further support or resources Haig recognised that offering unity of command, under Foch, was the only realistic chance of resolving the crisis of the *Kaiserschlacht* advance. A dual command, that forced the British to fall back to defend their communications with the Channel ports, whilst forcing the French to fall back in the other direction to cover Paris, must end in disaster. In his clear-headed assessment of the need to prevent that divergence, which would lose the war, Haig offered the opportunity that Foch would seize and use to win it. The reserves were found, and then held back; Foch was calm in the face of the German advances and could discern the loss of momentum that made violent counter-attacks unnecessary in the immediate aftermath of them.

Villers-Bretonneux and the Australians

Michael was not quite over but the gamble for Germany's future was already lost. The advance had come to a halt north of the Somme, and to the south of it progress was becoming harder and harder. Despite this, Haig and his staff were swinging away from the state of perpetual optimism that owed much to the Panglossian interpretations of his Intelligence Chief, Brigadier General John Charteris. As *Michael* ground on, slowing down but approaching ever closer to Amiens and the nerve centre of the BEF's presence in France, Haig may be considered to have panicked. He did so at a critical moment in 1914 at Le Cateau, leaving his fellow Corps Commander to rescue the BEF from defeat, and his Army Order of the Day of 11 April 1918 suggests that he had lost his nerve again:

'There is no other course open to us but to fight it out! Every position must be held to the last man: there must be no retirement. With our backs to the wall and believing in the justice of our cause, each one of us must fight on to the end. The safety of our homes and the freedom of

King Peter I
SERBIA

The Summer of 1914

28 June – Franz Ferdinand of Austria assassinated by Serbian nationalists.

Austria-Hungary declares war on Serbia.

Russia mobilises in support of Serbia.

Germany supports Austria-Hungary and declares war on Russia and France.

Germany violates Belgium neutrality on way through to France.

4 August – Great Britain declares war on Central Powers in support of Belgium.

Czar Nicholas II
RUSSIA

King Albert I
BELGIUM

CENTRAL POWERS

Emperor Franz-Joseph
AUSTRIA-HUNGARY

Kaiser Wilhelm II
GERMANY

TRIPLE ENTENTE

King George V
GREAT BRITAIN

TRIPLE ENTENTE

President Poincaré
FRANCE

"YOUR COUNTRY NEEDS
YOU"

Secretary of
State for War,
Field Marshal
Earl Kitchener
appeals for
100,000 men.

A scene typical throughout the British Isles: men with Bibles in their right hand being sworn into the military.

British troops arriving in Boulogne in August 1914. This is a Scottish regiment, who wore their glengarry bonnet until replaced by steel helmets in late 1915, and the kilt almost to the end of the war.

r by train
etable:
rman
ops bound
the
gian
rder.

Ausflug nach Paris

Elsaß-Lothringen
33644
6m

Au f Wiedersehn
auf dem
Boulevard

German infantry advancing in Belgium in the early days of the war. At this stage mobility was still possible.

German *Uhlans*, light cavalry, advancing in the hot summer of 1914. The heat and dry weather made conditions very difficult for all armies, which all depended on horsepower for every aspect of warfare.

By November 1914 lines of trenches stretch from the Belgian coast to the Swiss border a Basle.

Left and above: British and French infantry are in their trenches opposite the Germans (below). It is already clear that the Germans are taking the building of their trenches mor seriously than their opponents. This was normal throughout the war and all along the Western Front.

Above: British troops landed at Gallipoli in April 1915, after delays caused by having to reload all the ships in Alexandria Harbour. The delay was largely responsible for the failure of the Gallipoli campaign, along with poor leadership after the landings.

Right: Australians encamped on the cliffs above ANZAC Cove in May 1915. Having failed in the original intention to capture the high ridge that runs up the centre of the Peninsula, the invading forces could do little more than cling onto the small beachheads that they created in the initial landings.

Field Marshal Sir John French was British Commander-in-Chief until December 1915. He was instructed to cooperate with the French but always to remember his responsibility to his own government. At times this dual responsibility was difficult to reconcile.

General Sir Douglas Haig was in command of First Army after it was formed in late 1914. This army fought the Battle of Neuve Chapelle in March 1915. It was the first of many battles that promised much to begin with but delivered very little. Sir Douglas replaced Sir John French as Commander-in-Chief in December 1915.

British dead after an attack during the Battle of Neuve Chapelle in March 1915.

French infantry have captured a German trench during the fighting in the Artois region in 1915. Despite Moroccan troops having advanced onto the top of Vimy Ridge during these attacks, General Ferdinand Foch, commander of the Northern Group of French armies was unable to hold onto local gains. Vimy Ridge would finally fall to the Canadians two years later. Foch ended the war as Generalissimo of the Allied forces.

In February 1916, Erich von Falkenhayn launched the Battle of Verdun. After the war he claimed that he never intended to capture the city, but that he intended to 'bleed the French army white' in their determination to hold the city. He was to be replaced by Hindenburg and Ludendorf later in the year. A new German weapon, the flame-thrower, appeared at Verdun.

The Battle of The Somme 1916. The British bombardment began on 23 June and continued for a week. British artillery fired about 1.7 million shells during this period, equivalent to eighty shells per yard of the length of the assault frontage.

The Hawthorn Redoubt mine was fired at 0720 on 1 July, and many others were fired at 0728. The infantry assault began at 0730. There was little urgency about the advance to the German trenches and the advancing lines of British troops were easy targets for the German machine gunners.

Manfred von Richthofen, The Red Baron. He was the greatest 'ace' of them all, and his 'Flying Circus' was the outstanding air unit of the war. He was always able to obtain the latest models of fighter planes for this *Jagdgeschwader*, (fighter wing) and the Albatross Dr 1 was the most famous of them.

British aces like Mick Mannock and Albert Ball were individually celebrated as knights of the skies and gave a glamour to the desperately dangerous business of aerial warfare. However, aerial warfare was to become a matter of numbers and equipment, as this 1917 picture of British Sopwith Camels, being manufactured at Ruston, Procter & Co. shows.

Air ships made flight a possibility in the last part of the nineteenth century. German Zeppelins conducted bombing raids over British coastal towns in the early months of the war. Airships proved very vulnerable to artillery fire and were helpless in the face of faster and more manoeuvrable fighter aircraft.

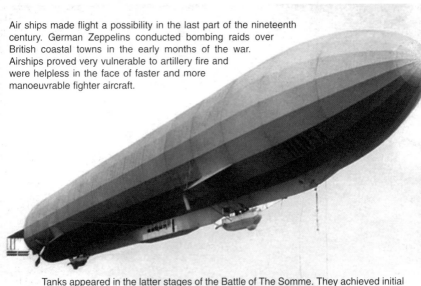

Tanks appeared in the latter stages of the Battle of The Somme. They achieved initial success through their surprise value. Later models were successfully used in a variety of roles. The Germans never built tanks in any quantity, and lack of raw materials probably prevented them from developing this arm of warfare

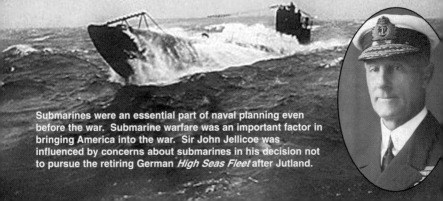

Submarines were an essential part of naval planning even before the war. Submarine warfare was an important factor in bringing America into the war. Sir John Jellicoe was influenced by concerns about submarines in his decision not to pursue the retiring German *High Seas Fleet* after Jutland.

Lieutenant General Sir John Monash. The highest-ranking Australian of the war. A part-time soldier whose fellow officers said he never spoke a word about anything except how to win the war, from its beginning until its end.

Lieutenant General Sir Aylmer Hunter-Weston. Known as 'The Butcher of Helles' his performances at Gallipoli and the Somme were the low points of a bad war for him. He would appear on most lists of the war's least competent generals.

Lieutenant General Sir Arthur Currie. The highest-ranking Canadian of the war. Another part-time soldier, who rose to command his country's troops on the Western Front. As a civilian he was a failure in business, but he proved to have a natural gift for making war.

Lieutenant Walter Tull. The first man of 'negro or coloured blood' ever commissioned in the British Army. He fought at Ypres, on the Somme in 1916, in Italy in 1917 and was killed on his return to the Somme in 1918.

Captain Noel Chavasse. The only winner of two VCs during the war. In this pre-war portrait he wears the lapel badges of his own corps, the Royal Army Medical Corps, and the glengarry of the regiment he served with, the Liverpool Scottish.

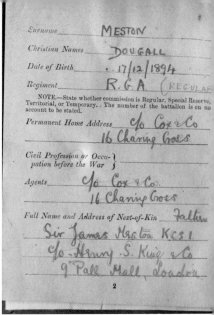

British 8-inch howitzer in action on the Western Front.

War Service record book. Every soldier carried his service record book with him. It recorded personal details, next of kin, details of units with which the individual had served, overseas postings, promotions and wounds.

The war service record of Captain Dougall Meston is typical of the experience of many young officers of the Royal Garrison Artillery. He served throughout the war on the Western Front, and was wounded at Ypres during the Second Battle in 1915. After six months' recovery, he was at the Battle of The Somme, where he was gassed in actions after the night attack of 14 July. He returned to active service in time to take part in the Third Battle of Ypres. During this last battle he fought in four separate battles of the campaign, including the Second Battle of Passchendaele, where he was gassed again. By the end of the war, Meston had fought in three of the great battles of the BEF's war, and had been wounded three times.

After the war, Meston stayed in the army and fought in the Third Afghan War in 1919, and in two subsequent campaigns on the North West Frontier.

After leaving the army had a distinguished career as a barrister, which lasted almost until his death in 1984. Meston became Lord Meston of Agra on his father's death in 1943.

SERVICE.

AT HOME			ABROAD					
Unit.	From	To	With Expedy. Fce. From	To	Elsewhere From	To	Wounded (date)	Sick (date)
G.A.	14/8/14	1/12/14					12/6/15	
Siege Bty RFA	1/12/14	12/6/15	20/4/15	1/7/15				
161 RFA	20/10/15	6/12/15						
3 Res Bde Exeter R.F.A.	6/12/15	12/1/16						
DAC. RFA.	12/1/16	3/3/16	12/1/16	16/8/16				16/8/16 to 12/12/16
87 RFA 19th Divn	3/3/16	16/8/16						
Bty RFA	12/12/16	4/3/17						
DA.C. RFA	4/3/17	27/4/17	4/3/17	3/11/17				
87 RFA 19th Divn	27/4/17	3/11/17						3/11/17 to 9/1/18
Res Bde Swanage RFA	9/1/18	25/6/18						
DA.C. RFA.	25/6/18	22/7/18						
Res Bde, Deepcut.	22/7/18	12/12/18						
G.A. Portsmouth Command	12/12/18							

British soldiers, temporarily blinded by gas, line up for evacuation to the rear.

Collecting casualties and removing them to the aid posts and clearing stations was dangerous and difficult work. It is no surprise that the most decorated soldier of the BEF was a stretcher-bearer, William Coltman, VC, Distinguished Conduct Medal and bar, Military Medal and bar.

German Stormtroopers operating a mortar during the Spring Offensive in 1918.

Major Osborne, whose defensive action with the Royal Sussex in Aveluy Wood near Albert marked the end of the German advance in the *Michael* Offensive in 1918.

A captured British supply dump is rifled by German troops during their offensive.

When the German offensive stalled it was the Allies turn to advance, this time to final victory. A British gun team pulls an 18-pounder across the Canal du Nord at Cambrai, September 1918.
Gun teams were down from six to four horses to help supply the Americans.

American troops, nicknamed 'Dough Boys', arrive in 1917, in time to make a difference. This staged picture was probably an official photograph for home consumption.

Portuguese troops formed an expeditionary force that fought in many of the key battles of the Western Front.

11 November 1920. The funeral cortege of The Unknown Soldier passing The Cenotaph, unveiled and dedicated on that day. The body of the unknown soldier is honoured for the tens of thousands of soldiers whose bodies were never found or identified.

mankind alike depend on the conduct of each one of us at this critical moment.'

The key feature defending Amiens is a long ridge to the east of the town, below which lies the small town of Villers-Bretonneux. The centre of Amiens can be seen from ridge's crest and on 24 April the ridge fell, the Germans employing thirteen tanks of their own to support the infantry advance. That same day Second Lieutenant Frank Mitchell's tank successfully engaged a German one in the world's first tank-versus-tank engagement. That night a strong Australian force of two brigades, with a British one, counter-attacked and recaptured the ridge. The northern flank of the *Michael* Offensive had run out of momentum at Aveluy Wood, so had the southern flank attack ended on this ridge.

This counter-attacking action was subsequently to be recognised as a supreme feat of arms. The Australian national war memorial in France is sited on top of the ridge and in every school classroom of Villers-Bretonneux is a plaque above the teacher's desk – *'N'oublions jamais l'Australie'* (We Must Never Forget Australia). Residents of Villers-Bretonneux have said that this is no mere form of words; the Australian action that day is a living part of the village's history.

Gough is Dismissed

The Fifth Army had fallen back, conducting a bitterly fought retreating action over a front over 20 miles wide, in some places ending up 30 miles behind their positions at the beginning of the German offensive. However, the line never actually broke to allow the Germans to achieve their objective of getting behind the BEF's line and rolling it up towards the sea. Gough's fifteen divisions had prevented eighty German ones from achieving their objectives, but the cost in territory given up was too great for the politicians to let go unnoticed. Even as he subordinated his position to that of the new Generalissimo – Foch – Haig needed a scapegoat. As an army commander Gough was sufficiently senior to be a suitable sacrificial offering to Downing Street. The fact that he had consistently warned Haig of the outcome of the battle, and of his intention to conduct it as it actually turned out, mattered not at all. He had to go.

The Fifth Army was re-formed as a new Fourth Army, under Rawlinson. This latter had been out of a job since the break up of his own old Fourth Army when the plan for an amphibious invasion of the Belgian coast in conjunction with Gough's breakout from Ypres in 1917 was abandoned.

Georgette and *Blucher/Yorck*

Even as *Michael* was running down, Ludendorff launched *Georgette* on 9 April, an assault whose name, changed from *George*, suggests a lessening of expectation. The Germans were about to have some good fortune. *Georgette's* axis was north-west, driving from east of Arras into the side of the pocket formed by the English Channel on one side and the front line on the other. Preparing for *Michael* further south, and then reacting to it, Haig had called heavily on Plumer's Second Army for reinforcements, and troops were thin on the ground in the north. *Georgette* struck at the positions of the Portuguese division, holding too much line with too few troops. This division and five British ones were badly cut up in resisting the advance. The Portuguese had been in the line continuously for a year and were already exhausted. *Georgette* made substantial progress, never actually capturing Ypres city but moving the front line well to the west of the city in the south side of the old salient. The highest point in the region, Mont Kemmel fell into German hands for the first time since 1914. Plumer decided that the Messines and Passchendaele Ridges to the north-east, taken at such cost only months before, were no longer tenable after this loss, and he withdrew his forces off the ridges and back to the edges of Ypres.

To the north the impassable obstacle of the still-flooded lowlands were held by the Belgians. Ypres was the way into the Pas de Calais, and an isolated Belgian Army would be irrelevant in the greater events now unfolding.

Foch now used his supreme command effectively. He moved fresh French divisions north to replace four spent British ones, who in turn went south to face the German lines overlooking the River Aisne along the Chemin des Dames.

Since the failed Nivelle assault in early 1917 the front on the River Aisne had become almost the quietest sector of the whole Western Front. It was a 'rest cure' for exhausted French units and was meant to serve the same purpose for these depleted and exhausted British ones.

Safely arrived and settling into the comfort of their new positions, between the River Aisne and the German positions on the Chemin des Dames, the British prepared to re-build and re-fit. They were in no condition to resist the next, *Blucher/Yorck*, phase of Ludendorff's programme. On 27 April, scarcely two weeks after being cut up in the north, these same units were overwhelmed for a second time. Again the Germans made startling advances. They had been about 70 miles from the Arc de Triomphe as *Blucher/Yorck* opened, and were within 30 miles by its ending, but with their momentum spent and beyond the safety of their artillery's protection. This battle, the Third Battle of The Aisne, rates as a particular British misfortune. Faulty intelligence had failed to identify German intentions and from an Allied perspective the battlefield was singularly unsuited to attack or defence. The Germans, inevitably, held the heights of the Chemin des Dames, and as always Allied military politics dictated that their positions be pushed forward as close to them as possible. It seemed unimportant that the River Aisne and its canalised section, running parallel to the Chemin, were therefore behind the Allied front lines. This Allied positioning ensured that transport of supplies and reinforcements, indeed all movement from rear areas to the front or in the other direction, was funnelled into the areas surrounding the few remaining bridges. The German observation posts overlooked the entire front, less than two miles from the bridges. The Germans could scarcely have asked for more favourable circumstances.

The British divisions were to suffer terribly from their posting into what had been almost the quietest sector of the Western Front since the Nivelle Offensive a year before. Coming down from the Chemin des Dames, the Germans would only cease their advance when they had outrun their resources of stamina, transport and artillery.

One action during these desperate days deserves mention. Lieutenant G.W. Bright was by now the senior officer of 4th Battalion, King's Shropshire Light Infantry, there being only five officers left and all junior to him. The Commanding Officer and all the majors and captains were casualties. Despite much greater numbers opposing the battalion, Bright led a brilliant action to recapture a key feature, the Montagne de Bligny. Without regaining that hill the British could not hope to hold any of the surrounding ground. With his battalion already down to 300 men, Bright led a charge of four waves of men, each wave led by one of the other four remaining lieutenants of the battalion. Pausing at the foot of the hill, and collecting up the remnants of two more battalions, from the Cheshire and North Staffordshire Regiments, but still being the senior officer, Lieutenant Bright took the hill in the face of astonished German opposition who managed to retain a foothold in an adjoining wood. Despite orders to retire from the *montagne* so that a proper full-scale attack could be launched on it, Bright held on until reinforcements arrived. Bright himself, Private Greaves – a stretcher-bearer who had worked all through the attack in the open ground overlooked by German positions – and Serjeant Poole were all awarded the *Croix de Guerre* by the French. The battalion too was decorated with the rare unit award of the *Croix de Guerre avec Palme*. The French awarded BEF units the honour of this decoration only eleven times during the war, and three of the eleven awards are the direct result of the charge and defence led by Lieutenant Bright.

This was undoubtedly a grim time, with German advances everywhere achieving more than all the assaults of all the armies of both sides had achieved on the Western Front in the previous three and a half years. More was to come; the attack code-named *Gneisenau* in June enlarged the salient south of Amiens, and the final attack of *Blucher/Yorck* in July east of Reims moved the German line forward and placed Reims at the apex of another uncomfortable pocket. Despite appearances at the time the successes had been tactical and no vital strategic points had been uncovered let alone lost to the Germans. However, in failing to reach their strategic objectives, the German high command could see that the war was now lost. The last German offensive had originally been code-named *Reims* but was nick-named *Friedensturm* – the Peace Offensive – with no greater hope than to force the Allies to peace negotiations before the Americans were ready to fight. That option being rejected, Germany had little choice but to hang onto what territory had been gained and hope for some unforeseen help.

Chateau-Thierry and the Americans

A year after declaring war America was at last ready to fight and indeed it was not a moment too soon. Foch had to deal with constant demands for support, for more troops, for reserves to support weak points, and was running out of resources. In early June the first American units fought as an American army, first in a modest defensive action at long range near the town of Chateau Thierry and then three days later in attacking a wood outside the town. Pershing's insistence on keeping his army separate from the Allies' was not immediately obviously successful. No experienced French or BEF troops under battle-wise officers had advanced to attack in parade-ground order for a year or more. The effect on the inexperienced Americans was exactly the same as it had been on the British at the Somme and in every other attack until new tactics had been developed. Tactics that had disappeared from other armies two years earlier brought the same 50 per cent casualty rates and lack of any progress over the ground that the BEF and French had suffered in every attack of the first two years of the war. Nonetheless, America was now in the ring and punching, raw and inexperienced but with resources of men and matériel of which others could only dream.

Charles Mangin returns

Mangin was Nivelle's associate at Verdun and was in local command for Nivelle's final disgrace following the disaster at the Chemin des Dames in early 1917. He had been dismissed from his command after Nivelle's fall, but he re-emerged in command of the French Tenth Army later in the same year. He now presented a plan to his Commander-in-Chief, Pétain; a violent blow into the side of the German salient that pointed directly at Paris following the German's April breakout at the Chemin des Dames. The plan had been shelved a week or so earlier, Mangin's forces might have been needed to deal with the Germans elsewhere. However, in that one week Foch had detected that the moment was ripe to switch from defence to attack. Mangin would launch his attack.

Mangin's plan was simple: two thrusts, one north into the right side as he looked at the pocket, and the other eastward into the left side. A third attack, at the point of furthest development of the salient, would be a distraction that Ludendorff could not ignore. Mangin launched his three-pronged attack on 18 July and achieved all the success that could have been asked of it. His forces took 25,000 prisoners and inflicted heavy casualties. The salient from Soissons to Reims, previously jutting as far south-west as the line from Chateau-Thierry to Epernay, was closed again, and Ludendorff was forced to retire back almost to the start line of *Blucher*, on the line of the River Aisne. Mangin had used his forces well; he had learned a lot from his experiences under Nivelle.

Foch's Grand Idea

As Ludendorff fell back on the Aisne, and the Americans moved east of Reims and beyond Verdun to take over the eastern end of the Western Front, other great decisions were afoot. Advised by Henry Wilson, Lloyd George had decided to wait to replace Haig until the defensive battles were over – much though he might have wanted Haig to go, the Prime Minister could only accept the advice that there was nobody better qualified to fight the defensive battles then taking place. Apart from any other consideration, Lloyd George knew that he could not himself survive as Prime Minister if he sacked Haig and his replacement proved no more adept; Haig had many friends in high places. In the meantime, Foch was in charge as Generalissimo, and despite being so disappointed when he had trusted Nivelle, Lloyd George had confidence in Foch's ability to control Haig.

Foch articulated his strategy, a colossal assault along the whole Western Front, from the Channel to Switzerland's border. Millions of men, their supporting artillery, tanks and transport, their medical support and all the impedimenta of war would point themselves at the western German town of Spa, the headquarters of the Kaiser's command and the centre of the rough circle of which the Western Front now formed a large arc. A series of individual armies' actions would tie in together to press against every segment of the arc, Americans in the east, French in the centre, BEF in the north, Belgians and French under command of the King of Belgium on the coast. Foch's plans and expectations were essentially simple – *Tout le Monde á la Bataille* – the general advance to overrun the enemy at all points that would win the war.

Given the recent successes of the Germans, the inexperience of the Americans, the less-than-certain morale of many French formations, and the recent losses of ground, and of men and matériel by the BEF, this decision that the time had come to end the war may seem a little premature. However, Foch was neither a gambler nor a foolish optimist. He had very solid reasons to back up his decision. He was fully aware that a number of German units had surrendered en masse rather than fight and die, a phenomenon that had never been known until recently. He knew about the increasing shortage of raw materials of all kinds in Germany. He knew that the German conscription programme was trawling ever more frantically for the middle-aged, the young, the unfit and the unsuitable in order to keep up its numbers. He also knew that the corps of non-commissioned officers, always the core of German military hierarchy, had more or less disappeared. These men with years of training and experience were used to commanding at levels far higher than those seen in other armies. They were irreplaceable. Above all, Foch knew of the increasing urgency with which German envoys to neutral countries were urging their hosts to carry messages and negotiations to the allied powers, offering terms for an armistice and negotiation about the future allocation of territories. He knew that Germany was led by a weakened monarchical government and a military class who could see that negotiations for peace were necessary and urgent.

The Spanish 'Flu

Another enemy, as deadly as any seen so far in the war, was also abroad. An unknown strain of influenza had appeared in America. It had been identified at Camp Funston in Kansas, close to the local reporting centre for army recruits, with whom it had travelled across the Atlantic. The first outbreak in Europe was soon identified in Lancashire and then amongst troops on the Western Front. Inevitably it crossed no-man's-land and was soon ravaging Germany, both in the army and at home. The results of the blockade – a shortage of food, fuel and medicines – certainly helped the disease's spread in Germany, but in fact the world was experiencing the outbreak of the largest health crisis since the Black Death. Over the next three years truly fantastic numbers of people, by no means only the elderly and weak, would die of Spanish 'Flu. Estimates at the time suggested about twenty-five million deaths, but more recent and sophisticated studies indicate twice that number. Typically the 'flu killed 2 to 4 per cent of those affected and the pandemic was worldwide. The Fiji Islands lost 14 per cent of the population, Western Samoa lost over 20 per cent. In India there were no accurate records beyond local estimates that add together to indicate seventeen million deaths, 5 per cent of the whole sub-continent's population.

> **Why was it called Spanish Influenza? Spain was the first neutral country to acknowledge the existence of the disease; every belligerent nation treated its existence as a military secret not to be reported in the Press. Thus as knowledge of the pandemic began to spread it was easy to associate its origin with the only country that had acknowledged the existence of it.**

Clemenceau and Wilson

Beyond all these factors, and it is difficult to know how much he knew about the last, even if he was certainly aware of its existence, Foch knew that behind him, utterly clear in his political philosophy, stood the Prime Minister of the Republic, Georges Clemenceau and his philosophy: '*Je fait la geurre*' – 'I make war'. Clemenceau believed in the absolute necessity of pursuing the war to its end, and to achieve victory he would do everything to put the means of success in Foch's hands, not least in supporting the argument that a unified command was essential to success.

In the meantime President Wilson in Washington was working tirelessly towards a negotiated peace treaty. He believed that offering a fair peace would help all sides to end the war. It would be based on resolution of pre-war grievances, open trade and some colonial re-alignment. He made no mention of war reparations, and none of allocating blame. Whatever the US Congress may have thought about the Fourteen Point Plan, it was unacceptable to Lloyd George, Clemenceau and Italian Prime Minister Orlando. They wanted blame and reparations in addition to the grievances addressed and the wrongs righted. Wilson's offer died in an atmosphere of suspicion among the Allies about his previous pacifism that was still part of his character, and among the German and Austro-Hungarians in suspicion of an attempt to destroy their nations as well as their colonies.

Tout Le Monde á La Bataille

After Mangin's success there was a necessary pause. Foch was determined on a war of movement on a scale that had simply no precedent on The Western Front. It would take time to plan, prepare and rehearse the actions to end the war. Much pressure came on Foch to relieve the impact on Paris of the great German gun '*Kaiser Wilhelm Geschütz*' – 'Emperor William Gun' – dropping its shells indiscriminately around the city from 70 miles away. However, Foch would not go before he was ready.

If we include Mangin's attack as the overture to the final campaign of the war, Foch's plan would have six separate elements:

1. Mangin pinching out the German salient Soissons-Reims achieved by the *Blucher/Yorck* Offensive.
2. Driving back the German advance achieved by Michael and Gneisenau centred at Montdidier.
3. Closing the long-established German salient south of Verdun at St Mihiel.
4. Clearing the Argonne Forest between Reims and Verdun.
5. Taking the Scarpe, the ground north of Arras.
6. Retaking all the ground lost in Georgette and clearing the Belgian coast.

The tempo would start off at a measured pace but would pick up as the phases unfolded; once started, no-one was to stop to await the arrival of units on either flank, this campaign that would only end with German defeat. After Mangin's Phase One in mid-July there would be a pause of three weeks before the next five phases, with the last beginning on 28 September. Foch was planning for six inter-linked battles and expected of each one greater results than any French or British offensive had achieved in four years of trying. Foch allowed seventy-three days to switch from the defensive crises of the *Kaiserschlacht* to being actively on the offensive along a front of 250 miles.

Phase Two – Amiens – 8 August

Rawlinson had arrived to take over the demoralised Fifth Army, re-numbered Fourth. He began by preparing defensive positions that reflected latest thinking about fluid defence in depth, keenly aware that Amiens remained vulnerable to a determined German attack. However, it quickly became clear that the German troops opposite his sector of the line were incapable of any assault that could have any chance of success, and indeed a large-scale trench raid by Australian infantry soon made clear that these Germans were also unlikely to be able to mount any defence against a determined attack either. Rawlinson considered, and his subordinates agreed with him, that an attack against this enemy on the grand scale had a very good chance of achieving much at acceptable cost. The army's three corps were first class, including the ANZAC (Australian and New Zealand Army Corps) and Canadian Corps. Not only had Rawlinson learned how to handle an army effectively, he commanded two corps considered by the Germans as the finest of any they had met in battle, commanded by two of the outstanding commanders of the whole war, Sir John Monash of Australia and Sir Arthur Currie of Canada.

Despite interference by Haig, who as usual saw the breakthrough and ride to Berlin, and Foch, who wanted the French on Rawlinson's right to be involved, Rawlinson was able to plan and execute his own battle. It was perhaps the first all-arms battle of the modern era. Aircraft were in plentiful supply, 2,000 of them in roles as varied as any that we take for granted in the modern air arm. They obtained and sent back unrivalled reconnaissance and battlefield information, dropped ammunition to advancing troops, bombed enemy gun positions and swept the opposing 400 German planes from the sky. 342 fighting tanks supported the infantry, and more specialist tanks brought up fresh troops, ammunition and other supplies. To provide further support, Rawlinson had over 2,000 pieces of artillery available, whose plan was that each would fire four rounds per minute – about 130 shells per second on a front of about 30 miles. Both Monash's and Currie's corps were under-strength, but the supply of matériel compensated for this lack of men.

Fighting over difficult ground on the left, in the wasteland of the old Somme battlefield, the British corps made less progress than the ANZACs and Canadians to the south, who advanced 8 miles and inflicted 27,000 casualties in the day. The presence of these latter troops, fit and full of confidence, had come as a complete and most unwelcome surprise to the Germans. Some small Canadian units had been moved, with deliberate indiscretion, to Ypres, and the move of the remainder to the Amiens area was completely unsuspected. After the war Ludendorff wrote about the day in his memoirs, 'August 8th was the black day of the German Army in the war. This was the worst experience.' After the war, the German official history was equally alive of the importance of the day: 'The greatest defeat suffered by the German Army since the beginning of the war.' Although he was not yet to know the true numbers, Ludendorff was aware that many of Germany's casualties on that day, probably as many as 18,000, had not been lost in battle but had surrendered, frequently whole units together.

Naturally Haig wanted more, but Rawlinson knew his business well, and whereas he had been forced into planning the Somme in 1916 as a breakthrough battle, by 1918 he would not take on more than he could achieve. The second phase had succeeded exactly as Rawlinson, Monash and Currie had planned, and Foch, able to accept the wisdom of the commanders on the ground, was content to let the battle end when Rawlinson insisted that it should.

In the same sector, on Rawlinson's left, Byng's Third Army was ready to advance, and made good pace as it harried retiring German forces along much of his front. Rawlinson began to move again and within a few days Horne's

First Army was on the move as well. Three of the four British armies were now moving forward together. They would soon begin to suffer heavy casualties, not least because the advance was over ground made dangerous by German booby-traps, unexploded shells and the other hazards of a battlefield that had suffered almost four years of modern industrial-scale warfare. Nonetheless, advances were made and towns like Albert were recaptured. Although nothing like the 20-mile advances of the Mangin Offensive were achieved, the British were again back on the Somme battlefield at its northern end.

Phase Three – The Americans at St Mihiel

On 12 September the Americans launched their largest and most ambitious offensive of the war so far. The large German salient at St Mihiel to the south of Verdun still threatened that city and offered Germany the tantalising possibility of a breakthrough into north-eastern France. The area of the salient stretched back from the town of St Mihiel on the River Meuse, south of Verdun, north-eastward towards the Moselle river system and the ancient city of Metz. The land is flat and dotted with lakes and watercourses. Ranges of hills dominate to north and south and were strongly held by the Germans, who as usual had spent much time and effort on ensuring the effectiveness of their defences.

Pershing's plan was to pinch out the neck of the salient and then press on to capture Metz, about 30 miles behind the furthest point of the salient's penetration into France. Lacking adequate air or artillery support he borrowed freely, from the French in particular. When the battle began he had an air force of over 1,000 machines, mostly flown by French pilots. His artillery was almost exclusively French. The infantry was almost exclusively American, and as they made up the bulk of the numbers involved and the offensive was American-commanded this may validly be claimed as the first major engagement of American forces in a European theatre of war.

A number of factors were quickly identified. The Germans, aware of the impending attacks, were already in the process of withdrawing from the salient when the attacks began. It was later claimed that the half-hearted speed of the attacks to the mouth of the salient prevented a far greater success for the offensive. However, the road system was simply inadequate to cope with the stresses of a large-scale advance against an enemy conducting a fighting retreat, destroying bridges across the many streams and small rivers as they went. Equally, it was impossible to keep moving the artillery fast enough to keep up with advancing infantry. As with so many other offensives, operations that had begun with successful advances, the logistical problems overwhelmed the fighting opportunities. Metz was clearly out of range, but perhaps that was a good thing; the city was considered the most formidable fortified centre in

Europe. However, Pershing could justifiably stop the offensive on the fourth day, having closed the sack, claiming equality of cost in terms of manpower, and advantage in terms of captured matériel. Most importantly he could proclaim that the US Army was ready to take its place in the bigger battles yet to come.

> Seven thousand casualties on each side do not make this a 'great battle' in the terms of this war. Its significance lies in its confirmation to Germany that the war could not be won, under any circumstances, now that the Americans were taking their share of the strain.

Phase Four – The Argonne Forest

Scarcely had Pershing closed down the St Mihiel Offensive than he was ready for the next American contribution. The Forest of Argonne lies between Reims and Verdun, hilly, wooded and offering every advantage to the defender. Strategically the Germans were bound to defend this area, because the main supply routes of the eastern end of the German front lay behind it. It was also the only route that the Germans could take if they needed to draw back towards their border river systems. The city of Sedan, humiliatingly lost to Prussia in 1870, was the hub of this communications network.

Only eleven days after St Mihiel's ending the Americans were in action in this dangerous sector on 26 September. To begin with they made good progress; on Day One they took the key strongpoint, the fortified hill-top village of Montfaucon d'Argonne, situated in the middle of the gap between the forest itself and the River Meuse, and advancing 7 miles in the first two days. However, as the Americans moved further into the wooded areas they faced the problems that had bedevilled so many previous attempts to break through; getting ahead of the artillery, meeting the stronger defensive lines behind the lightly-held front and naïve leadership by American junior officers. By the end of the first week, the Americans were exhausted, running out of men and supplies and facing fresh German divisions sent to reinforce the threatened area. Even by this early stage the weaknesses of Pershing's argument to fight American troops as a unified US army were becoming manifest. He was already dependent on British and French air superiority, and almost totally dependent on French artillery, both as to guns and gunners. The inexperienced American logistics units were unable to manage traffic on the few narrow roads in the forest. There was simply too much traffic; artillery following up behind infantry, wounded soldiers being bought back from the front, food and water being taken forward, as well as all the ammunition, animal fodder and other essentials of an army on the move. In some places whole units simply abandoned the advance and made their own way back from the front to find food and water.

After a lull to bring experienced British and French logistics management to the rear areas, and despite being able to field only half of the almost 100,000 reinforcements that he needed, Pershing was anxious to press on. This was no longer an action to pinch out another shallow salient; it had become a head-on attack against strong German defences. Like so many previous similar offensives, this one took on a life of its own. Foch wanted the offensive to be maintained; other offensives had begun further north and he needed the Germans to be distracted in as many places as possible. The American army under Pershing became two armies and by the end of the offensive, which lasted until the last day of the war, over 1.2 million soldiers, including airmen, had fought on this front under Pershing's command. Of the American Expeditionary Force, 26,000 had been killed and 96,000 wounded, half the total number of battle casualties that the United States suffered during the war.

Although this was one of the few great offensives of the American war, and it is commemorated as such, it cannot be denied that this was another failed attempt. The strategic objective, to cut German communication lines, was not achieved, and it is highly doubtful whether the casualties suffered by the Americans were justified, even if one allows for the similar number of German ones, as well as the relief afforded in the other offensive actions further north. Undoubtedly German military leaders were more shaken by the relentless ferocity with which American units pressed home their attacks than by their results. Nonetheless, one may question whether that moral factor alone, allied to the meagre results, justifies any thinking of this battle as a success.

It is perfectly possible that in due time history will place the Argonne Offensive alongside Verdun, the Somme, Passchendaele and the Chemin des Dames in 1917 as America's modest but still notable first contribution to the list of some of the greatest, most costly and least successful battles of the early twentieth century.

Phase Five – The Scarpe

The River Scarpe is the river system immediately north of the Ancre/Somme river complex. On the day after the Argonne Offensive opened, Foch's next blow was struck. Byng's Third Army started in the newly-regained ground to the east and north of Albert, and with the devastation of the old Somme battlefield behind him, Byng was ready to launch the second great British offensive of 1918. The French offensives already taking place would ensure that Germany could throw in no sudden counter-attack delivered by fresh reserves. This British offensive made spectacular gains, re-taking the Somme villages, driving forward through the heavily fortified Hindenburg Line, and so towards that never-yet-seen country, the open ground behind the German lines. With complete air superiority, tanks in abundance, and the advantages of superior resources of all kinds, the Ride to the Rhine was underway.

Phase Six – Ypres and Belgium

On 28 September, the day after the opening of the Scarpe Offensive, Haig launched the third British offensive. The objective was to clear the Belgian coast and drive towards Brussels. First fighting was as hard as always, and casualties heavy whilst the Germans were being cleared back from their close positions around Ypres, and took two weeks. Then the impetus of advance began to develop; within another three weeks Lille and Bruges had fallen to the British advance, and still the whole Western Front rolled forward. The western end of the front had moved from the coast at the beaches at Nieuport, north of Ypres, to the Dutch border near Ghent, 50 miles nearer to Germany.

In counterpoint to his earlier General Order of 11 April, the 'Backs to the Wall' appeal, Haig caught the moment perfectly. After the first British contribution to *Tout le Monde á la Bataille*, generals were freed, encouraged and even ordered to take risks that would have seemed unthinkable only a month earlier. Indeed, Haig's General Order of 22 August made this clear: 'Risks which a month ago would have been criminal to incur, ought now to be taken as a duty.' It was perhaps a pity that he also used the same order to establish a 'new' principle; 'Reinforcements must be directed on the points where our troops are gaining ground, not where they are checked.' However, the war was now obviously in its end phases and Haig was less concerned with arguments about the urgent need to scale back the British war effort in 1919 than he was with ensuring that incessant pressure all along his part of the Western Front would bring victory in 1918.

'Reinforcements must be directed on the points where our troops are gaining ground, not where they are checked.' A competent student of military history could have made that latter point at any time in the previous four years. If he could have convinced Haig, which would have been no easy task, he would have saved Britain and the Empire over one million casualties.

The Beginning of the End

As the last days of October passed the German effort was clearly coming to its end. Civil unrest was too widespread to be ignored in Germany itself; the combination of Spanish 'Flu and food shortages was taking as much a toll on German morale as the actual fighting. The weak German parliament was never as important in Germany as the rule of the Hohenzollerns, but it was increasingly vocal and inclined to interfere in matters hitherto outside its areas of authority. The iconic figure of Hindenburg, the victor of the East, was not to be blamed, but his first co-equal Ludendorff was forced to resign. His prophetic forecast in the last days of October did not help his cause: 'In two weeks we shall have neither Emperor nor Empire'. He was accurate to the day, and on 9 November it was announced in Berlin that the Kaiser Wilhelm II had abdicated.

On 29 October a small number of sailors in the German navy reacted to preparations that had begun the previous day. These were movement of ships to offshore anchorages in preparation for a last desperate attempt to clear the North Sea of the British. It was a plan hatched by Naval High Command, and the government had not approved it, as indeed they could not because they had not been told of it. A small local refusal to obey orders to raise steam for sailing and to weigh anchors was soon followed by widespread mutiny. Naval High Command abandoned the plan to sail, but the damage was done. Within a week the main naval bases of Kiel and Wilhemshaven were in the hands of councils set up by mutineers, a mix of sailors, soldiers sent to put down the mutinies but joining them instead, and local munitions and dockyard workers.

The government now had to seek peace, on the best terms that could be arranged, or failing that on any terms that would be offered. The flow of emissaries between Germany and neutral countries increased, and at last a group representing the newly empowered parliament crossed the lines of opposing armies to meet the allied deputation to discuss peace terms. There was little to discuss; the allied demand was for unconditional surrender and, after a few days argument, an agreement was signed. There would be an Armistice, a cease-fire. The fighting would actually end at eleven o'clock in the morning, noon in Germany, on 11 November. The actual peace treaty and imposition of reparations, division of the spoils of war and other details would be for later conferences.

The End

At two minutes before 1100 on the morning of 11 November 1918, Private George Price, a Canadian soldier, looked out over the parapet of his trench. Firing had more or less died away in anticipation of the coming cease-fire. A

German sniper fired a single shot and Price died instantly, shot through the heart. Many men would die of wounds in the years and decades to come but Price was the last man actually killed in action on the Western Front. He was buried in the nearest military cemetery, at the nearby village of St Symphorien. In the same cemetery, buried within a dozen yards of him, lies the body of the sixteen-year-old John Parr, the first British casualty of the Western Front. He too had been buried in the cemetery closest to where he fell. Thus the British war on this front ended, with a terrible coincidence of location, exactly where it had begun, 1,442 days earlier.

Fighting in The Great War, the 'War to End All Wars', the war from which the armies of 1914 would be home by Christmas, had ended. There would be a grand conference at Versailles to set the terms of German surrender and indemnity. On 28 June 1919 the war formally came to an end, five years to the day after Gavril Princeps had fired the shots that killed Franz Ferdinand and set the war in motion.

The End of Five Empires

Four Empires collapsed and disappeared as the immediate consequence of the war: The Russian, Austro-Hungarian and Ottoman Empires had been in decay for years, and the war merely accelerated the process of their dissolution. The German Empire had never been a genuine empire, being little more than a few leftover territories from older empires' colonial expansion in Africa. Germany was now a republic.

At the beginning of the war the British Empire was the largest and richest the world had ever known. Less than thirty years after the war's end the bulk of that empire was gone. The Dominions – Australia, Canada and New Zealand – were independent states under the Crown. India was an independent republic. Fifty years after the war's end the whole edifice of empire was reduced to a few Crown colonies with a residual tie to the Crown in the form of The British Commonwealth. The age of European domination of the world, where a handful of countries in mainland Europe owned and managed much of the rest of the world, was truly over.

In the Far East the war had scarcely touched the Japanese Empire, which was to survive to fight on another world war and lose, but keep its emperor throughout.

APPENDIX I

The Cast

Individuals fought the war, and some have appeared in the narrative of this tale. Some, like Walter Tull and Colonel Driant won personal reputations that will not fade with time. Their stories transcend the story of the war itself and have become legends in their own ways.

Colonel Driant's name is recalled at St Cyr, the French equivalent of the Royal Military Academy Sandhurst. Every intake of aspirant officer cadets is given an intake name, called after a hero of French military history. Every 'Colonel Driant' intake visits his grave during their training and leaves a plaque recording their privilege to be another intake named after his memory.

Walter Tull was brought back into the public eye in 2006 when a statue of that footballer and soldier, and ambassador for black people everywhere was unveiled at Northampton Town, the club he served with distinction before the war.

Others, like Lieutenant Bright and Noel Chavasse, are remembered and honoured by their own corps and regiments, and in their home towns.

The enduring questions are never about men like these, whose reputations and honour are unassailable. Instead the questions are always about the generals, the men who planned, led and commanded the greatest military enterprise the world had ever known. Who were these generals? Were they the 'donkeys' of that cruel remark of Ludendorff – 'The British have an army of lions led by donkeys'? Were they actually very competent soldiers thrust without experience or training into the great enterprise? Or was there some mixture of both the donkey and the competent, some being more obviously donkey and some less so? One cannot list, let alone analyse, the competence of the many hundreds of officers of dozens of armies who held general's rank at some stage of the war. Instead the following is an arbitrary short selection, with a Western Front bias, and that means ignoring many who would appear in any list of significant generalship of the war. Thus the Russian general Brusilov, whose Easter offensive of 1916 was one of history's great victories, gets no mention. Kemal Ataturk, the father of modern Turkey and the victor of Gallipoli is another.

APPENDIX I

THE BRITISH AND THE EMPIRE

The British provided the bulk of the generals in the BEF and the eventual size of that force dictated that hundreds of officers would hold general rank during the war. This selection is limited to those who feature large in this book. Thus there is no room for Kitchener, despite his towering contribution to the creation of the armies that fought and won the war. The worst general of them all, Sir Charles Townshend, led the infamous total failure that was the Mesopotamia expedition to capture Baghdad. His omission from further consideration in this list allows him to keep a degree of anonymity that he does not deserve. Other army commanders deserve to be considered, as do naval men like Fisher, the creator of the Royal Navy that Jellicoe commanded at Jutland, and Beatty commanded thereafter. Trenchard, the father of the Royal Air Force, deserves more than a mention. There are lists of hundreds of short biographies on websites and a book like this cannot try to compete with them.

Sir John French

Sir John French was Commander-in-Chief of the original British Expeditionary Force, the BEF. He proved inadequate to command the force of 100,000 men at the outset, and was to prove progressively less adequate as the army swelled in numbers. He was temperamental, scheming and a fierce believer in the importance of social distinction. His ability to nurse grudges for years was well-known and that character trait came to work against the well-being of the army during the critical months that led up to Le Cateau and Loos.

John French was born in 1852, lost his father before he was three years old, and his mother was confined in a mental home shortly afterwards. He joined the Royal Navy at the not-unusual age of fourteen before transferring to the army aged twenty-two. He had been appointed Field Marshal in 1913 at the end of his term as Chief of the Imperial General Staff (CIGS), the senior appointment of the British Army. French blotted his copybook badly over the Curragh Mutiny. In March 1914 a number of officers based at the principal Irish garrison, The Curragh, outside Dublin declared that they would defy any orders given to march into the six counties of Ulster to prevent a rebellion against Home Rule from Dublin that was proposed for the whole of Ireland. French backed the would-be mutineers in their refusal to support the government in their proposed actions against the Ulster Loyalists. His part in this complex moment in Anglo-Irish politics caused French to become bitterly estranged from his sister, his only living close relative.

Sir John French was forced to resign as CIGS in the aftermath of the Curragh Mutiny and played no part in military affairs for some months afterwards, although Field Marshals never formally retire. However, he was brought out of his effective retirement to command the BEF on the outbreak of the war.

Sir John was famously indiscreet with women, not least with the wives of fellow-officers. It is quite probable that when he had borrowed the large sum of £2,000 from Sir Douglas Haig some years before the war, he had needed the money to buy his way out of social disgrace. Both to borrow and lend money in this way were prohibited by King's Regulations.

Sir John was probably the source of much of the information leakage that plagued British military affairs in 1914 and 1915. He was extremely unwilling to give adequate information to his political masters, the government, but he gossiped freely to Colonel Repington, the correspondent of *The Times*. As a result readers of *The Times* knew before the government that French blamed the failure at Loos on shortage of shells. There were other instances when the government fighting the largest war in British history was obliged to depend on a newspaper correspondent for information about events at the front.

After the early failures of 1915 the government replaced Sir John French as Commander-in-Chief. After his dismissal he was appointed Commander-in-Chief of Home Defence, and in this role was able to maintain some influence, which he rarely used to assist the Field Commanders in their endless debates and arguments with the politicians and the War Office.

Sir Douglas Haig

Sir Douglas Haig was unusual in the officer corps of the British Army of his time, especially the cavalry. He was too closely associated with trade, and his family's prominence in the distilling trade brought wealth but little social distinction. However, his military record was good. Despite later criticism, Haig's record was not that of a junior officer owing most of his promotion to political manoeuvring and fortunate circumstances. He attracted notice as result of some distinguished service in South Africa, and in particular he took the attention of Lord Esher, who was then setting in train some long-overdue reforms of the army after the fifty-year reign of the deeply traditionalist Duke of Cambridge as Commander-in-Chief.

Esher was known to favour rich, good-looking and young bachelor officers, and took Haig into the centre of military affairs as a key member of his reforming commission.

Haig's sister was at the centre of Court affairs as a lady-in-waiting attending Queen Alexandra at the new King's Court. Haig had been appointed an Aide de Camp to the new King Edward VII in 1902 on returning from his successes during the Boer War. King Edward was not concerned about the origins of money so long as his associates were rich, hospitable and respectful. In 1905 Haig was a guest at Windsor Castle for Ascot Week. He wasted little time, meeting and proposing to Dorothy Vivian, another lady-in-waiting, within three days and marrying her less than a month later. 'Why not?' he asked. 'I have frequently made up my mind about more important matters more quickly than that.' Apart from his own honorary position as an Aide de Camp to the King, Douglas Haig was now firmly established as an intimate in Court circles.

Haig's connections had already been useful when, having failed the exam to get into Staff College, he was nominated for entry as one of the Commander-in-Chief's non-examined protégés. However, 20 per cent of places at Staff College were allocated by nomination, and passing in by nomination carried no stigma. A late starter, a captain at thirty-eight and overtaken by many contemporaries, Haig had fought a good war in South Africa, was a success on Esher's commission and a success at Court. In the space of five years, from 1899 to 1904, he was steadily promoted to become almost the youngest Major-General in the British Army. It is difficult to argue against his being worthy of this change in his career's fortune, and at the time few did so.

Haig was Lieutenant General and Commander-in-Chief at Aldershot Command before the war. That posting carried the automatic appointment as Corps Commander of I Corps in the event of European War.

> **Haig was widely caricatured as being almost inarticulate, especially in the presence of large numbers of soldiers. At the last Aldershot Command athletics meeting before the outbreak of the war, he presented the prizes to the winners before addressing all the assembled competitors: 'You have all run very well, I trust you to run as well in the presence of the enemy.' No harm was done, his reputation for inability to find the right phrase was too well-known for there to be any surprise.**

As a Corps Commander Haig was not distinguished, and we have already seen how he panicked at Le Cateau. However, he had established a correspondence with the King, but it must be said that this was at the King's own invitation. Haig used the channel to his own advantage. Rarely overtly damning of Sir John French, Haig was quick to point out weaknesses of character and competence, never doubting that Sir John was doing his best, but noting that Sir John's best was not good enough. His assurances of his own desire to serve in whatever capacity might be thought best were a trifle ingenuous under the circumstances. When French was sent home in 1915 there was little surprise that Sir Douglas was appointed Commander-in-Chief of the BEF in his place.

Having never commanded more than a corps of about 50,000 men at the beginning of the war, Haig needed time to learn how to command what would become the incomparably larger force of five individual armies, each consisting of more than three times the number of men of the original BEF. The learning process was undertaken against the backdrop of the constant demands of the ever-changing day-to-day war, with no pause for analysing what had been learned so far. In addition to learning the business of commanding two million men in battle, Haig also had to assimilate the lessons of new weapons and methods of waging war as well as learn to handle his political masters.

Just two examples serve to illustrate this point.

At the beginning of the war it had never for a moment been imagined that for most of the war there would be almost two million men from all over the world living in the open air in northern France for four years. Every item of supplies had to be brought to them, not just military stores but each mouthful of food, each drop of water that wasn't drunk out of a shell hole that might contain within its stagnant pool a corpse or two, a few drowned rats and the leaking contents of an unexploded gas shell. No general, anywhere, had ever had to face the consequences of such demands, let alone face them with no experience whatsoever, and with no staff remotely equipped by training or experience to deal with the problems. As a result, administration and logistics were initially exactly as poor as any army faced with such challenges would suffer.

Haig spent much of the war under the handicap of having David Lloyd George as Prime Minister. There can be no doubt that they were temperamentally polar opposites. Whilst Lloyd George was a long-time Member of Parliament, and in touch with his working-class constituents, he was also one of the most gifted orators of his time, perhaps of any time. He was called 'The Welsh Wizard' for a reason. Lloyd George distrusted Haig and his acceptance of colossal casualties, but lacked the courage to sack him, not least because he had no general available who could be expected to do the job better. Thus Haig struggled for most of his period in command knowing that he did not have the support of his political masters at home.

As an aside David Lloyd George was also called 'The Welsh Goat' behind his back, again with reason; his working arrangements with his secretary Frances Stephenson were widely know in political circles. They were to marry in 1943, after the death of Lloyd George's first wife two years earlier. Frances had been his mistress for thirty years.

Haig suffered from an inability to manage his involvement in subordinates' affairs. At the Somme in 1916 he interfered in detail inappropriate to his position and drove his local commander Rawlinson to seek greater results than Rawlinson himself ever believed possible. Cambrai offers another example of this tendency. Then at Third Ypres in 1917 he failed completely to insist on Gough's adherence to the agreed strategic plan. The tragedy of Passchendaele stems directly from this failure. Thus, at times too interfering, Haig was also capable of shameful lack of control over those whom he commanded.

Haig's apologists claim for him the credit for commanding the greatest victories in British history; the remarkable successes of the last 100 days of the war, the advances along the whole British front, from the coast and along over half the whole Western Front. His detractors point out that by this stage the French were back in the war and that the Royal Navy's blockade had already weakened Germany beyond the point of no return. Beyond those immediate factors, the collapsing Austro-Hungarian Empire was demanding German resources and most tellingly, to German consternation, 20,000 American troops were arriving in France every week.

Haig has suffered more than any general of his time in the process of revision of history. Immediately after the war he was honoured and respected by old soldiers everywhere. In 1928 it was reported that 100,000 soldiers who had fought during the war attended his funeral or lined the route to his last resting place at Dryburgh Abbey, near the Haig clan ancestral home, Bemersyde, in the Scottish borders. In 1961 that respect was blown away in an instant by Alan Clark's attack on First World War generalship, *The Donkeys*. This scathing attack was largely directed at the command of Haig's predecessor, French, during the failed battles of 1915, but has since been used as a convenient weapon to attack almost any senior officer of the time, and Haig in particular. In 1963 John Terraine set out the counter-argument in *Douglas Haig, The Educated Soldier*. Then a series of powerful attempts in books, theatre and television set out to demolish any lingering respect for Haig as a soldier or individual with any spark of care for the men he commanded. As is so often the case, the truth about Haig's place in history lies somewhere between the extremes of opinion. In some aspects, Haig was the man for the hour, undaunted by adversity, willing to accept every responsibility and fearless of the cost. In other aspects he was unable to listen to debate, suspicious of disagreement and a woeful chooser of those who worked for him. His Chief of Intelligence for most of the war, Brigadier-General John Charteris, gave a damning assessment of both Haig and himself when he admitted that he did not generally bring bad news to Haig's attention for fear it might upset 'The Chief'. A few of Haig's diary entries in the latter years of his period in command confirm that he saw himself as a man chosen by the Higher Power to fulfil his destiny, and few around him saw fit to question this rather dangerous self-delusion.

Let the reader choose. You may conclude that Haig was an over-promoted bungler, so inept that it was a political necessity to conceal his failure from the eye of history for ever after. Or you may decide that he was a general of considerable distinction, a fast learner who held highest command with general distinction in the greatest crisis of history since Trafalgar and Waterloo. Whatever you decide, there is a scholarly body to support your opinion. Change your mind every ten years or so, and you will find good company in that as well.

Haig left behind one lasting achievement. Well before the war had ended he became very conscious of the nation's obligations to the men who had fought in the war, and he had begun to turn his attention to what he foresaw would be a great and long-lasting need. Using his considerable prestige he was able to persuade a number of the many charitable funds and organisations that were already springing up to unite as the Earl Haig Fund and the British Legion. Both remain in recognisable form today.

Sir Henry Rawlinson

Rawlinson was an infantry general in an army whose senior officers at the outbreak of war were predominantly cavalry men. He was, in the jargon of the day, 'a card'; a slightly raffish and irreverent officer, a man not afraid to speak his own mind and certainly more willing to learn than his later reputation would indicate. It is his misfortune that his name will forever be associated with the Battle of The Somme. Few give him credit for the speed with which he changed from being the inexperienced commander of the almost totally inexperienced Fourth Army into a capable and generally successful manager of large-scale battles. In 1916 he was in command of inexperienced soldiers fighting against good troops well settled into some of the strongest defensive positions on the Western Front. Even his critics can acknowledge that he achieved more than most others could have done in like circumstances. However, his sheer determination and his willingness to accept unbelievable sacrifices of life in the pursuit of the objectives set by Haig fall heavily on the negative side of the ledger. The records of the time indicate that Rawlinson was unable to argue either the generality or detail of objectives set by Haig, even when at times he was fully aware of the implications of them. We have to wait until 1918 to see Rawlinson win any argument for scaling down offensive plans to fit the reality that large plans almost always led to large casualties and small achievements. Naturally this weakness has been held against him

Rawlinson was certainly not a great general, but he was equally certainly not the mindless executioner whose only concerns about casualties were that he could be constrained by lack of men from fighting his war in the only, wrong-headed way that he could imagine.

Sir Herbert Plumer

Another infantryman, Plumer was so much a picture of the archetypal tall, drooping and heavily moustached general that it has often been assumed that he was the inspiration and model for Colonel Blimp, cartoonist David Low's caricature of the elderly and reactionary retired army officer of the 1930s. It is almost certainly a convenient fiction, although Plumer was an ideal candidate to be Colonel Blimp. After the war he was a Colonial Governor, President of the MCC and an active member of The House of Lords. However, nobody ever doubted that he was one of the few outstanding military leaders of his generation and his appearance belied that fact.

Appointed Corps Commander of IV Corps shortly after the outbreak of war, Plumer was the commander of Second Army for most of the war, given responsibility for the Western Front in Belgium, and thus particularly for Ypres. He was methodical, careful and essentially a calm man. In 1917 he was not needed for the great breakout from Ypres to clear the Belgian coast; Haig wanted a less cautious and more dashing leader, choosing Gough for the task. Thus Plumer was at a loose end whilst another general took over to deliver the knockout blow. It was fortuitous that he was available, he was needed in Italy to command the British force sent to help the Italian leadership recover their balance after the disastrous Battle of Caporetto. It was equally fortuitous that before the end of the long and tortured series of battles that made up Third Ypres Plumer was back, able to take the ridge at Passchendaele and close down that front for the winter.

In this war, leadership was taken to mean the determination to press on to achieve objectives regardless of the human cost. Haig did not believe that Plumer had that determination, and saw weakness in Plumer's preference for limited operations with defined objectives and concern for the demands placed on his men. He would undoubtedly have replaced Plumer with a man more in his own mould if he had felt able to do so without damage to himself.

After the war, the newly ennobled Viscount Plumer of Messines was always at the centre of an admiring crowd of former Second Army soldiers, whether at home or abroad. He was known to his army in a way that was rare for the time, and was one of the few generals able to earn any sort of affectionate nickname, and his first 'Old Plum' would later be replaced by the ultimate admiring nickname, 'Daddy'.

Sir Edmund Allenby

'The Bull' was by no means liked or even much admired as a Western Front general. He had been commander of the Cavalry Division at the beginning of the war and had been first Commander of the Third Army at its formation. His legendary explosive bad temper did not encourage subordinates to offer advice or suggestions, especially if such words conflicted with Allenby's known position on any subject. His relationship with Haig was scarcely better. It would be difficult to say who was the more relieved when Allenby fell out with Haig after the Battle of Arras and was sent to Palestine.

In Palestine Allenby became a truly different figure. He commanded in a fast-moving and open war, a cavalryman's war. He understood the use of long and vulnerable lines of communication and was never averse to the unconventional methods of a number of British officers who knew and understood the tribal and national politics of the region. Of these irregular soldiers T.E. Lawrence – Lawrence of Arabia – was the best-known. During the course of his period of command Allenby captured Gaza, was the first Christian leader to enter Jerusalem since before the Crusades, and took the critically important cities of Damascus and Aleppo. His greatest contribution at the time was the extraordinary and unsuspected sensitivity that he brought to the political and religious problems of being the conqueror of Jerusalem. His first entry into the city was on foot like a pilgrim, with a minimum of ceremony. His first acts were to ensure protection of the holy sites, gaining cooperation from their traditional religious guardians drawn from three religions. His proclamation of martial law in Jerusalem and its surrounds is a model of thoughtful writing.

Within the context of this book, Allenby is certainly not a leader to be liked or admired, but as a leader on a different stage he is an outstanding figure of his time.

If later leaders had paid more attention to how Allenby undertook his duties, a very different Middle East might have emerged in the remainder of the twentieth century.

Sir Hubert Gough

Gough was the epitome of the dashing cavalryman, and he needed to be dashing if he was to live up to family tradition. His father and uncle had both been generals and both had won the Victoria Cross during the Indian Mutiny. His brother John had also won the VC, during the South African War. All three had been alive during Hubert Gough's years as a 'coming man' before the war.

Hubert Gough was born into a distinguished Anglo-Irish family with Unionist beliefs. He first came to public notice during the Curragh Mutiny in March 1914. He was Brigadier General commanding a brigade of cavalry based at the Curragh, the principal British army garrison in Ireland, outside Dublin. It was inevitable that he would be caught up in the controversial decision by the government to order the general commanding the Curragh to prepare plans to march into Ulster to act against the Ulster Volunteers, a political group opposed to Home Rule for Ulster from Dublin. Gough let it be known that he would be unwilling to act on such orders, and of the seventy officers under his command only thirteen did not make similar declarations. The recently retired Chief of the Imperial General Staff, Field Marshal Sir John French, came out in favour of the would-be mutiny but such was the ambiguity of feeling at all levels about the rights and wrongs of the Ulster Question that neither French nor Gough suffered any long-term impairment to their careers.

Brigade Commander on the outbreak of war, Gough was rapidly promoted during the early period: Divisional Commander in 1914, Corps Commander at Loos in early 1915 and Reserve Army Commander by mid-1916. This became the Fifth Army and was to bear the brunt of the German offensive of 1918.

Gough could have been removed from command several times during the war. He was reputedly careless of life, risking the lives of men under his command as he had fearlessly risked his own in earlier wars and in the hunting field, and was justifiably criticised for it. He was politically naïve, as at The Curragh. One misfortune is that as a friend he had considerable access to, and influence over, Haig but lacked skill to use that influence to good effect. His brother John Gough was a supreme realist, an ideal chief of staff to Haig, and he was almost alone in being able to make Haig listen to argument. John's death in action in February 1915 removed one part of that influence, leaving only the more volatile brother with the ear of the Commander-in-Chief.

Gough could most reasonably have lost his command after the Battle of The Ancre in 1916, the failure that brought the Somme to its close. He should have lost it even before the Third Battle of Ypres began. Gough more or less ignored the direction of attack that Haig had specified, and the attack so nearly failed, only coming to achieve any success at all after Plumer had taken command. That had not been the only instance of the cavalry general as a thruster taking his own counsel rather than listen to what was being asked of him. However, the one battle for which he did not deserve to lose his command was the fighting retreat of 1918. That had been an outstanding feat of arms, and Gough would live long enough, dying as late as 1963, to have much of his good name and reputation restored.

Sir Aylmer Hunter-Weston

Whatever anyone thinks about the overall quality of generals and generalship in Britain during the war, there can be no doubt about this general's contribution to the later commonplace statement that all First World War generals were incompetent and merciless butchers. It will be recalled that the 31st Division in Hunter-Weston's VIII Corps at Serre were among the greatest sufferers from mismanagement on the first day of that battle. Fewer people remember that his contribution in Gallipoli had already earned him the name 'The Butcher of Helles' even before the Somme battle had been thought of. At the Battle of Gully Ridge in 1915 he had launched the 52nd (Lowland) Division into an assault, unsupported by artillery or diversions, against a well-defended Turkish position. Over one-third of the division, about 5,000 men, were killed, wounded or taken prisoner in a matter of hours. His description of the event as 'Blooding the Pups' was deeply resented, especially in his native Lowland Ayrshire, where he had recently become 27th Laird of Hunterston.

Hunter-Weston was a political general, elected a Member of Parliament in October 1916 as the Somme battle was winding down. This was doubly unfortunate in that it made him almost impossible to sack for incompetence and it gave him a position of some influence in political circles, one of the few generals with a voice in the councils of the nation. He did not pursue his political career with any grand plan in mind; his main objective seems to have been to preserve his name and reputation from any criticism that might appear either in the forthcoming Official History of the war or in other memoirs. He remained an MP until 1935, and died in 1940 in an unexplained fall from a high turret at Hunterston Castle.

> **Hunter-Weston appears on any list of the outstanding British generals of the war, in his case because he was so extraordinarily incompetent in every aspect of his career as a general that his continued remaining in command has formed part of many 'proofs' of the incompetence of all generals.**

Sir Arthur Currie

So many myths and stories surround this Canadian general that it is almost impossible to believe that all can be true. He was a failed some-time stockbroker, a failed land salesman, and about to be prosecuted for fraudulent misuse of client funds when the war conveniently broke out. He was also under investigation over missing army clothing funds. Despite the failure of Currie the businessman, he had a successful parallel career in the local militia in the years before the war. By 1914 he was commanding officer of his regiment, and thus one of the few senior Canadian officers to go to Europe at the beginning.

He was very tall, slack-shouldered, badly turned-out in uniform and later to run into trouble again with problems concerning about £10,000 missing from army funds. Haig and others wanted him dismissed for this, but his government would save him. They considered that his value as an economical and Canadian commander of Canadian troops – by then he was commanding the entire Canadian Corps – was more important than a few missing thousands of pounds.

The Canadians were without doubt the equal of any national group who fought anywhere during the war. They had no experience of previous colonial wars to guide them, no encrusted military traditions to hamper them, and only the smallest of professional military establishments to plan for them. Despite these perceived handicaps, they were natural soldiers, eventually to be led by a natural general.

Currie's Canadian Corps' achievements in 1917 confirm a record of economical success equalling or surpassing any that could be boasted by any formation during the whole war. The capture of Vimy Ridge, followed later in the year by the capture of Passchendaele Ridge, were two of the outstanding achievements of the entire middle years of the war.

> **One of the enduring strange things about the Canadians in the war is that about half of them were not native-born Canadians at all; they were immigrants, and the majority of the immigrants came from the Home Countries. The same stock as sometimes seemed inept in British uniform appeared to flourish differently under the 'amateur' leadership of the Canadian Corps.**

A modern thesis has it that Currie was under active consideration for appointment as overall Commander-in-Chief when Lloyd George was casting around to replace Haig. This is an interesting story, especially to Canadians, and indeed Lloyd George mentioned the plan in his memoirs. In truth Currie was simply too junior, a Corps Commander and not an Army Commander, and with no experience of command at the highest levels. None of that should detract from the fact that Currie was an outstanding soldier; successful, deeply conscious of his responsibility to his countrymen and government as guardian of their army and a man who grew in moral stature as that responsibility grew.

Currie was not afraid to speak out, and indeed he was largely responsible for the Canadian stance that the corps would prefer not to serve under Allenby or Gough, whose styles did not suit their own. Haig, who valued the Canadians more highly than any other soldiers, accepted that wish. In truth, Haig had little choice; as the senior Canadian commander, although not yet commanding the whole corps, Currie had the ear of his government and answered to his political masters for the welfare of their soldiers.

By late 1918 Currie was opposed to Armistice. He wanted to fight on until the German Army was so roundly beaten that it could never again offer a threat to world peace. He believed that without such a comprehensive victory there would be a second war. Germany would rally to the idea of never having actually lost the first war on the only ground that mattered, the field of battle. He was only wrong in his timing; he thought Germany would be back for the second round shortly after 1940, not shortly before. He died in November 1933, having seen the beginnings of the movement that would bring his prophecy to bear fruit.

> **The memory of Currie remains strong in Canada. His personal slogan was 'Pay the price in shells, not blood' and it is part of the folk memory of this remarkable man.**

Sir John Monash

Just short of his fiftieth birthday on the outbreak of the war, Monash was another civilian in part-time military clothing. He was an engineer by profession, with Bachelor's and Master's degrees and a Doctorate of civil engineering. In his middle age, before the war, he was also a studious and rounded colonel of militia artillery who set himself the task of understanding every branch of the profession of arms. He studied artillery as much as he studied his own profession of engineering, and infantry tactics as much as he studied either. He spoke and read perfect German and studied any German publication about military matters that he could find. People who worked with him during the war said that from the beginning of the war until its end they never heard him say a single sentence that was not about the war and how to wage it more successfully.

Monash's study was imaginative and he learned from what he read and saw. He saw war as a unified whole, with all arms working together to achieve the common goal. The infantry were part of the whole, not the point of the spear thrust forward by other hands. He was an early believer that with good training and better equipment the interaction between artillery and infantry could improve the advantages of the bombardment. This would enable the infantryman to work closely behind the artillery barrage without risk from it. He was passionate about preparation and planning to maximise the possibility of results without casualties, and in this he was like Currie.

Monash came late to higher command, and took command of the Australian Corps in May 1918, after its success at Villiers-Bretonneux and before the offensive *Tout le Monde á la Bataille*. He handled his command skilfully and with great success during the last 100 days. As with Currie, some supporters like to claim that Monash was under consideration for appointment as Commander-in-Chief, but if Currie's claim founder on his relative lack of seniority and experience of higher command, Monash's are even less convincing, given that he was no more than a Divisional Commander in mid-1918. Lloyd George mentions him in his memoirs as the man to be Currie's Chief of Staff when the latter was promoted to replace the sacked Haig. However, Lloyd George was not averse to glossing his actions and thoughts, or making them up altogether, if it suited his own purpose. By the time he wrote his memoirs it did suit him to claim how open-minded he was in looking to replace Haig in 1918.

Monash's German-Jewish family had fled persecution during the nineteenth century, but despite his German origins and the prevailing anti-Semitism of the times Monash was never to suffer from the prejudices that would have made success in the British Army of the times improbable. Equally, like the Canadians, the Australians never suffered the worst of the leadership misfortunes that befell so many British troops under sometimes indifferent, and sometimes worse, management and leadership.

> **Monash is buried beneath a headstone that bears two words and nothing more: 'John Monash'. It is typical of the man, modest in life, modest in death.**

Sir William Robertson

William Robertson began his career as a seventeen-year-old trooper, a private soldier, in the 16th Lancers. At the age of twenty-four he was already a serjeant major, and in 1888, when he was twenty-eight, his Commanding Officer Colonel Maillard put him forward to be granted a commission as an officer in the cavalry. For any person to rise through the ranks to gain a commission was unusual, although exceptions were made to ensure a supply of competent quartermasters and other administration officers. Robertson's was a much rarer case, a man from the ranks who obtained his commission as a squadron officer in a cavalry regiment. He could not afford to stay with the expensive 16th

Lancers, with the enormous officers' mess bills associated with being posted at home. Colonel Maillard used his range of contacts to arrange that instead of returning to the Lancers, Robertson would join the 3rd Dragoon Guards, based in India, where lower costs of living were combined with generous local allowances. Maillard did all in his power to help Robertson achieve his commission in the Dragoon Guards, and then he rallied the 16th Lancers to help in assembling the equipment that Robertson would need. Maillard himself gave a sword, another officer paid for the complete set of saddlery that a cavalry officer would require. The serjeants of the 16th Lancers gave a silver-mounted dressing case. Others helped in their different ways, and the result was that by joining a cavalry regiment in India, with higher pay and lower costs, Robertson was on his way.

As a new but not-so-young officer, Robertson made a fortunate marriage, to Mildred Palin. Her father Lieutenant-General Palin was openly disappointed that his daughter had chosen a penniless ex-ranker of no family and no money, instead of the promising young officer whom he would have wanted. He became reconciled to the marriage when his son-in-law passed him in seniority on his way to the top.

As a newly enlisted young cavalry private soldier, Robertson had to cope with receiving his mother's first letter to him. Among her many anguished sentences about her shame of seeing her son join the army, one stands out: 'I will name it to no-one, I would rather bury you than see you in a red coat.' Despite this he never lost his family ties, and he kept this letter for the rest of his life, noting in his autobiography its impact on his determination to succeed. Perhaps these sentiments encouraged him to keep up the studies that had marked him out at the village school that he had attended, and enjoyed, up to the age of thirteen.

Robertson was a dedicated student of his profession. As a young lieutenant in India he became fluent in Hindi and achieved proficiency certificates in five other native languages, the better to understand his surroundings and the native troops with whom he came into contact. The fact that each language proficiency certificate brought added pay was an added incentive to an ambitious young man without means or connections. As a half-pay colonel, without a formal job for a year before the war, he worked his way, helped by a dictionary, through German technical manuals about the employment of artillery in the forthcoming war. He had previously taught himself French in order to achieve the all-round proficiencies needed for entry to the Staff College, without which he could not achieve his ambition.

William Robertson was a competent fighting soldier, and took part in the Chitral Relief Expedition of 1895, during which he was wounded and earned the DSO. However, his greater skill was as a staff officer, especially in the Intelligence branch before the war but more generally as he progressed. He was the first officer commissioned from the ranks ever to attend the Staff College at Camberley.

We met 'Wully' as French's Chief of General Staff in the aftermath of Neuve Chappelle, with his handling of the dismissal of Smith-Dorrien. When Haig became Commander-in-Chief he needed a reliable man to protect his political interests in London, and Robertson, a loyalist to his military family, was the man. Thus he became Haig's eyes and ears as Chief of the Imperial General Staff in London. Nominally the professional head of the army, Robertson never doubted his role as the protector at home and occasional mouthpiece of the military command in France. It was his misfortune to serve as the interface between GHQ in France and the politicians in London throughout most of the period of greatest mistrust between Lloyd George and Haig.

Robertson fell victim to Lloyd George's distrust in mid-1918. He was removed from the War Office and given the largely nominal role of Commander-in-Chief, Eastern Command, Home Forces. He was soon promoted to be Commander-in-Chief of all home forces, but if he was in any doubt about the significance of this appointment, Robertson only had to recall that his predecessor in this position was Sir John French after his dismissal from the post of Commander-in-Chief of the BEF in France.

THE AMERICANS

'Black Jack' Pershing

As benefits a nation that joined the war even as some of the main protagonists were already dropping out of it, the USA produced only one notable general, John 'Black Jack' Pershing.

Pershing's pre-war career would have resonated with many British generals; long periods of colonial wars, some on home territory in the American Indian territories, others in Mexico, The Philippines and Cuba. He had been professor of military studies at the University of Nebraska and was proud to recall that he had commanded the Corps of Cadets of West Point Military Academy when that body formed the guard of honour at the funeral of Ulysses S. Grant.

The USA could put fewer than 25,000 men into the field on their declaration of war in 1917. Within days of the declaration the army was growing by a larger number than that every week, and by the end of 1918 Pershing could call on the largest army of all, about 2.5 million men under arms.

Pershing's greatest achievement was to realise that the Americans would not fight well as drafts brought in to support the armies and formations of their allies. There had to be an American army, and the Allies would have to wait until that army was ready to fight before Pershing would commit it. Initially this segregation extended to almost all aspects of the American contribution, but Pershing was a pragmatist and soon realised that he needed help from his allies, which he was not too proud to accept. In particular, in answering the call for infantry, Pershing accepted that he could not go into the field without the support of British and French artillery and logistical specialists. There simply was not time to train these specialists to the levels that were now taken for granted in the other armies.

> Pershing was fifty-seven when his country went to war, fifty-nine when he became Chief of Staff and about the same age when he was appointed 'General of the Armies'. He was the first general so honoured. There would not be another until Douglas Macarthur was similarly appointed on his seventy-fifth birthday in 1955. George Washington was posthumously appointed to the same rank in 1976. Legislation was subsequently passed to ensure that no future general could ever in future out-rank Washington, and the title has therefore disappeared.

THE FRENCH

For forty years before the Great War, the French officer corps was driven by one objective; recovery of the lost provinces. Every officer looked forward to playing his part in the war, and prepared and trained for the event. The offensive would triumph over defence in the advance to battle to right past wrong, and avenge past shame.

From 1894 onwards the French Army was riven by the *Affaire Dreyfus*. Alfred Dreyfus was a young and highly promising officer. His arrest for alleged spying for Germany, conviction, re-convictions and subsequent pardon and honouring by the Republic was cause of a deep and lasting rift. On one side stood the right wing, old family or aristocratic, largely Christian and Catholic members of the traditional officer class, who believed the Jewish officer to be guilty of treason. On the other stood the left wing, lower class officers, often anti-clerical and stoutly republican in sympathy, who saw the *affaire* as an anti-

Semitic plot. To have the misfortune to serve with officers on the opposite side of opinion about Dreyfus could be both lonely and damaging to one's career. Personal animosities and divisions were carried forward from twenty years of peacetime struggle for the moral high ground in the *affaire*. Such was the background to the career of every officer.

We met Plan XVII for the French conduct of the war, but for years before the outbreak its constant revision and attention to its detail was so obsessive that it entirely ignored any assessment of what Germany might do on the outbreak of war. Thus the Schlieffen Plan came as a surprise; the invasion of Belgium and the trap into which the French neatly stepped by advancing into the lost provinces had never been imagined. If von Moltke had been marginally more competent France might have lost the war in 1914 without ever putting up a struggle.

Joseph Jacques Césaire Joffre

As a classically profiled success as a staff officer where his apparently imperturbable calm was valued, Joffre achieved the appointment of Chief of Staff of the French Army before the war.

Joffre was a trencherman, a man for long undisturbed nights, regardless of any event that might disturb the sleep of a lesser man. He wanted to abandon Verdun and other fortresses; he wanted heads to roll when the same fortresses proved to be so stripped of defences as to be indefensible. In the first months of the war he sacked more than fifty generals, especially those who seemed to lack that offensive élan that was the essence of French military spirit. Even before the war had begun he had purged the army of many senior officers lacking the necessary attitude. It was fortunate that his colleague Foch had been chief instructor of the Staff College before the war, where he had instilled into a whole generation of younger senior officers exactly the beliefs and theories that both men wanted to see in battle. As a result Joffre was able to call on this body of believers to fill many positions of senior command.

In 1914 Joffre's calmness was crucial to the recovery after the retreat from the Belgian frontier to the Marne. His success at the Battle of The Marne, and the recovery back to the northern frontier, before the trench line stabilised, ensured that he would be admired. Despite the costly failures of French offensive operations in the Champagne region in 1915, Joffre might still have survived but for the overwhelming catastrophe of Verdun. So he was replaced in December 1916. Like Sir John French before him, he received other appointments, and was given the honorary title of Marshal of France. For the next two years he was seen as travelling plenipotentiary and France's military representative on various bodies, but in reality without power.

Joffre made a brief comeback as chief of the Supreme War Council, a body supported by Lloyd George in one of his attempts to take commander-in-chief of the BEF away from Haig. The council had little authority until the crisis of March 1918, but by that time Joffre had already been supplanted. His successor had also been replaced, by Foch, the general who ultimately would come to have the power that the council had been supposed to have from the beginning.

After the war Joffre retired to his estate near Versailles, worked on local non-governmental affairs and his war memoirs until his death in 1932. He was buried there, an unassuming end for one of the key figures of French history of the twentieth century.

Robert Nivelle

Charming and speaking fluent English learned from his English mother, Nivelle enjoyed a meteoric ascent once the war began. An artillery colonel approaching retirement in 1914, he was commanding a brigade before the year-end, a division within six months, a corps within another, an army by early 1916 and the Northern Group of armies by the middle of that year. On 31 December that year he replaced Joffre as Commander-in-Chief. His charm and command of English made him most acceptable to the British government, and during this time Lloyd George first proposed that the BEF be subordinated to his overall command.

Nivelle's career was shattered within months of taking the role of commander-in-chief. The colossal failure of the Chemin des Dames battle, the 'Nivelle Offensive', was followed by the French Army mutinies of 1917. By May he was gone, posted to North Africa, where he served, away from the public eye, for the rest of the war. His brief time in supreme command marked perhaps the lowest point of French military history since 1870 and would only be equalled again by the surrender of France in 1940.

Nivelle died in March 1924 and is today almost forgotten, being almost ignored as a subject for scholarly study or biography.

Philippe Pétain

This is the life of such contradiction that even today, almost sixty years after his death, it is impossible to be clear about his place in history. To write about his undoubted achievements as a general in the First World War can only show half the picture, because he became President of France as a puppet of Nazi Germany during the Second.

Pétain was never afraid to be his own man. He spoke out in the years before the first war, never believing the Grandmaison rhetoric and never hiding his opinion of those who espoused the doctrine of *La Revanche* without ever thinking about its practicalities. He thought about the coming war, and about how the industrialisation of warfare must change the nature of battle. He distilled his philosophy of war into just two words: 'Artillery kills'. On the basis of that belief he developed a view of how the relationships between the soldier, his weapons and the land must be developed to something more realistic than the dramatic speech-making that had created Grandmaison's influence.

In terms of political stance, Pétain tended to the left wing, ostentatiously ordering meat for dinner on Fridays, especially when it would be noticed by Catholic officers, and earning a reputation for enjoying a distinctly un-Catholic attitude to the pleasures available to an active bachelor in garrison towns.

Before the war, Colonel Pétain's 33rd Infantry Regiment stationed at Arras attracted a cadre of young officers who wanted to be at the forefront of developments. Notable among these was Charles de Gaulle, a young man who would spend the rest of his life thinking that his capture at Verdun had shamed him, and the honourable course for a Frenchman at war with Germany was to fight, fight and carry on fighting. De Gaulle so admired his first commanding officer that he named his first son Philippe in his honour.

We have seen Pétain as commander at Verdun, then again as Commander-in-Chief after the Nivelle failure. He served on after the war until 1931 until retiring and entering politics, already seventy-five years old. It was his misfortune that his personality and reputation set him up to be the dominant personality of the government at the time of France's surrender in 1940, and he soon became Head of State of the unhappy Vichy Republic. In this role he was rather more willing to cooperate with his country's occupiers than was wise.

After the fall of Germany in 1945, Pétain was tried for treason and condemned to death. In a twist of fate the decision to confirm that sentence fell upon the new Prime Minister, Charles de Gaulle, the former disciple of Pétain's doctrines in the years before 1914. De Gaulle was unwilling to confirm the death sentence, but commuted the sentence to life imprisonment. The ninety-year-old former hero of France would spend the rest of his life in the small prison of the Ile d'Yeu off the Atlantic coast, eventually dying there senile, incontinent and still loved by Mme Hardin, the war widow whom he had married late and who remained true to the man she married.

Pétain is buried in the place where he died, in the small churchyard of the church of the parish church of the Ile d'Yeu.

Ferdinand Foch

Another man of the Pyrenees, like Joffre, Foch was a devout Roman Catholic in a largely secular army. He had been a staff officer, instructor at the Staff College, and its commandant in the years before the war. His influence as a thinker and writer of two widely acclaimed books about the theory of modern war was considerable.

Foch began the war as a corps commander during the Battles of The Frontiers. He was promoted in rapid succession to army commander and then to Commander-in-Chief of the Northern Group of armies. Thus he was the man charged with re-vitalising Plan XVII after its early failures. In this role, Foch was the man on the spot, most directly responsible for the failures of 1915, and then for Verdun in 1916. Foch was removed from command on 29 December 1916, just two days before the dismissal of his own mentor, Joffre. Foch himself was not dismissed altogether; Italy needed military advice and Foch was seen as a good man to give it. Thus he disappeared from the Western Front.

As 1916 turned into 1917, Robert Nivelle had been briefly the coming man. After his failure on the Chemin des Dames and the mutinies, his going had caused another shake-up. Pétain had been promoted Commander-in-Chief of the French Army, and needed a new Chief of Staff. Foch was called for again and took the job, second only to Pétain in the French military hierarchy.

The great crisis of March 1918 had led to the meeting at Doullens and the creation of a joint supreme command. The only acceptable choice would be a Frenchman, and Pétain could not be spared, nor was he the right man. Joffre would have liked to have had the job but was better employed in a figurehead role. So it was that Foch, French Chief of Staff and on the spot, was appointed Generalissimo of the Allied forces, Marshal of France, and the man who would orchestrate the series of six phases that ended the war in the following seven months.

Foch accepted the German surrender, was appointed a British Field Marshal and received many other honours. He argued that the new frontiers of Germany should be on the Rhine, with military encampments across the Rhine, and that Germany had to be kept in a state of inability to start another European war.

> **Over-ruled by the politicians at the peace negotiations Foch was depressed by what he saw as the weak line taken by Allied politicians. 'We have not signed a peace treaty but only an armistice for twenty years.'**

Already sixty-eight by the time of the Armistice, Foch died before his prophecy was realised. He had been one of the great figures of France during the war, and on his death in 1929 he was buried alongside Napoleon in *Les Invalides*, a hero of France to the end.

THE GERMANS

As befitted an army based on Prussian principles, the German Army was the best prepared in all respects for the war. National military service was more professional, lasted longer and training was more realistic than in any other army. Studying the profession of arms was a high calling, and military theorists studied and argued with a freedom that was unseen in any other European army of the day. The result was that when war broke out the Germans had the best-equipped army, with the best idea of what could be achieved and what could not. The national will was aligned with militarism in a way that would only come to other countries as the war developed.

The only false note in this national military chorus arose from a peculiarity of Prussian military history. The Kaiser must command the national army and men of sufficiently noble birth must command the armies and army corps. As an aside it is notable that at the annual war games concluding the training season the Kaiser, as supreme War Lord, always commanded one side. By coincidence, in every year's manoeuvres his side always ended the war game having surrounded and overwhelmed the opposition.

To compensate for the need to qualify for command by birth, the hierarchy gave unusual authority to each noble commander's Chief of Staff. Thus, the Kaiser was Commander-in-Chief, but his Chief of the General Staff von Moltke held the real power. When Hindenburg became Chief of Staff he should have been the most important military figure in Germany, despite his nominal role as Chief Staff Officer rather than Commander. However, in Hindenburg's case the situation was complicated further by the fact that he had been a noble commander of armies with his own Chief of Staff, Ludendorff. The latter was offered the new title of Second Chief of Staff. He saw himself as second to nobody and instead took the title First Quartermaster General, in which role he became the de facto supremo of German army activity for three years.

> The difference between titular command and real command was not important when campaigns were going as planned. The commanders got the public credit that their status required, and the professional soldiers got the promotions, medals and professional recognition that their efforts deserved. As a result, this selection of German figures has to choose between the two types.

Helmuth Johann von Moltke

Von Moltke was born to succeed in the German Army. His uncle, Helmuth Karl von Moltke, known to history as von Moltke the Elder, had been Chief of Staff of the Prussian Army for thirty years. He had masterminded the series of wars, including the Franco-Prussian and Austro-Prussian wars that had cleared the way for Bismarck's successful unification of Germany under Prussian leadership. Helmuth Johann von Moltke, the Younger, was a dedicated, personally courageous, soldier. After graduating from Staff College, a training academy for mid-ranking officers created by his uncle, he was appointed as his uncle's personal adjutant, senior personal staff officer, at the reasonable age of thirty-four. In this appointment he caught the Kaiser's eye and on his uncle's retirement became Aide de Camp to the Kaiser.

Steady progression thereafter gave him a lieutenant general's command at the age of forty-four. There was no suggestion of over-promotion, he was a success at every level in his career, and it was only when he became Chief of Staff of the whole German Army that doubts were raised about his suitability. However, his principal rival for the appointment did not doubt von Moltke's qualification for the position.

After the outbreak of war, and the failure of the Schlieffen Plan, von Moltke was faced with the very circumstances that all German military planning had sought to avoid; France undefeated in the west and Russia able to mobilise in the east. This crisis placed von Moltke under intense strain, and towards the end of 1914 during the final stages of the German retreat from the Marne back to the borders, at the age of sixty-six, his health broke down. He retired from the army and died within eighteen months, on Waterloo Day, 18 June 1916.

As a postscript, Helmuth James von Moltke, the only child of his father Helmuth Johann's marriage to a South African mother of British descent, was a respected international student of law. He was an early opponent of National Socialism and after the July Plot on Hitler's life in 1944 was one of the 5,000 or so persons rounded up and one of the 200 executed. Paradoxically, as an opponent of Hitler he had argued against the assassination attempt, fearing that it would fail and only expose those who might have been the future leaders of a democratic government. He was correct in this analysis.

Erich von Falkenhayn

Prussian, with some experience of fighting in China during the Boxer Rebellion of 1899-1901, von Falkenhayn was Prussian Minister of War by 1913, and succeeded von Moltke as Chief of the General Staff of the German Army in September 1914.

Von Falkenhayn is remembered for his sponsorship of the Battle of Verdun, and the concept of that battle as nothing more than a means of killing Frenchmen. The battle cost Germany 320,000 casualties, 'human resources' as they were called for the first time. Those resources would have been better spent in other activities. The Battle of Verdun prevented Germany's successful prosecution of war against Russia in the east, where instead of facing defeat Brusilov launched his offensive to relieve France so successfully that it effectively destroyed Austria-Hungary's ability to contribute to the fighting yet to come in the east.

Having lost the support of the Hindenburg and Ludendorff partnership in the east, and of his army commanders in the west, von Falkenhayn was removed from his appointment as Chief of the General Staff and took command of the Ninth Army in the east, where he was successful in actions that knocked Romania out of the war. Following that success he was sent to the Middle East, where he was matched against Allenby. As with his period in overall command, von Falkenhayn reverted to type and his lack of offensive drive was no match for Allenby's mobile style of campaigning based on use of cavalry and railways. The decisive Battle of Gaza was his undoing, and he went home to Germany, to retirement and early death in 1922 at the age of sixty-one.

Paul von Hindenburg and Erich Ludendorff

It is not easy to see these two commanders in isolation. Paul von Beneckendorff und von Hindenburg was the noble commander, whilst Erich Ludendorff was the staff officer who crafted the victories. The former had already retired by 1911 but came back after von Prittwitz's failure of nerve to lead the German armies in eastern Prussia. The latter had been a chief staff officer during the stages of the Schlieffen Plan advance through Belgium, promoted and appointed to head Hindenburg's staff before the end of 1914.

Whilst Hindenburg was a competent but not particularly distinguished general on the retired list, Ludendorff was already known as one of those rare men for normal concepts of bravery or courage simply do not apply. Being completely without physical fear or moral doubts, he simply did what he thought should be done with no concern for his self or for the consequences of his actions.

After their remarkable successes in the east, the partnership was the natural team to take over the General Staff once the Kaiser had lost confidence in von Falkenhayn in late 1916. They were to remain as Chief of the General Staff and First Quartermaster General for the remainder of the war, Ludendorff the brilliant but occasionally over-confident planner and Hindenburg the older and calmer steadying influence.

Both men would play significant roles in the rise of Nazism to political acceptability. Hindenburg would become President of the Weimar Republic in 1925, and as a very aged figurehead President would appoint Hitler as Chancellor of the first National Socialist government.

Ludendorff was an early supporter of Nazism, and took an active part in the Munich putsch of November 1923. He saw National Socialism as Germany's best hope for the recovery of military self-respect and re-armament that would lead to the Second World War. Given his belief that the purpose of nations is to provide their armies with the means to wage war, he would have been gratified by the way in which Hitler used his ascent to power as a means of fulfilling that purpose. He died in 1937, three years after Hindenburg.

Colonel Georg Bruchmuller

In a review of the contributions of the commanders and leaders, Georg Bruchmuller earns his place because of his achievements rather than his rank. Retired before the war, Bruchmuller came out of retirement as a staff lieutenant colonel in an infantry division. For three years he was the undisputed artillery expert on the Eastern Front, but was back with Hindenburg and Ludendorff in a central role by the end of 1917. By the end of the war he was the leading practitioner of artillery warfare in any combatant army, and despite his relative lack of seniority was in demand throughout the Western Front for the war's remaining major battles, as the inspirational planner of the use of artillery in attack or defence. His greatest single achievement in a war where artillery dominated all was seen in the destruction of advanced defensive positions as well as disruption of communications behind the front at the beginning of each of the phases of the *Kaiserschlacht* campaign of spring 1918. He retired again in 1919 and wrote a number of artillery textbooks before dying in 1948.

Crown Prince Rupprecht of Bavaria

The Kingdom of Bavaria remained a state within the German Federation, and whilst lacking the purity of militarism that characterised the Prussian state, still produced the exception to the practice of the noble commander who led whilst a less noble chief of staff actually managed the business of war. Crown Prince Rupprecht was a dedicated, competent and successful soldier. He was commander of the *Sixth Army* at the outbreak of the war, and handled the French advance into Lorraine with considerable skill, allowing the French to break the momentum of their advance on his defence in depth before the counter-attacks that cost the French at least half of the 200,000 casualties of the Battle of The Frontiers. He was subsequently promoted Field Marshal and took command of the northern group of German armies on the Western Front for the rest of the war.

> **Rupprecht lost his right to the Bavarian crown with the abolition of the monarchies in Germany after the war, and like von Moltke the Younger was opposed to National Socialism from the beginning. He fled Germany and lived in exile in Italy from 1938 onwards. He managed to escape arrest and trial after the German occupation of Northern Italy in 1944. His wife and children were less fortunate and were sent to concentration camps. He died in 1955.**
>
> **Through his mother's line Rupprecht of Bavaria was the Jacobite Pretender to the United Kingdom throne.**

Crown Prince Wilhelm of Prussia

As the oldest of the Kaiser's five sons, the Crown Prince was naturally educated in a militaristic environment, and was given command of an army upon the outbreak of war. Initially he was humiliatingly ordered in public by his father to accept without question the 'advice' of his Chief of Staff. Wilhelm gradually became his own man, a competent but not inspired general in his own right, eventually commanding a group of three armies in the eastern sector of the Western Front. The attack on Verdun in February 1916 fell to his command, and as army commander he was the first to see the fatal flaw in von Falkenhayn's order to limit the initial attack to the right bank of the Meuse, the eastern side of the Verdun Salient. His advice was soon followed and the attacks encompassed the entire northern perimeter of the salient after this intervention.

In August 1916 Wilhelm asked his father to overrule the general staff and order a cessation of the pointless attacks at Verdun, and had managed to persuade the Kaiser to do so, albeit only after von Falkenhayn's dismissal during that month. In fact nobody has ever refuted his later claim that he first proposed to halt attacks at Verdun on the day after the seizure of Fort Douaumont.

Wilhelm was the first senior figure in Germany to recognise that the war was lost. In 1917 he told the Chancellor, Bethmann-Hollweg, that Germany's only hope of an honourable peace was to seek an end to hostilities without delay. He was rebuffed.

He fought on in his command, achieved successes during the advances of 1918, suffered reverses in the final Foch Offensive and retired after the

Armistice. It is clear that Wilhelm bitterly resented the perception in Germany and abroad that he was the 'Laughing Butcher of Verdun'. In his later writing he made no apologies for his role in the war but sought to make clear that the Battle of Verdun was not of his choosing and had been fought against his advice.

> Although his father was not permitted to return to Germany after the war, ex-Crown Prince Wilhelm was allowed to do so in 1923. He lived until 1951, occasionally writing but otherwise living completely privately with his family. He refused to endorse Hitler in his rise to power, holding to his undertaking to play no part in political life for as long as he remained permitted to live in Germany.

APPENDIX II

Composition of an Army

The infantry battalion was the basic unit of the British Expeditionary Force throughout the First World War. The soldier's battalion was one of two or three in a regiment, closely tied to a particular county or city, and commonly reinforcing ties by incorporating the county or city name in its title. The regiment itself was not a unit in the line of battle; it was the 'parent' of a number of battalions, usually two. In pre-war days one battalion would be based at home and the other based in the colonies, usually India, Africa, the Caribbean or in the East. The regiment was the soldier's 'family' unit, to which he owed his primary military loyalty and to which he returned throughout his career. During the war the regiments raised battalions according to the ability of their regional connections to support them. Thus The London Regiment, The Durham Light Infantry and the Manchester Regiment raised dozens of battalions, whilst other regiments were able to raise fewer.

The battalion had its own command structure for all management purposes. For the individual soldier this structure started with his section.

The platoon section was the most basic level of command, eight or ten men under command of a corporal. This group, a sub-unit, was the daily horizon of the private soldier, and if the regiment was his family, his section comrades were his siblings. In a tight-knit local regiment a man might and often did find himself serving in a section with men he had known from his school days. Three sections formed a platoon.

Each infantry platoon or cavalry troop was commanded by a lieutenant or more junior second lieutenant. The infantry platoon was about forty to fifty men, in three sections, with a small platoon headquarters. The platoon commander led the platoon, assisted by his platoon serjeant, who managed it. It was usually a newly commissioned officer's first appointment, whereas a peacetime serjeant would commonly be a veteran who had enlisted when his officer was a small child. Few serjeants aspired to be officers, and the social gulf was rarely bridged.

The infantry company, cavalry squadron or artillery battery was commanded by a major or senior captain and had its own headquarters team, also dealing with logistics. The primary role of this unit was to put rifles or guns to work. This level was the command centre for managing four platoons of infantry or troops of cavalry, or two half-batteries of artillery. Apart from controlling the fighting operations of four platoons, company headquarters provided a vital link between those fighting platoons and the supplies of ammunition, food and the other necessities of warfare.

The battalion. A lieutenant colonel in command was assisted by about thirty other officers in the command of almost 1,000 men. There were four rifle companies and various specialist groups as part of battalion headquarters. The adjutant was a senior captain responsible for daily management of battalion headquarters. The regimental serjeant major, the senior non-commissioned officer, was responsible for day-to-day discipline as well as management of the serjeants and other senior ranks who managed the battalion under the officers' leadership. The quartermaster and his staff ran the stores, catering and other logistics. Communications were a personnel-intensive part of battalion headquarters, because the only way to deliver orders and information was to employ 'runners'. The battalion had a small medical staff attached to its headquarters, typically a doctor who was an officer in the Royal Army Medical Corps, perhaps a medical serjeant from the same corps, and a small number of medical orderlies. In battle the demand for stretcher-bearers would always be very heavy, and it was the traditional role of the battalion's peacetime bandsmen to serve as stretcher-bearers when the need arose.

The cavalry system was a little different. A cavalry regiment was smaller, about 600 men, but with identical command functions. The major difference was of course that the cavalry regiment was wholly dependent on horses. The demands of over 600 horses, with attendant farriers, vets and feeding needs, were at least as complex as providing for a like number of men. It has been said that the movement of forage was the largest single logistical undertaking of any army in the war. The cavalry regiment was composed of squadrons and troops instead of the companies and platoons of the infantry.

Artillery was different again. The artillery was dispersed across the whole army, with brigades, batteries and troops or half-batteries, instead of battalions, companies and platoons. A significant further difference was that whilst infantry and cavalry units were rarely broken up to serve in small numbers, the artillery battery was very often a semi-autonomous unit serving in support of an infantry division or brigade. Batteries of light artillery had six guns or howitzers, in two half-batteries. Light artillery generally meant Royal Horse Artillery supporting cavalry brigades or Royal Field Artillery supporting infantry brigades. Heavy artillery of The Royal Garrison Artillery was found at divisional or corps level and usually had four or six guns in two half-batteries. By August 1915 the first giant railway guns or howitzers had been delivered to France, and these batteries had two guns or howitzers, usually of 12-inch calibre. The long-gun designs were adapted from those used in the dreadnought class battleships and had an effective range of 25,000 yards.

The brigade was a brigadier general's command, the first level at which generals exercised day to day control, and where command was exercised outside the 'family' structure of the unit. The brigade is the first level at which the group is called a formation rather than a unit. The brigade consisted of four infantry battalions or three cavalry regiments commanded by a small headquarters team. At the beginning of the war the whole brigade headquarters might be as few as four or five officers, although the demands of a horse-based officer corps might bring a dozen or more grooms, soldier-servants and other supporters. Brigades tended to be closely-knit; the Guards brigades absolutely did not have any non-Guards battalions in them, likewise the Ulster brigades of the New Army were exclusive to Ulster battalions. With its four battalions, a brigade was about 4,000 strong, although the increasing need for specialist warfare skills raised this 'establishment' number to nearer 5,000 as the war progressed. Some brigades were almost an extension of their battalions in local affiliation. As an example, 92 Brigade, which suffered at Serre on 1 July 1916, the first day of the Somme, was composed of four battalions of the East Yorkshire Regiment. The 10th, 11th 12th and 13th Battalions of the regiment were the four Pals battalions raised in Hull, so when the brigade suffered heavy casualties the effect on the people of Hull, coping with about 1,600 casualties as the result of one morning's action, was very severe.

A division is the formation that controls brigades, but importantly is the first level at which the concept of combined arms warfare comes into the picture. A major general, the commander, had three brigades, say 12,000 men, a separate pioneer battalion, another 1,000 men, substantial elements of artillery of different kinds, and elements of engineers, signals units, supply train, veterinary and medical support. In total the divisional commander had about 18,000 men in his division. This is a relatively stable formation, and brigades within divisions tended to stay together for the duration of the war. As with brigades, some divisions had strong ties to particular local regions. This particularly applied to the 36th (Ulster) Division.

The army corps is the next level in the upward chain of command. At this level of command a lieutenant general is a significant battle manager, in terms of his control, the scale of his responsibilities and the resources available to him. These resources were less defined than those available to lower-level commanders. A corps might have one, two, three or more divisions under command for a particular action, and then lose some of them or acquire others as events developed. It would have its own artillery, as well as that of divisions under corps command, and then be allocated yet more, for a specific offensive, but then lose its own to a more pressing demand elsewhere. Before a major offensive action, the corps might receive added numbers of railway troops, pioneers, medical resources and perhaps a cavalry division to exploit the breakthrough following an attack. It might lose many of those resources again as demands ebbed and flowed. Thus a corps might number anything from 40,000 to 100,000 men or more.

An army is a fully functional freestanding entity. The general is a highly important figure, with influence over all aspects of the battle, from planning to execution and exploitation. He is responsible for every aspect of conduct of the battle in his area of command. The army commander may have one or two or more corps under command, and he is responsible for the whole conduct of war in his area of responsibility. For example, the medical chain now stretches back from the regimental aid post with a unit at the front, past the casualty clearing stations of the larger formations and right back to the field hospitals. Railways and canal transport, battle training schools, repair workshops and even bakeries and butcheries all came under an army's command. Air operations came firmly into the picture at army level, even if tactically controlled further down the chain of command. The British Expeditionary Force began as a single army with two corps and a mounted division. By the halfway point of the war there were five British and Empire armies on the Western Front alone. Each was four or five times the size of the original BEF.

Within the context of any set-piece battle, it is worth comparing the difference in responsibility between a divisional commander's and his superior's on the first day of the battle. For example, for the Somme battle General Sir Henry Rawlinson, as army commander, was responsible for planning and directing a battle, which at different times involved fifty-two infantry divisions spread over a front of about 14 miles. He was responsible for every aspect, both logistical and fighting. Logistics included supplying food, water, shelter, fuel, animal fodder, ammunition, and every last item needed by men living in the inhospitable climate of the front line and its support areas and care of the wounded from regimental aid post to delivery to base hospital or back to the UK. Under GHQ's strategic direction, he managed artillery support, the use of the air service, front-line attack, and defence of captured objectives. All this lasted from the first planning to implementing Haig's final decision to 'close down' the battle five months later. At any moment, a divisional general would have one task to undertake, perhaps to capture a village or strongpoint on the first day of the battle, before others would take over the next part of the plan. Many generals found that the leap in responsibility, as they went from peacetime command of a battalion or even a company to war-time command of a brigade or division or even higher formation, was too great for their abilities. It was not the fault of the man but an inevitable fact that the whole British and Empire war effort had developed at a speed and to a scale that had been unimaginable to all but one person, Kitchener, at the beginning, and everyone was learning as they went along.

The final, highest level of field command was the Commander-in-Chief, originally Sir John French but latterly Sir Douglas Haig. He had the strategic responsibility for conducting the war on the Western Front and the final tactical say in terms of approving plans for major offensives and actions. However, he also answered to the nation and government for the employment and safety of the whole British army and had large responsibility for joint conduct of the war with his French and other allied commanders. The Commander-in-Chief was also heavily aware of his responsibilities to the many nations whose soldiers fought under his command. We know well the Canadian, Australian and New Zealand achievements, but overlook all too easily the front line contributions of India, Portugal, South Africa and other nations. Chinese, Indian and Egyptian labour corps also fell under his responsibility. Haig's was a truly imperial force.

A large General Headquarters supported the Commander-in-Chief. The BEF headquarters was at Montreuil, near Le Touquet. As the war developed, the number working here increased to about 2,000 as the BEF itself grew and as the complexity of war increased. The Commander-in-Chief depended on this staff for the flow of information and expert advice that enabled him to conduct the war on the Western Front.

The senior staff officer was the Chief of the General Staff, the Commander-in-Chief's right-hand man, who was responsible for the efficient management of GHQ. The Adjutant General was responsible for administration, personnel matters and organisation throughout the BEF. Heading the branches of the staff were heads of individual arms, such as air service, artillery and infantry, heads of support arms such as engineering, medical services, intelligence, transport and logistics, legal services and many other disciplines.

A feature of Haig's GHQ was that he himself was never reluctant to employ 'civilians in uniform' as heads of department if he thought he could improve the efficiency of his staff by doing so. One of his key heads of department was Eric Geddes, Deputy General Manager of the North Eastern Railway Company, but with no military experience. In mid-1916 Haig arranged for him to be commissioned as a major general and gave him charge of all transport resources of the BEF. It was a much-needed appointment, because for all Rawlinson's planning and attention to detail, the railways and other transport links were overwhelmed by the demands placed on them as the Battle of The Somme developed into its second and later months.

APPENDIX III

Other Arms

Military Flying

Flying was not popular in senior cavalry circles and had certainly not impressed Haig before 1911, when he suggested that the future of aviation lay only in sport. Few cavalrymen thought it possible that airmen could supplant the cavalry in the essential role of reconnaissance. Therefore, it was typical of that home of enterprise and adventure, The Corps of Royal Engineers, that they sponsored the first military flying in the British armed forces. The Royal Engineers had been interested in ballooning since 1863 and formally responsible for the School of Ballooning since 1888.

> **Whilst many leading soldiers discounted the possibilities of military flying in the pre-war years, all recognised the importance of the Royal Flying Corps as soon as its use in wartime conditions was demonstrated.**

In 1911 military flying took its next steps, when the Italian army successfully used heavier-than-air machines in their war against Turkey. One result was the formation of the Air Battalion, Royal Engineers. Officers of all arms were invited to apply to join the new Air Battalion. All had to have a flying certificate issued by the Royal Aero Club, and all had to pay seventy-five pounds to take part in military flight training. Those who failed the course did not obtain a refund, but those who passed were reimbursed.

Only one year later the Air Battalion was reorganised into the Royal Flying Corps (RFC). There were two wings, naval and military, although the latter became the separate Royal Naval Air Service in July 1914.

As the war developed, so the changed nature of the air war was recognised. Towards the end of the war, only six years after its formation, the RFC was undertaking most of the functions that we associate with a modern air force. These included reconnaissance, tactical and strategic bombing, and re-supply from the air. The changed nature of the air service was formally recognised with the formation of a new service, the Royal Air Force, on 1 April 1918.

Throughout the war the balance of superiority in the air changed from time to time. Numbers of aircraft and the amount of training received by pilots were important factors, and the development of tactics was vital. However, the balance of superiority was often swung by development of aircraft types. Speed, manoeuvrability, ability to take the height advantage and flying time duration all improved regularly as aircraft engineers on all sides worked to improve the machines available.

Royal Engineers

The Royal Engineers (RE) managed much of the range of services that were required to keep an army in the field. As the war developed and needs became more sophisticated, the extent of RE services expanded beyond that of any other part of the whole army. Just fewer than 6 per cent of the original BEF wore the RE cap-badge. By mid-1918 that percentage was just under 12 per cent, of a vastly larger overall number. Nineteen-fourteen's worldwide total of 25,000 members of the RE, only 12,000 of them regular soldiers, had expanded to 314,000 four years later.

Among their roles, Royal Engineers were responsible for:

- signalling, including telephones, pigeons, post and mail
- building and maintaining roads and bridges
- building standard and narrow gauge railways
- inland waterways and some sea-port operations
- cross-Channel barge trains from late 1917 onwards
- building ammunition dumps and other stores
- building hutments for troops in the UK and behind the Western Front
- creating reserve lines of trenches
- boring wells for water, laying pipes and managing water supplies
- drainage
- quarrying and forestry to deliver stone and wood for army needs
- handling and discharging gas
- camouflage design, training and creation in two rear areas factories
- demolition works

Towards the end of the war, about 140,000 tonnes of engineering stores were passing through RE depots every month.

Labour Corps

The urgent need for labourers was always a problem half-solved. The divisional pioneer battalions were an early attempt to provide the resources needed for the endless digging, road-laying, building defensive and offensive works and other tasks that proliferated as the war took on its static nature. All fighting soldiers were also resources to be called upon in this way, and a period of 'rest' behind the lines often meant nothing more than substituting rifle for pick and shovel.

As time went on and the calls for labour multiplied, the RE labour battalions, the pioneer battalions and Non-Combatant Corps labour companies proved insufficient. By 1916 prisoners of war were used by both sides as non-combatant labour. The French signed an agreement with the Chinese government in 1916 and 50,000 Chinese men from eight provinces were shipped to labour for the French Army. Great Britain followed suit and by 1918, 98,000 Chinese were enrolled in the Chinese Labour Corps. Add in a further 100,000 Egyptians, 21,000 Indians, 20,000 South Africans of the Native Labour Corps and other contingents from all across the Empire, the non-combatants and prisoners of war, and the total Labour Corps manpower reached about 300,000 by the end of 1918. Nearly 2,000 Chinese labourers died in France, many as victims of the Spanish 'Flu epidemic. All are buried in CWGC cemeteries, treated exactly as any others cared for by that organisation.

> **The Chinese Labour Corps remained in France after the Armistice, employed in clearing battlefield debris, including unexploded shells.**

Army Service Corps

Logistics are vital to any gathering of people. Food, water, clothing and the means of shelter and protection have to be gathered, delivered to the gathering and then distributed.

The armies on the Western Front inevitably had logistical needs beyond any previous expectation. By 1918, 500,000 horses had to be fed, shod, sheltered and yoked or saddled. This alone required a monthly delivery of 15,000 tonnes of forage. A force of three million men needed a monthly delivery of over 40,000 tonnes of bread alone. Artillery demanded ever-larger amounts of ammunition, and that ammunition became less easy to transport as the war required ever-larger calibre guns. The infantry needed constant supplies of bombs, grenades, and cartridges for machine guns and rifles. Static warfare also demanded defence stores such as barbed wire and pickets, and supplies of wood and metal sheeting to build and maintain trenches and shelters. Men needed food, their daily tot of rum, water, shelter, clothing, as well as their mail and parcels from home.

Delivering all these goods and supplies needed new railways, both full-gauge and narrow and new roads. Building these required yet more supplies, stone imported from Cornwall, timber sleepers and steel rails, coal and diesel to fire the locomotives.

Although the Royal Engineers played a major role in many of these activities, the Army Service Corps and Royal Engineers cooperated in logistics management. However the prime responsibility for logistics delivery fell upon the Army Service Corps, generally described as Line of Communication Troops. As with the Royal Engineers, this corps expanded beyond any expectation as the war developed. By the end of the war it numbered a little over 300,000.

Women's Service During the War

The services' demand for men led to a change in the role of women. As manufacturing industries turned to meeting the needs for war matériel, so factories were losing their manpower. As a result, female labour began to appear in factories, and especially in the munitions works. Offices, farms and shops that had hitherto been male preserves had to recruit female workers in order to survive, and women were released from the drudgery of domestic service to work in a variety of other activities. The demand for munitions in particular meant that new armaments factories were often largely staffed by women throughout the shop floor.

> **Manufacturing smoke and illuminating shells required working with phosphorus. The dangers of this work were not recognised at first and the disease 'phossy jaw' was not rare among these workers. Workers took their lunch to work, where their food would be contaminated by phosphorus. This would be absorbed in the teeth and gums, causing abscesses and rotting. In time phossy jaw affects the jaw bones themselves and then the brain. It causes terrible disfigurement and a lingering painful death.**

During the South African wars at the turn of the century, medical services had been primitive and relied largely on volunteer assistance. A small professional military nursing corps was formed in 1902, consisting of the 300 or fewer members of Queen Alexandra's Imperial Military Nursing Service (QAIMNS). However, from the first days of the 1914 war, women were determined to play a part regardless of the strict criteria laid down for joining

QAIMNS. At the same time, the lack of sufficient established medical services led to leaders of society, like the Duchesses of Sutherland and Westminster, to form private hospitals in France. To begin with the army resented and tried to ignore these initiatives, but when the official medical establishment was clearly unable to cope with the unprecedented casualty rates, the private initiatives were gradually brought into the mainstream of medical provision. QAIMNS had over 10,000 nurses in hospitals in the UK and on the Western Front by the war's end.

The First Aid Nursing Yeomanry (FANY) had been founded in 1907 as a horse-mounted paramedical service staffed by female volunteers in the field. Members were trained in riding, first aid and signalling, and were expected to work in the front line of a mobile battlefield. Each member was required to provide her own horse, which ensured social exclusivity. In August 1914 six members with only £12 between them travelled to France with the first troops. Initially the senior military establishment resented their interference, but they were welcomed by the Belgian Army, and by the British Brigade of Guards. By 1916 their first hospital was treating several hundred casualties every month. In addition, FANYs were driving ambulances, delivering rations and doing other non-medical jobs.

The FANY ethos, a club-like approach to recruitment and membership, was too unwieldy to be a solution to the needs of the army to employ women in large numbers. The Women's Auxiliary Army Corps (WAAC) was formed in 1916 to offer the opportunity for women from all walks of life to serve in France. From the outset the Adjutant General Sir Nevil Macready supported the new service in every way he could. He believed that women should be given all possible opportunities to serve and that they should be treated as far as possible the same as their male comrades. Traditional prejudice prevented the sort of integrated service that Macready believed in, and which we take for granted a century later, but his support enabled the service to achieve far more than would otherwise have been possible. By 1918 over 6,000 WAACs were serving in France. Of that number, and despite every fear of the authorities about allowing women into the battle, only twenty-one became pregnant whilst on service in France and only thirty-seven were dismissed for incompetence or disciplinary reasons. By the war's end WAACs were the largest and most visible female military presence in France. Members became mechanics, drivers, cooks, bakers, signallers, waitresses at headquarters, and were frequently seen in the forward areas of the battle zone, delivering supplies and rations, operating shower, bath and de-lousing stations and assisting in forward medical facilities.

Macready was responsible for repealing the army regulation that required all officers to grow moustaches. He was known to hate his own and shaved it off on the day the regulation was repealed. Perhaps his willingness to think unconventionally came from the fact of his father being a celebrated actor and his mother a member of a family that included a number of artists among the more conventional naval and clerical sons.

Medical Services

Medical services began the war with little in place beyond the unit medical officer and his assistants and stretcher-bearers. This situation changed as soon as war broke out. Behind the Regiment Aid Post or its equivalent came Field Dressing Stations, and then Casualty Clearing Stations, Base Hospitals and evacuation to England.

Specialist hospitals were created, such as the one where Noel Chavasse was treated for his abdominal wounds, behind Ypres in 1917. Specialist nerve doctors set up hospitals for treating shell shock and other psychological conditions. Provision of artificial limbs began the slow process of development from peg-legs to proper prostheses. These specialist centres took development of treatment to unknown levels of expertise. Survival rates rose to levels that were not reached again after the war until penicillin became available in the last days of the Second World War. Modern principles of immediate action to treat wounds were understood as being crucial to successful casualty management. Despite the difficulty of moving casualties across broken ground during battles like Third Ypres, and despite the problems of managing the treatment of sheer numbers of casualties, the chance of a casualty surviving his wounds rose remarkably for each year that the war continued.

Voluntary hospitals sprang up all over the country. Great country houses and other buildings of all kinds were made available. County hospital associations, St John Ambulance, The Red Cross and others provided equipment, training and experience. The matrons were frequently the ladies whose families owned the houses. Local businesses and individuals gave ambulances and specialist equipment. In Shropshire alone, thirteen new hospitals were opened for war wounded before the end of 1915. Another eighteen would follow before the war's end. Most were country houses, a few were former schools or similar premises.

Military morale is influenced by many factors, and the soldier who thinks that he will receive prompt and skilled attention to his wounds will have higher morale and be more willing to face risk than will a soldier who lacks such belief.

APPENDIX IV

Weapons

Artillery

In essence, artillery could be divided into three categories. Long-gun artillery is characterised by long-barrelled weapons that are designed to deliver shells accurately over considerable distances. This artillery is ideal for precise operations, such as attacking targets at some distance behind front lines. Railway and road junctions, bridges and command positions would be typical targets. Long-barrel artillery has particular value if it can out-range other artillery and be effective in neutralising the enemy's batteries without itself being involved in local duels. This last function is called 'counter-battery' work.

Short-gun artillery is characterised by the typical picture of the Great War gunner working around the heavy short-barrelled howitzer, muzzle pointing skywards as it launches a heavy shell to land a mile or ten in front. Heavy shells, plunging almost vertically downwards from thousands of feet above, fused to explode a split second after hitting the ground, were the ideal weapon for destroying trenches, bunkers and local communications. The largest such guns created the giant shell holes that one still sees on the battlefields; some are large enough to be confused with small mine craters.

Both these types of artillery use rifled barrels. This means that spiral grooves are cut into the barrel; the opening sequence of James Bond films shows how these spirals appear if one looks through the barrel of a rifled gun or pistol. The shell itself fits into the gun, not tightly, but around the base of the shell is a band of soft metal, such as copper or zinc, that itself has a ribbed surface that will engage the spiral grooves of the barrel. As the gun is fired the ribbed driving band begins to turn with the spiral of the rifled grooves, and this spinning motion transfers to the shell itself, giving it stability in flight that permits accuracy and distance. A rugby player spinning the ball in his pass is achieving exactly the same aerodynamic effect.

The third type of artillery is the mortar. This a short-barrelled, smooth-barrelled weapon, necessarily less accurate than other artillery, but having the advantage of being simple, often portable and small enough to be taken right to the front line. Trench systems frequently incorporated large bays where a mortar could be set up within yards of the enemy front line, to hurl high explosive, gas or illuminating shells over the enemy lines as the need arose. Although mortars were common in all armies, some aspired to technical excellence whilst others aspired to simplicity. Of the latter, one of the commonest was the Stokes mortar, a weapon designed to be used in the front line trenches, throwing a 3-inch bomb anything up to 800 metres. The weapon was a powerful addition to the defensive armoury, with an experienced crew capable of sending up twenty-five bombs per minute. The local effect on attacking infantry caught in the open was devastating. Over 1,600 Stokes mortars were in operation on the Western Front at the end of the war.

The Livens Projector was another front-line mortar, an invention of Captain Livens, Royal Engineers. He commanded an RE company set up to devise a means of delivering gas efficiently to enemy areas. Simply laying hose lines out into no-man's-land and connecting them to canisters stored in the front line trenches was not good enough. He was also interested in the ancient Greek weapon of flaming projectiles. His first design project was to create a weapon that could hurl a fused drum containing 2 gallons of flammable liquid, and the projector was the result. In essence it was a metal tube 4 feet long and about 8 inches in diameter, buried in the ground and pointing at an angle towards the German target, less than a mile away. A charge was laid in the base, the projectile lowered in on top, and the device would be fired electrically. Because the charge was only intended to throw the projectile a short distance, there was no need for a sophisticated and strong barrel. As a result, Livens projectors were extremely common throughout the British sectors of the Western Front. By the end of the war they would be set up in long rows in trenches especially constructed for the purpose, and hundreds could be fired simultaneously, each throwing a 30-pound container of poison gas or flaming oil into enemy territory. In the attack following the detonation of the seventeen mines at Messines Ridge in 1917, 1,500 projectors were fired almost simultaneously, to give extra cover to the assaulting infantry.

Attitudes to artillery were by no means uniform before the war began. The French Army, as late as 1911, believed that only very light and mobile field artillery was needed in modern warfare. A modest number of large calibre guns were needed for fixed fortifications like those of Verdun. Thus they took the trouble to develop one of the outstanding artillery weapons of the war, the light 75mm field gun. It was mobile, reliable, accurate and quick-firing. The BEF was content with similar, standard, light artillery, notably the 13-pounder horse-drawn field gun developed using lessons learned from the need for such mobility during the Boer War. This artillery was the stock-in-trade of the Royal Field Artillery. A separate branch of the army, The Royal Garrison Artillery, was responsible for heavier 'siege' artillery. The British and Germans mixed both types of artillery, light field artillery travelling with quick moving troops and heavier siege guns to be brought up to bear on fortifications such as those standing at Liege, across the advance route through Belgium.

As the war progressed and became a trench-based stalemate, defensive fortifications became stronger and stronger. Concrete shelters and defensive positions made their appearance, and these were impervious to the offensive power of small-calibre field guns. By the end of the war both sides were using guns that could fire shells with diameters up to 420 millimetres and weighing almost one tonne. These were more accurate over longer distances than had been thought possible at the beginning of the war, and were effective against all but the very strongest defensive strongpoint. By the war's end, the extreme examples of the development of heavy artillery were the German train-mounted ultra-long-range guns used to shell Paris from over 75 kilometres to the north.

The ultra-long-range guns that shelled Paris were the *Paris-Geschütz*, the Paris Guns. They were immense weapons, with barrels 30 metres in length and a range in excess of 75 kilometres. The actual shell weight was a modest 90-100 kilograms, less than one tenth of the weight of the largest howitzers used by all sides on the battlefield. Wear on the barrels was so great that shells had to be made in numbered series, each shell slightly larger than its numeric predecessor, to ensure that they could grip the rifling of the barrel as it was worn off by the preceding shell. Very few guns were made, and perhaps only three were ever fired. One exploded on first firing, leaving only two to threaten Paris. As Germany approached defeat, the guns were taken back to Germany and destroyed. The plans were burned and as far as possible the Germans did all they could to ensure that the weapons could not be used or rebuilt to be used against their own cities.

Artillery generally fired a variety of shells, according to the needs of the firing plan and the nature of the guns:

Shrapnel. The shell consists of a core of high explosive packed around with hundreds of small lead balls about 6 millimetres in diameter. The shell had a fuse timed to explode it above the enemy and propels the balls in all directions, including downward. The effect is especially useful when attacking enemies sheltering in trenches, or when defending against large numbers of attackers in the open and in close formation. Artillerymen and generals alike believed that shrapnel could cut barbed wire, and went on so believing until the definitive failure of wire cutting by artillery in the preparations for the Battle of The Somme.

High Explosive. The shell is packed full of high explosive and can be fused to explode on contact with the ground, or shortly afterwards, the former being useful for destroying troops and equipment at ground level and for cutting barbed wire, and the latter being useful for destroying trenches and shelters below ground. Developments in fuse technology continued throughout the war, and by the end fuses were available that were so sensitive that they would explode instantaneously on grazing contact with a strand of barbed wire, but before touching the ground.

Gas. Early gas attacks depended on the attackers carrying canisters to no-man's-land in front of their own lines, opening a valve and hoping that wind would do the rest. The French solved the problem of delivering gas more effectively than this by inventing artillery-fired gas shells that were able to reach areas far behind enemy lines. Gas attacks like this were effective in creating confusion and delays in the movement of soldiers and supplies during attacks.

Smoke. Smoke is valuable in attack, masking the vision of defenders, and reducing the efficacy of defensive fire.

Star Shells. These deliver an intense light over a large area and are invaluable to the defence when countering attacks at night or seeking to drive off reconnaissance patrols.

> **Artillery was the dominant arm of battle during this war, on all major fronts and with almost all armies.**

Gas

The first gas attack on the Western Front was during Second Ypres in April 1915. Common industrial chlorine was easily obtained and easy to handle. However, the first antidote was also easily obtained, when soldiers quickly realised that breathing through a folded handkerchief on which one had urinated caused a chemical reaction that neutralised some of the effects of chlorine.

More effective gases quickly followed, phosgene and mustard gas in particular. Phosgene has no instant effect, but reacts in the moistness of the lung to form carbon dioxide and hydrochloric acid, which dissolves the membranes of the lungs causing a slow and horrific death. Most of the many varieties of mustard gas causes deep, intensely painful and incapacitating blisters on skin exposed to it, but are generally not fatal, being so in only about 1 per cent of

APPENDIX IV

cases. From a military point of view this is an advantage because wounded men absorb more resources than do dead ones. Mustard gas was certainly being made in Germany by 1860, was written about by an English chemist in the same year, and may actually have been made experimentally as early as 1822. Perhaps it is surprising that it took so long to be seen as a useful weapon of war.

In all, at least seventeen different gases were used by different armies at different stages of the war. All armies used poison gases, with the chemical advantage ebbing and flowing as new gases were countered by improvements in anti-gas defence. Gases fell into a number of categories but principally were asphyxiating, blistering or lachrymatory. Although the general aim was often to incapacitate rather than kill, survival was often a matter of living death rather than escaping scot-free.

Gas was a significant feature in both attack and defence for all sides as the war went on. Early gas attacks relied on canisters of gas carried to the front line and connected to hoses with very long nozzles that were pushed out into no-man's-land. Thus the gas was usually discharged closer to those using it than to those intended to suffer from it, and a tiny variation in wind direction could bring gas into the users' trenches. More sophisticated delivery systems were developed, including artillery shells and Livens projectors. By 1918 about one quarter of all shells fired on the Western Front contained gas rather than high explosive. Meteorology dictates that in the early stages of the gas war on the Western Front the Allies had an advantage over the Germans. The prevailing wind came from behind the Allied lines and blew gas towards the German ones. Thus in default of any local or short-term wind-shift the advantage of releasing gas lay with the Allies. This was not always to be relied upon and the use of gas at Loos in 1915 proved a very mixed blessing to the BEF.

Fire and Flame

The concept of flame as a weapon was first recorded as the ultimate weapon of its time in about 570AD. It enabled the Byzantine Empire to maintain pre-eminence for a century, and the composition of the burning agent was the closest-guarded military secret of the age. The secret of 'Greek Fire' was lost at some stage in early history, but over centuries military thinkers developed means of delivering fire. Some involved catapults that threw flaming tar-impregnated animal bodies over the walls of besieged cities; others involved developing leather hoses with metal nozzles attached to simple pumps. These latter were especially usefully in the galley-based naval wars of the Mediterranean civilisations.

The first use of flame as a weapon in this war was by the Germans in the British sectors in July 1915, in the Ypres Salient at Hooge. A leisure park now

185

stands on the exact site. The initial effect was all that the Germans could have expected, and it took a strong counter-attack to repair the hole in the British line that appeared following the appearance of this unknown weapon.

Although all sides used flame-throwers as weapons for the whole war, their general use tended to deliver diminished returns. Operators of flame-throwers were conspicuous by the bulk of their apparatus and their appearance in attack or defence was the signal for every rifle and machine gun to turn on them. In addition, German infantry operators were members of special units, with their own death's-head badges. There no recorded instances of anyone wearing that emblem being taken prisoner. Flame-throwers were used as auxiliary weapons on tanks, and in that role proved effective against bunkers and pill-boxes, but always suffered from having very limited range, never more than about 30 yards in the case of hand-held devices and 60 to 75 yards when they could be mounted on tanks towards the end of the war.

Machine Gun

All machine guns during this war were derived from an invention by American-born British citizen Hiram Maxim in 1885. Before Maxim's invention, a variety of mechanical guns generally worked on the principle of a hand-operated crank mechanism that rotated a number of barrels past a single firing chamber, with a separate mechanism to unload and reload each barrel in turn. The best-known mechanical multiple-barrelled gun was the Gatling gun, used by both sides during the American Civil War.

Maxim's machine gun was the first practical gun to operate by harnessing some of the energy unleashed by firing one bullet, a 'round', to operate a mechanical process that reloads the gun ready to fire the next round. If the operator keeps the trigger pressed, and the supply of rounds is maintained, the gun will fire an incessant stream of bullets. By 1914, machine guns were reliable, accurate for distances up to a mile and capable of firing up to 600 rounds per minute. There was a problem; guns overheated and jammed when fired for prolonged periods. This had been addressed by encasing the barrel in a water-filled jacket, in turn connected to a separate reservoir. Maxim's brother had made the invention of a smokeless propellant his own project and by 1914 smokeless charges were used by all armies. By 1912, the Vickers Company had bought out Hiram Maxim's interest in a company formed to exploit the invention. The company refined the principles of the Maxim gun, reduced its weight, improved its reliability and extended its killing range. The newly named Vickers machine gun was now available to the British Army.

The Vickers machine gun had an effective aimed range of between 2,000 and 2,500 yards, but against massed troops was effective at longer distances, up to 4,000 yards at its maximum range. Firing non-stop the gun would fire about 600 rounds per minute. The bullets would fall in a predictable lozenge pattern, whose size would depend on the distance to target. This is the 'beaten zone' and at extreme range could cover an area 200 yards long and 50 wide. Firing non-stop to create a fully beaten zone was only an option in extremis; despite the water-cooled jacket surrounding the barrel, the gun overheated too quickly to offer sustained fire as a routine option. In general the gunner would fire a four-second burst of about thirty or forty rounds, then swivel the gun mounted on its tripod very slightly to left or right. Thus the gunner could shift the gun's beaten zone to overlap the previous one, and cover the width of his area of defensive fire in measured degrees.

When the war began machine guns were served by sections of ten men operating two guns, with one section in each infantry battalion or cavalry regiment. Many cavalry regiments resented having a machine gun section; they felt that it detracted from the smartness of the regiment on parade and could only hinder the regiment in its two key roles, reconnaissance and the hard-riding exploitation of the breakthrough. By the end of 1915 the tripod-mounted heavy machine gun was an arm of war of itself, controlled by the newly created Machine Gun Corps. A machine gun company was attached to each infantry or cavalry brigade, with another as part of each division's resources.

As the heavy machine gun became an arm of war, alongside the artillery, removed from local control, a new 'light' machine came into being. The Lewis gun was half the weight of the Vickers, had fewer parts, could be carried into the attack, fired on the move and any infantryman could be trained to use it. It was very widely used, with up to fifty issued to each infantry battalion.

Both heavy and light machine guns used the same ammunition as that for the ordinary infantryman's rifle. This eased manufacture and supply and made it possible to use the same ammunition in all the hand weapons of the battalion. However, later in the war a new version of the Vickers gun was introduced, firing bullets with a calibre of 0.5 inches, instead of the standard 0.303 inch bullet in general use. This was now called the heavy machine gun, and the .303 version weapons were re-named as medium machine guns.

Tanks

'Success has many fathers, failure is an orphan.' The list claiming paternity of the tank is a long one. The concept is the joining of many different developments, made possible by the caterpillar track, without which an armoured vehicle could not move across broken ground. Under the enthusiastic patronage of Winston Churchill, light armour plating had been added to civilian motor cars on which machine guns were mounted in 1914. The internal combustion engine offered a workable means of propulsion. Breech-loading weapons offered offensive capability to the crew inside the armoured shell of such a tracked, armoured and self-propelled machine.

Self-propelled armoured vehicles were not a practical proposition before the war; the technology was primitive and unreliable. A machine that could only move at less than walking speed, when it was able to move at all, did not appeal to a generation to whom the cavalry offered speed and proven worth.

The idea of an armoured land-ship, armed with light field guns, came from Major Ernest Swinton, yet another imaginative Royal Engineer. He was pondering the question of how to get men close enough to enemy machine guns to be able to destroy their positions. His idea for an armoured mobile weapon went before the Imperial War Committee but they rejected it. However, the First Lord of The Admiralty, Winston Churchill, was a member of the committee. He took up the idea and sponsored it within his department. The Landships Committee was formed in great secrecy, Churchill knowing that neither Kitchener nor the War Office appreciated incursion by sailors into the land war. The Royal Naval Division, already fighting as infantry in Gallipoli and France, were commonly seen as Churchill's private army, used by him to interfere in strictly army matters. However, successful demonstrations to the Ministry of Munitions, under Lloyd George, and to others persuaded the War Office to acknowledge and adopt the development from prototype to a vehicle that would be practical on the battlefield.

Early tanks were essentially weapons platforms designed to get light guns close to enemy positions and overwhelm them with close range fire. Later versions were designed to mount a single heavier piece of artillery, and one design was adapted to be able to carry an infantry section of ten men in armoured safety.

Tanks were also used in dual roles, as armoured gunships that also towed armoured trailers containing ammunition, barbed wire and other supplies needed by the infantry to enable them to hold against counter-attack positions that they captured.

Grenades, Clubs and Others

The demands of trench warfare led to a variety of developments that encompassed all aspects of life in the trench.

The hand grenade was used in siege conditions in the Napoleonic wars. The Germans were the first to develop a practical grenade for the coming war and had a substantial stockpile of both hand grenades and others that were projected a slightly greater distance by an adaptation fitted to a standard rifle. The British

Mark 1 grenade was unreliable and risky to use, frequently detonating within the confines of the thrower's own trench. In 1915 the Gallipoli campaign saw the improvised 'jam pot' grenade, literally a jam tin filled with explosive, with a match-lit fuse attached.

All sides saw the grenade as the ideal assault weapon for trench warfare, and by the end of 1915 the Mark 5 grenade, the Mills Bomb, was in service on the Western Front. By the end of that year the armaments industry was manufacturing an average of 250,000 such grenades every week, and that number was later to rise yet more. During an attack or raid a bomber could carry up to twenty-four grenades, weighing a little over a pound each, with more carried by other members of a bombing party. It has been estimated that over seventy million Mills grenades were thrown by Allied forces.

Trench raids sometimes wanted to capture prisoners, and in such cases the use of rifles or grenades would be self-defeating. As a result a variety of homemade clubs and coshes became part of the armoury of every front-line unit. The rifle is in any case too cumbersome for use in the fast and desperate struggle of a hand-to-hand trench raid. There was no standard model for the improvised weapons of the trench raiding party, and every museum on the Western Front offers an exhibit of the nail-studded clubs, handy coshes, sandbags and knives that were the preferred weapons.

Tunnelling

Strictly speaking, tunnelling is not a weapon. However, tunnelling was simply another means to deliver large amounts of explosive to a particular point for a particular purpose at a particular moment, and can therefore be thought of as a weapon in every way.

Tunnelling companies were a new part of the array of forces available to commanders. The original BEF had no tunnelling capability but by early 1915 tunnelling companies were being formed as units of the RE. The early ones were formed by taking experienced miners out of infantry battalions, the first two coming from miners enlisted in the Monmouthshire Regiment. About 500 men formed a tunnelling company. In due course the recruitment and training of tunnellers became appropriate to the highly specialised nature of this warfare. By 1916 there were both a School of Mining and a Mine Rescue Company, supporting over twenty-five front-line tunnelling companies. In addition to the twenty or so British mining companies there were two Australian companies, two Canadian and one New Zealand. Australia also provided a specialist Mining Service Company to maintain the equipment used in all companies.

Tunnelling had three separate but inter-locked purposes:

1. The major purpose was to dig under enemy lines, to create a small cave or chamber at the end of the tunnel to be filled with an explosive charge. Electrical fuses would be fitted to the charge and lines run back to the opening of the tunnel, which would be back-filled to direct explosive power upwards, to the enemy positions above.
2. The second purpose was counter-tunnelling, digging out from one's own line solely with the purpose of intercepting and destroying enemy tunnels that might be coming inwards.
3. Not unnaturally, a third purpose of tunnels arose, tunnelling to prevent counter-tunnelling and to establish listening posts under enemy lines.

The extent of tunnelling activity can be understood by an awareness of two facts.

Although Haig was committed to the Somme in 1916, he still wanted Plumer's Second Army at Ypres to prepare its own offensive plan in case a change of plan became necessary. Plumer's building of twenty-four mines under Messines Ridge involved about 3 miles of deep tunnels. This work demanded so much manpower that all other strategic preparations in the Salient were diminished by demands for tunnellers and labourers to remove spoil.

Haig met the French President, Prime Minister and Minister of War at Montreuil on 31 May 1916. The French claimed that the BEF was not suffering the same intensity of German attacks as the French, which was true given Verdun. Haig replied that since 1 January that year, a matter of 152 days, the Germans had fired 653 mines, an average of thirty per week, under BEF positions. Most would have been relatively small mines, attacking local outposts or tactically important defensive positions, but the number indicates the importance that both sides attached to mining as part of their overall conduct of offensive and defensive warfare.

> **When tunnels and counter-tunnels intersected there would be small and violent clashes between enemies, sometimes at depths of 60 feet or more underground. In the dim light of candles or lamps, and using cudgels or knives, tunnellers fought in desperate hand-to-hand combat.**

The technical challenges of tunnelling depended on the geological formations in different parts of the line. In Flanders, around Ypres, the topsoil was sandy river deposit, water-logged once the war had broken the ancient drainage system. Beneath that is a thick layer of heavy, sticky London blue clay, the eastern end of a stratum on which London also lies. Tunnels here had to be lined with cement to ensure stability and waterproofing. Boring machines were brought over from the London Underground building programme but proved ineffectual in the wet soil and clay. Tunnelling reverted to hand digging, usually in near-darkness, total silence and foul air conditions. In the Somme *département* the subsoil was chalk, where tunnelling was relatively easy, could be undertaken quickly and did not require the engineering support that was essential in Flanders. Here, tunnels and counter-tunnels proliferated.

Appendix V

Hints for Visitors

When you go to France and Belgium to see these places as a first time visitor, whether alone, as part of a family party or within an organised tour group, you will need to think about some aspects of these visits that may not always be obvious:

- Some of the most interesting sites are not conveniently sited on dry tarmac roads and a pair of reasonably sturdy shoes is desirable even on the driest days. Waterproof shoes or boots are essential in any wet weather, which can be at any time of year; mud and wet weather played a major part in some battles.
- Although they are much rarer than they used to be, unexploded shells and grenades do still turn up, especially during the ploughing season. DO NOT pick them up, they were designed to kill someone and even after ninety years that someone might be you. A hand grenade recently turned up in a batch of potatoes sent from Belgium to Lincolnshire to be processed into potato crisps. During the 2007 ploughing season I saw a tractor driver marching across a ploughed field beside Delville Wood on the Somme carrying a large unexploded shell that his plough had turned up. That same morning only a mile or so away another plough brought to the surface the last remains of yet another of those bodies that were lost under the mud for ninety years.
- The battlefields are spread across open country and are frequently some distance from shops, cafes or lavatory facilities. Be prepared for this.
- Remember that lunch is eaten at midday and that country restaurants in particular will not offer much to the British visitor who wants to eat at one o'clock English time, two o'clock in France or Belgium.
- The most common mistake is to try to do too much in the time available. Before you go to the Western Front read up about a few sites and visit them with time to spare, and try to get the feel of them rather than seek

to tick as many names on an itinerary as possible. This is important when visiting the museums that are increasingly a part of the visitor's experience. There is a list of some of these museums, with some personal comments on them in Appendix VI.

- Take a pencil or pen. At the entrance gate of every Commonwealth war cemetery is a small bronze cupboard door set into the wall and behind it is a visitors' book. Record your visit and comments; they are important to other visitors and to the Commonwealth War Graves Commission who maintain the cemeteries. On two days in September 2011 the Commission buried the remains of six unidentified soldiers of the war, all found that summer. Their work is not just about the cemeteries as they are today.

- If you are a first time visitor, and equally if you are returning, take time at some moment in your journey just to walk around and look at the headstones in one cemetery, any cemetery. You may see a name, a date, a regimental badge, or something else that encourages you to find out a little more about what happened and how or why. The internet is full of sites that will help you on your way. Above all, as you walk around, stop and wonder. It is almost impossible to imagine such men doing such things ever again, and it humbles the soul accordingly.

APPENDIX VI

Visiting the Western Front

Without trying to pass judgement on the importance of any event that occurred, and aware that this is a wholly subjective approach, there is a small abbreviation at the end of each entry in this appendix. They are MV (must visit, the most important sites for a first-time visitor to the area), SV (should visit) and V (visit if you have time, but perhaps on a second or later visit). Just nine sites merit AMV, Absolutely Must Visit.

CEMETERIES IN GENERAL

There are British war cemeteries, including Empire and Dominions, all along the Western Front: 613 are in Belgium and 2,940 are in France. All are maintained by the Commonwealth War Graves Commission (CWGC). This body is funded by some of the national governments of different parts of the Empire and Dominions who lost soldiers in the war. Great Britain pays about 80 per cent, Canada about 10 per cent, with Australia, New Zealand, South Africa and India contributing the remaining 10 per cent. Some cemeteries are huge national memorials and some are very small, but each tells a story about an action, a series of events. Within 6 miles of each other in the Ypres Salient lie Tyne Cot Cemetery, the largest British war cemetery in the world, and the smallest, a cemetery with no graves but the headstones of the men of 177 Tunnelling company buried alive on 28 April 1916 under the hill on which their memorial stands.

Some have become famous and are visited by many every day, others are inaccessible and the records of the visitors' book show that perhaps fewer than ten people a year visit them. The point is not just to visit cemeteries but to visit the places where actions and the consequences are visible. The seasoned traveller will have a few personal special sites, places that call him or her back again and again. Every cemetery, however small, has a central point of focus, the Cross of Sacrifice that stands about 4 metres high on a pedestal in the most prominent position in the cemetery. Larger cemeteries containing over about

400 burials also have a Stone of Remembrance, a large Portland stone carved in a block shaped like a catafalque or empty tomb.

There is a deliberate 'feel' to all Commonwealth war cemeteries. From the beginning the Imperial War Graves Commission recognised that many people in the years to come would visit the cemeteries to see the graves of family and friends. The commissioners wanted every visitor to see the cemetery as an extension of an English garden, planted with shrubs and flowers that would be familiar to the visitor and the dead buried there.

Every grave has a headstone, carved from Portland stone and all identical in size and shape. At the top of the stone are listed the name, rank and unit in which the buried individual served. Whenever possible one body is buried in each grave. Exceptionally, one or two bodies were found so inter-mingled that separate identification proved impossible and joint burial was the only answer. To walk along a line of graves in any cemetery can tell a visitor a lot about local history. Are most of the burials associated with a single regiment, or do they have a date of death common to many burials? The answer will tell the visitor what happened, when and to whom, and the quest for the other answers, how and why, can begin.

When it was impossible to identify an individual body it was sometimes possible to identify a rank, or the force in which the individual had served. Whatever detail that was known is recorded on the headstone. In almost every cemetery there are all too many that simply bear the inscription *A Soldier of the Great War, Known unto God.*

Many first-time visitors and some who have never visited the Western Front wonder about the apparent obsession with cemeteries that form part of any itinerary of a visit. The reason is that most cemeteries are sited where men fell or died of wounds. Thus a visit to Passchendaele has to include Tyne Cot Cemetery because Tyne Cot is sited on the area of fortified bunkers and shelters that was the key objective of all the actions of the summer of 1917.

The gate into each cemetery has a small recess let into one pillar. This contains a book of remembrance for signature by visitors. A second list gives details of the burials in the cemetery and of the actions and battles in the area that caused the cemetery to be built.

GERMAN CEMETERIES

German cemeteries are different in many ways. They are sombre and give a feeling of the Teutonic finality of death. This is the deliberate policy adopted by the *Volksbund Deutsche Kriegsgräberfürsorge*, the voluntary charity that undertakes the care of German war dead, as does the CWGC. In Germany there was neither money nor the will at government level to undertake such work in 1918 and 1919, with starvation and social collapse at home. In December 1919 the *Volksbund* was formed to care for the bodies of the war-dead. Visitors will also note that there is usually more than one body in each German war grave, unlike British and Commonwealth ones. This reflects another philosophy, that of comradeship in death as in life.

There are far fewer German cemeteries on the Western Front. After the Second World War the Volksbund faced new demands on their limited resources. Following national agreement with Belgium in 1954, about 125,000 bodies were collected from small local cemeteries and brought to the four regional 'collection' cemeteries, at Hooglede, Langemark, Menin and Vladsloe. The 192 German cemeteries in France are mostly in the centre and east. They contain about 750,000 burials. As in Belgium many cemeteries are collection cemeteries. Collection cemeteries are all much larger than Tyne Cot at Passchendaele, the largest Commonwealth war cemetery in the world.

THE YPRES SALIENT

Menin Gate, Ypres at 8.00 pm is the supreme living moment of any visit to the Western Front. Every day of the year, at exactly 8.00 pm the buglers of the Ypres Town Fire Brigade play Last Post whilst standing in the centre of the great arch that spans the road north east to Menin. The ceremony was begun on 1 July 1928, but was discontinued after about four months. It was restarted on 11 November 1929 and has continued every night ever since. During the Second World War the ceremony in Ypres was discontinued when the Germans occupied Ypres on 20 May 1940. On that and every subsequent night the ceremony was carried out at the military cemetery at Brookwood, Surrey. On 6 September 1944, whilst heavy fighting continued in the outskirts of the city of Ypres, a Polish bugler stood in the middle of the road under the arch and played Last Post. The ceremony has not been missed once since that day. It also continues at Brookwood, played at 4.00 pm GMT on the first Sunday of every month.

The Menin Gate itself is an archway across the road, a memorial to the men who died in the Ypres Salient and whose bodies were never identified. The names of the missing are cut into the stone panels that form the facing of the memorial. The 'official' number of names is about 55,900, but that decreases occasionally as a newly disinterred body, from a road works, or building site, or turned up by the plough, is identified. The memorial was designed by Sir Reginald Blomfield, one of the three leading architects employed to create the cemeteries and memorials that mark the dead and missing of the war. **AMV**

APPENDIX VI

In Flanders Fields is the finest single museum of the Western Front, anywhere. The museum is housed in the Cloth Hall, the building which itself was the old centre of the medieval cloth and wool trade on which the prosperity of the city and region was founded. Like almost every single building in Ypres, the Cloth Hall was utterly destroyed by the constant shelling of the city during the war and after the end of it was rebuilt exactly as it had stood before. It presents a magnificent introduction to the Ypres Salient, in its collection, in use of sight and sound. Although the presentation changes from time to time there are some unforgettable moments, including the presentation of perhaps the most famous war poem of all, Wilfred Owen's *Dulce et Decorum est*. There are other museums in this list but this is undoubtedly the most important and comprehensive to be visited by the British visitor. **AMV**

Langemarck German Cemetery lies in the north of the Salient, one of only four German 'collection' cemeteries in Belgium, which between them hold 126,000 bodies, in small group graves or mass hecatombs. Langemarck itself holds 44,286 burials, about 19,000 of them identified and 25,000 unidentified. The names of over 16,000 of the bodies in the central mass grave are recorded on granite slabs that stand around the grave. Like all German war cemeteries, Langemarck Cemetery gives the visitor exactly the impression that the designers of all the German cemeteries intended.

Langemarck was at the centre of bitter fighting in 1914, 1915 and 1917, the First, Second and Third Battles of Ypres. **MV**

St Julien Crossroads is the scene of the German gas attack on 22 April 1915. The Canadian government selected it to be the site of the Canadian National Memorial in Belgium. The memorial does not present the scale of Vimy Ridge, but it is an important marker of one of the crucial interventions by Canadian forces that are a recurrent theme in any history of the BEF. The crossroads was named Vancouver Crossroads during the war, just another example of BEF troops giving familiar names to the unfamiliar features around them. **V**

Sanctuary Wood was a small area behind the original lines of the Salient, a place where soldiers who got lost in the mêlée of battle could regain their senses and bearings before setting of to rejoin their units. Today the small wood adjoining Sanctuary Wood is one of the most-visited sites of the Ypres Salient. The road to Sanctuary Wood is Maple Avenue, located south of the Ypres to Menin road, about 3 kilometres from the Menin Gate and close to the Bellewaerde Amusement Park on the other side of the road. A large signpost to the Canadian Hill 62 Memorial identifies the access road. Sanctuary Wood lies on the left, eastern side of this road. A café full of relics and souvenirs of the war provides the entrance to a small museum or collection of more relics. Behind the whole is a small 'preserved' segment of trenches and shelters. The effect of the preservation work is perhaps more authentic than the trenches themselves, but nonetheless this is a popular stop on the Salient itinerary. It is a pity that there is no attempt to explain what there is to see, and very little effort is made to preserve the many artefacts in display. The stereoscope picture machines need little explanation. **MV**

The Canadian Memorial lies at the end of this road, about 100 metres beyond the café. It marks the Canadian defence, retreat and recovery of three small hills, Hooge, Mount Sorrell and Tor Top in June 1916. Hill 62 is part of Tor Top, less than an hour's walk from the centre of Ypres, which is within easy medium artillery range.

As one leaves the area to return to the main road, the first cemetery on the left, almost adjacent to the café, is Sanctuary Wood Cemetery. It is a collection cemetery containing BEF re-burials from the immediate area, and from German cemeteries further afield when all German burials in those were being collected into the large cemetery at Langemarck. The CWGC lists 1,989 burials here. Only 637 burials are identified, the remaining 68 per cent of burials are 'Known Unto God', a remarkably high percentage reflecting the difficulties of grave registration in the Salient.

These two sites together, **SV**

Hill 60 saw some of the most long-fought struggles for supremacy in the Salient. The site has been left as undisturbed as possible and contains many features that reflect its importance as a point from which the surrounding ground can be dominated. **SV**

Tyne Cot Cemetery lies on the top of the gentle slope that leads up from the flat lands between Passchendaele and Ypres itself. The Cross of Remembrance stands atop a large plinth of Portland stone enclosing a large German bunker that was one of the anchor points of the German fortifications in front of Passchendaele. Although the whole bunker is covered with the stone plinth, part of the concrete beneath was left exposed. Popular legend has it that this was done at the suggestion of King George V when he visited the cemetery during its building. To stand in front of the cross and look down towards the flatlands, with Ypres only 6 miles away, gives a clear impression of the importance of holding the high ground anywhere in the Salient, given the natural wetness of all the ground below. The advantage of having such a commanding view over the land is also obvious. Standing there one also looks over about 11,850 individual graves, bodies collected from all around the Salient. These are bodies of men who died in every year of the war, and in every significant engagement in the Salient, and from every regiment and nation of the Empire. They lie together, joined in recent years by the bodies of German soldiers disinterred in the area. Their numbers continue to increase, a few each year, as more bodies are reclaimed from the ground, by construction work or by the natural action of the soft earth gradually returning a body to the surface, for it to be uncovered by the autumn plough.

At the back of the cemetery is a long semi-circular wall on which are inscribed the names of yet more men killed in the Salient but whose bodies were never identified. The Menin Gate holds the names of those missing in the Salient before August 1917; the wall holds the names of a further 33,000 who died after that date and whose bodies were never identified. The names of 1,176 missing New Zealanders are also inscribed here. **AMV**

Spanbroekmolen is a mine crater, one of those created by the mining of Messines Ridge in 1916 and fired in the attack of 1917. Unlike Lochnagar, the most famous surviving crater on the Somme, this one is filled with water and forms a nearly exactly circular pool. It is surrounded by trees and shrubs and is now very aptly called The Pool of Peace. The land surrounding the crater was bought in the early 1930s by Lord Wakefield and was passed by his heirs to a local charitable trust for preservation. It is perhaps the most peaceful site of all those commonly visited on the Western Front. The soil thrown up by the mine's explosion forms a steep lip all around the central pool, the result of firing a mine containing 91,000 pounds of ammonal high explosive. Close by, the smaller twin craters of Kruisstraat are also clearly visible from the road, now used as farm ponds but still clearly the result of the Messines Ridge tunnelling war. **SV**

Bayernwald is a small section of trenches on Messines Ridge. It was left undisturbed for many years and now belongs to the Commune of Kemmel, who used the original German manual of field fortification when restoring the trenches to something like their original state. There is a small concrete bunker, and the head of a deep shaft sunk to give access to counter-mines dug in the area. It is an important site in any visit that seeks to understand the nature of trench warfare. **MV**

THE ARTOIS
Arras and Vimy Ridge are the best-known of several important sites in the immediate surroundings of the city of Arras, the centre of the Artois.

Notre Dame de Lorette is a major French national memorial park and cemetery. It sits on top of the hill where in 1914 and early 1915 the two Battles of the Artois were fought, at the usual great cost of life. The French attacks were intended to dislodge the Germans from their strong defensive positions in the triangle of land bordered by this feature, the slag heaps near Lens to the north-east, and Vimy Ridge to the south-east. There is a museum at the back of the memorial park and a visitor centre, but the dominant buildings are the basilica church and the smaller chapel, which holds the bodies of unknown soldiers from various French wars and the body of an unknown victim of the concentration camps. **MV**

German Cemetery at Neuville St Vaast is one of only three in the whole of the Western Front within France. Over 44,000 burials are laid in rows in a plantation of trees, with no central building or focus except the lines of stark metal crosses. Bodies from German battles throughout the war are interred here. The cemetery lies on the east side of the road from Notre Dame de Lorette to Arras. Every visitor to the front should visit at least one of the very few such cemeteries to understand the difference between the two sides in their commemoration of their war dead. **MV**

Vimy Ridge is the Canadian National Memorial Park, set below and on the ridge itself. Below the ridge one can take a guided tour of the only section of Great War front-line tunnelling that is left anywhere in a safe condition, visit the restored trench system, now immortalised in concrete sandbags and duckboards, and see the effects of some of the mines blown during the 1917 assault. There is a small visitors' centre.

The memorial itself stands on the top of the ridge, its twin pylons dominating the skyline with their gleaming white marble height of 30 metres above the platform on which they stand. The monument is built of Seget limestone quarried in Croatia and selected for its pure colouring. The whole stands on bed of 11,000 tonnes of concrete. The monument was restored over a period of two years and re-dedicated by Queen Elizabeth II on 9 April 2007, the ninetieth anniversary of the capture of the ridge.

The names of every one of the more than 11,000 Canadian soldiers who died during the Great War and whose bodies were never identified are inscribed on the walls surrounding the monument's platform.

From the memorial one can look east and see the view over the Douai Plain that stretches from there to Belgium and the Channel ports, and appreciate the strategic importance of the ridge as an anchor point for German forces in the area. **AMV**

The Lichfield Crater Cemetery is nearby, one of the very small CWGC cemeteries, containing only fifty-eight burials. It contains fifty-seven individually unidentified Canadian bodies in a central mass grave, which is actually a small mine crater. All were killed on 9 or 10 April 1917, the assault on Vimy Ridge. The names of those known to be buried there are listed on plaques in the walls of the cemetery. The fifty-eighth burial is of a soldier found buried beside the crater. **V**

Arras Memorial is the memorial to 35,000 BEF soldiers who died in the Arras sector between spring of 1916 and August 1918, and who have no known grave. Walter Tull is commemorated as one of them. In addition on the same site is the Arras Flying Services Memorial, commemorating about 1,000 men killed in the air and whose bodies were never identified. The cemetery contains about 2,650 burials. Behind the cemetery is the Mur des Fusillés, the site of a Second World War execution site where 214 partisans and Resistance members were shot. **SV**

THE SOMME

There are hundreds of sites to be visited on the Somme. Some are the sites that are visited by hundreds every day and by thousands during the peak months. Some are rarely visited. This list is a selection of the must-see sites that enable the visitor to understand something of the nature and scale of the Battle of The Somme. The list reads from north to south, left to right in modern practice as one faces towards the German trenches.

Serre is the site of the wreck of the attack by the Pals battalions in 31 Division. Standing at the gate into the memorial wood one is exactly on the line of the trench, still visible, from which the assault was made. Facing towards Serre village one looks up the open field towards the lines of trenches and fortifications of the village that are out of sight just over the crest of the hill. If you re-read the description of the task facing the division on 1 July (page 70), it is too easy to visualise the 3,600 killed and wounded lying in the area ahead, about 100 yards deep and stretching less than a couple of hundred yards to either side. **MV**

Newfoundland Park at Beaumont Hamel is the memorial to the men of the only non-British regiment to take part on the first day of the Somme. As subjects in a Crown colony the regiment's one battalion had preferred to serve as an integral part of the British Army rather than as a battalion absorbed into the

Canadian force. The park contains the area of the Newfoundlanders' failed assault and Y-Ravine itself. Cemeteries and memorials within the park testify to the intensity of fighting on 1 July and in later actions in the same area.

The Canadian government has a guides programme. Young Canadians are recruited and trained to guide visitors around the site, explaining the events of 1 July and later actions. Any visitor will learn more from their guide than they can achieve by trying to visualise events through studying books and walking the ground. **AMV**

Thiepval is itself the scene of the prolonged struggle that finally saw the spur on which the village stands captured at the very end of the battle in November 1916. It had been an objective to be taken on 1 July. The huge monumental arch designed by Sir Edwin Lutyens to commemorate the missing of the Somme stands on the crown of the spur, the highest point of the entire Somme battlefield. The walls are inscribed with the names of over 72,000 soldiers whose bodies were never identified. The location and size of this monument mean that it can be glimpsed from several miles away, in several directions. **AMV**

Ulster Tower commemorates the men of 36 (Ulster) Division and their actions on the ground that the tower dominates. It is modelled on Helen's Tower, a landmark of the Clandeboye Estate in County Down, Northern Ireland, where the division trained before leaving for the Western Front. The tower stands almost on the site of the Schwaben Redoubt, the Ulstermen's objective on 1 July. It is open to visitors and from the top of the tower there is a bird's-eye view of the local area of battlefield.

On the other side of the road is Thiepval Wood, where the division's front line ran along the front of the road, down to the Ancre River, and just across it. There is a substantial project underway to excavate trenches within the wood. This work in progress can be visited by arrangement with the staff of the Ulster Tower, but is not otherwise open to the public. **SV**

Aveluy lies on the road from the Ulster Tower to Albert. The small and atmospheric Lancashire Dump cemetery lies beside the road in the middle of the wooded area. Behind the wood lies Martinsart British Military Cemetery. This is most unusual in that the headstones are made of red limestone rather than the white Portland stone that we expect to see in all CWGC cemeteries. **V**

Albert lies at the heart of the British sector of the Somme battlefield. The legend of the Golden Virgin is brought to mind when the tower of the rebuilt basilica is seen, with the gleaming golden statue dominating the town. The Albert

Museum is in one of the old tunnels underneath the town. It is very easy to find, the entrance is directly beside the main door of the basilica, with a Second World War light artillery piece outside. This museum is full of battlefield artefacts, has some excellent representations of life in the trenches and a good selection of other exhibits, including the rifles and other different weapons used by all sides. For many people this is the most interesting museum on the Somme, not least because it is old-fashioned and unpretentious. **MV**

Lochnagar Crater lies behind the village of La Boiselle, to the right of the main road from Albert to Bapaume. The mine was fired at 0728 on 1 July 1916. The crater is almost the last dry crater still accessible to visitors to the Somme battlefield. Its dimensions are awe-inspiring, now being with a diameter of about 200 feet and a depth of 80 feet. Both are considerably less than when the mine was first blown because later attempts to fill the crater and return the land to farming continued until Richard Dunning bought the site to ensure that at least one of these craters would survive as testimony to the effects of mine warfare. This site is very vulnerable to the erosion caused by the number of visitors who want to walk around the lip of the crater, and there is concern for its future.

Lochnagar is now another of the must-visit sites on the Somme. It is a focal point for most group visits and there are always many wreaths of poppies laid there to mark the remembrance element of those visits. **MV**

The Devonshires' Trench is at Mansell Copse, on the D64, 500 metres south of Mametz village. Although it is a small cemetery, it is on many tour itineraries. The story of the attack of the Devonshires is told on page 80. The cemetery contains the grave of Captain Duncan Martin, who foretold the fate of his battalion in the 1 July attack. Close by is that of Noel Hodgson, whose poem *Before Action* was written on 29 June 1916, the eve of the original date planned for the assault phase of the Somme, and therefore just two days before his own death.

It is also instructive to visit Mametz village, and look back from the road outside the cemetery to see the view that the German machine-gun team in that cemetery had as the Devonshires climbed from their trenches and began to walk across the open ground towards their objectives. **SV**

Delville Wood is the most important South African site on the Western Front. The South African memorial and museum are in the middle of this important site. The cemetery containing many of the graves of those who died here is situated at the entrance to the wood on the opposite side of the road.

Many of the South African soldiers who fought and died here were from Boer families, who had been at war with the British only a dozen years before war broke out. The record of South African service in the war, both on the Western Front and in fighting in the German provinces and colonies of Africa itself, is remarkable. **MV**

Péronne lies to the east of the British sector of the Somme, in the French sector. It is a market town with a busy Saturday market. The chateau-fort in the town centre houses the *Historial de la Grande Guerre*. If the museum at Albert represents the old-fashioned approach to presentation, the *Historial* represents the modern. Some people are deeply impressed by the museum and indeed the presentation is scholarly and informative. Others find that visiting it is a clinical and detached experience. Whatever one's opinion, it is certainly one of the important visitor centres of the region. **SV**

Villers-Bretonneux National Memorial lies about 5 miles south-west of Albert on the road from Villers-Bretonneux to Corbie. The memorial stands on the site of the Australian actions under Monash that marked the end of the *Kaiserschlacht* advance on this part of the Western Front in 1918. It is another Lutyens design, completed in 1938 after the Depression had halted work for a period. The memorial lists the names of all Australians who were killed on the Western Front but who have no marked grave. **MV**

THE AISNE

The River Aisne lies in the French part of the Western Front beyond the Somme but not as far as Reims and the Argonne. Here, as around Ypres, there were great events that led to little movement on the ground. This was because the ground so favours defence that once the Germans had fortified the high ground and natural defensive features they had little need to move from it. On the French side offensive actions against such defences always failed, always at terrible cost.

In 1918 this sector was taken over by the BEF, manned by troops 'resting' after the German first assaults of the *Kaiserschlacht* in April. The *Blucher/Yorck* phase of the German campaign fell heavily on them as the Germans swept down from the Chemin des Dames heights above the River Aisne.

Memorials and cemeteries abound in this region, reflecting the intensity of fighting throughout the Great War and in wars before it and after. There are many BEF memorials among them, because the BEF came through here in the retreat from Mons in 1914, as well as bearing much strain of the *Blucher/Yorck* Offensive of 1918.

The Chemin des Dames is the road from Chavignon to Craonne, parallel with the north bank of the River Aisne. This road in the French part of the Western Front is as symbolic in French military history as the Menin Road is in British. At almost any point on the road one can stop, look south over the spurs and re-entrants that run down to the River Aisne and marvel at the folly of French generals who expected to capture the ridge from a well-fortified and prepared enemy. This strategically important site also features memorials relating to other wars. A statue of Napoleon marks the Battle of Craonne, a small but important tactical win for his forces in the lead-up to Waterloo. A group of tanks and light artillery records fighting in 1939. Memorials in the immediate area also record the contributions and casualties of Senegalese troops in 1914 and American and Italian troops in this small region in 1918. **MV**

The Caverne du Dragon is a museum and visitor centre housed in a former underground working expanded by the Germans and used as a bunker to house and shelter troops manning the defences of the area. It is sited on the Chemin itself, halfway between Cerny and Craonne. **SV**

Hurtebise lies only a few hundred yards beyond the Caverne, east towards Craonne. Within yards of each other are memorials to French troops who fought here in 1814-15, 1915-17 and 1940. **V**

California Plateau is closer to Craonne and is the start point of a trail through woodland, along which is a series of large dioramas setting out the story of the war in the area. This fairly easy walk helps understanding of the importance of this battleground in so many major wars. This place-name is taken from The California, a tearoom, saloon and tourist feature that existed on the site before the Great War. **MV**

VERDUN AND BEYOND

Much of the battlefield of Verdun was a closed area for most of the inter-war years. As a result, the area in remarkably rich in buildings such as forts and bunkers, trench systems that have decayed at nature's own pace, and memorials that are almost without equal in their impact anywhere on the entire Western Front.

Verdun is a city full of historical reminders. The approach along the *Voie Sacrée* is an important historical site. From the Second Word War, *La Route de la Libération* starts in St Mére Église in Normandy to follow General Patton's route through Verdun to Bastoigne and the German surrender in 1945. The kilometre posts of *La Route* can be seen on the road from Ste Menehould to Verdun.

The city is another of Vauban's fortified frontier cities and his designs included fortresses on a number of important hills that immediately overlook the city. Thus the concept of the fortified region was already established before the period of reinforcement that followed the Franco-Prussian War.

There are museums and memorials throughout the city. **MV**

Bois des Caures lies north of the city. Take the D964 towards Stenay and about 4 kilometres out of Verdun take the D905 towards Beaumont. The Bois sites are clear to see after 4 kilometres on this minor road. From the car park there are three sites: Colonel Driant's command post, a few metres along the road to Moirey-Flabas on a clearly marked path of about 50 metres. From there back to the Driant memorial, with the graves of young officers from his battalions surrounding his own. Then across the main road into the woods behind the car park, following the trail, which is clear, and pass the memorial marking where he was hit and killed. A little further following the trail takes one to his first burial place, so carefully marked by the Germans at the time of his death. **MV**

Douaumont Memorial and Ossuary. The National Memorial stands at almost the highest point of the Verdun fortified region. The long main building lies along the ridge, with a bell-tower rising from the middle of it. This building holds in its crypts the bones of 130,000 bodies collected from the battlefield of Verdun. Windows along the base of the walls enable one to peer into these crypts to gain some limited idea of what that colossal number of skeletal remains means in visible terms. Inside, the memorial is a long open space, dimly lit through orange glass and the walls lined with thousands of private memorial plaques commemorating French dead of this and other wars. It is truly one of the wonders of France and one of the great memorials of the world. The cemetery in front of the memorial contains about 13,000 graves. **AMV**

Fort Douaumont is close by. The fort is one of the two at Verdun that are preserved in such a way as to offer safe and informative visits. Some artillery remains in place and much work is under way to stabilise and preserve the fort and its artefacts. **AMV**

Fort Vaux is also close by. The defence of the fort by Major Reynal remains an epic of courage. As with Douaumont, the self-guided tour is helped by a clear explanation of what happened and what one is seeing. **MV**

Abri des Quatre Cheminées is on the plateau, as with most main sites, and very clearly signed. A bitter four-day action was fought here in June 1916 at a time when the *abri* was fulfilling its literal name as a shelter, in this case for hundreds of wounded French soldiers awaiting their turn to be evacuated from the Verdun Salient back into the city. It was not intended to be a fortified strongpoint but was a barracks, headquarters and shelter. **V**

Ouvrage de Froideterre is a counter-point to seeing the main fortresses like Douaumont. The *ouvrages* were relatively small fortified points, housing men who manned the trenches immediately nearby and mounting two or three machine guns in armoured turrets to provide area support. One can identify reinforcement work undertaken after the French recapture of the *ouvrage* in the later stages of the battle. **SV**

The Memorial is a small museum at the destroyed village of Fleury on the plateau, close to the Ossuary. There are displays of many aspects of the war, including artillery pieces, uniforms, infantry weapons and medical equipment. The centrepiece is a simulation of a very small piece of land looking as most of the area must have looked after the Battle of Verdun was over. **MV**

Fleury is one of the nine villages of the plateau that were obliterated during the battle and never re-built. Each has just a small chapel built on its site to mark that a village was ever there. The site of this village adjoins the Memorial and the village and its principal buildings are marked on the ground where they stood. To walk among the markers laid out in the shell-broken ground, now populated only by trees that have taken over the land, is to understand something of the nature of the battle that lasted here for most of the year of 1916. **V**

Leaving Verdun to drive south to St Mihiel, about 30 kilometres south, one travels alongside the River Meuse, its lateral canal, and the road and railway. It becomes clear that none is of any use to the defence of Verdun if the eastern side of this set of transport arteries is overlooked from the east, as they all were from 1915 onwards.

St Mihiel and Butte de Montsec lie at the western tip of the German salient. Passing through St Mihiel eastward one drives 15 kilometres into the heart of the salient and to the American Memorial on The Butte de Montsec. The butte is a volcanic outcrop standing between two lines of hills that demark the Plain of The Woeuvre and form the defensive sides of the St Mihiel Salient. The American Memorial stands on top of the Butte, overlooking the salient and battlefield. If any memorial on the whole Western Front deserves a 50 kilometre journey just to see it, this stands alongside the Ossuaire at Verdun as being it. No explanation of ground, or picture, can do justice to the panorama of the whole St Mihiel Salient that one sees from the memorial, which is itself a building worthy of its site. **AMV**

Tranchée de Soif can be visited on the return trip to St Mihiel, signposted south off the D907. This was the site of a French attempt to drive the Germans out of the salient in 1915. A French attack broke through four separate lines of German trenches, but was unable either to break into the fifth and final line, nor to retire under the bombardment falling behind them. No food, water or ammunition was able to pass through the German fire, but despite this Commandant André and his company of infantrymen held their position for five days until thirst forced their surrender. The trench system and immediate area are preserved as a memorial to this action. **MV**

APPENDIX VII

Casualties

It is impossible to compute casualty figures exactly. In a war where millions fought and were wounded or died, record keeping ceases to be an exact science. Many men were wounded twice or more times. Men listed as missing presumed killed had sometimes deserted and re-joined as new soldiers in a different regiment. Records were lost or destroyed, notably in the Second World War when enemy bombing by both sides destroyed huge archives. Russian totals, in particular have been drawn from various sources that do not pretend to offer more than estimates.

In round numbers here are some generally acceptable estimates. The second number under Killed is the civilian death toll of each nation. None of these figures includes the death toll from the Spanish 'Flu.

Country	Killed	Wounded /Missing	Total
Allied Forces			
France	1,400,000 300,000	4,250,000	5,950,000
Great Britain	885,000 110,000	1,660,000	2,656,000
Dominions	230,000 2,000	410,000	273,000
Italy	650,000 590,000	960,000	2,200,000
Russia	1,800,000 1,500,000	4,600,000	7,900,000

USA	117,000		206,000

Plus Belgian, Greek, Portuguese, Montenegrin, Luxembourgers, Romanian, Serbian and 415 Japanese.

Total	5,700,000	12,800,000	
	3,675,000		22,200,000

Country	Killed	Wounded /Missing	Total
Central Powers			
Germany	2,050,000	4,250,000	
	425.000		6,725,000
Austria-Hungary	1,100,000	3,600,000	
	465,000		5,165,000
Bulgaria	90,000	150,000	
	100,000		340,000
Ottoman Empire	770,000	400,000	
	2,150,000		3,320,000
Total	4,010,000	8,400,000	
	3,140,000		15,550,000

These figures do not include several other categories of casualties of the war. The Chinese and Indian Labour Corps casualties are not included, nor are the 300,000 or more Africans who died in territories affected by the war because of famine, resurgent endemic disease or tribal strife caused by the war.

It is sometimes claimed that one Dominion nation or another suffered particularly heavily over the course of the war as a result of British incompetence. As percentages of their home populations there is actually little to choose between Australian, Canadian or New Zealand mortality rates. As percentages of total population they are all about 1.4 per cent to 1.6 per cent. South African fatal casualties are lower, reflecting the different relationship between the population and Great Britain, as well as the prejudices against black men joining the army.

Relative to Dominion totals, fatal casualties of British troops amounted to 2.2 per cent of the, much larger, national population. French deaths amounted to 4.3 per cent, Italian to 3.5 per cent. Serbia, where the trouble all began, suffered fatalities of 725,000 from a population of 4.5 million, a loss of over 16 per cent of the entire population.

Food shortages claimed large numbers. Even in mainland Britain the War Office reported in 1922 their estimate that during the war years over 100,000 civilians died as a direct result of food shortage or malnutrition. The Ottoman Empire civilian death toll includes deaths from disease, starvation and inter-ethnic group fighting.

In round terms perhaps sixteen million people lost their lives as direct consequences of the war.

APPENDIX VIII

The War Poets

This was not the first war to draw a body of poetry around it. That started most notably with the American Civil War. However, this war led to some of the most recognisable poetry of the twentieth century, written by men such as John Masefield, the Poet Laureate, as well as by servicemen of all backgrounds.

The tone of poetry changed as the war progressed. In the early years acceptance of the consequences of war is expressed in poetry. By 1917 a harder note was prevalent, and Siegfried Sassoon's *The General* was an overt commentary on the fighting man's opinion of his generals and their staff officers. By the end of the war much poetry had taken on a bitter and accusatory note.

John McCrae

McCrae was a Canadian army doctor. In May 1915 he officiated at the funeral of a friend and fellow officer, for lack of a padre. That experience led to his poem *In Flanders Fields*, which he started to write that same evening. He was killed in 1918.

In Flanders Fields

In Flanders fields the poppies blow
Between the crosses, row on row,
That mark our place; and in the sky
The larks, still bravely singing, fly
Scarce heard amid the guns below.
We are the Dead. Short days ago
We lived, felt dawn, saw sunset glow,
Loved and were loved, and now we lie
In Flanders fields.

Take up our quarrel with the foe:
To you from failing hands we throw
The torch; be yours to hold it high.
If ye break faith with us who die
We shall not sleep, though poppies grow
In Flanders fields.

APPENDIX VIII

Wilfred Owen

Owen was born in Oswestry, Shropshire in 1893. Living in France, he joined the Army in 1915, after meeting wounded French soldiers.

Owen is the most famous and prolific of the Great War poets, inspired by Siegfried Sassoon to strive to improve his writing. The manuscript of *Dulce et Decorum est* contains suggestions for improvement, written by Sassoon, most of which appear in the final poem. Owen was killed in France on 4 November 1918.

Dulce et Decorum est

Bent double, like old beggars under sacks,
Knock-kneed, coughing like hags, we cursed through sludge,
Till on the haunting flares we turned our backs
And towards our distant rest began to trudge.
Men marched asleep. Many had lost their boots
But limped on, blood-shod. All went lame; all blind;
Drunk with fatigue; deaf even to the hoots
Of tired, outstripped Five-Nines that dropped behind.
Gas! Gas! Quick, boys! – An ecstasy of fumbling,
Fitting the clumsy helmets just in time;
But someone still was yelling out and stumbling,
And flound'ring like a man in fire or lime.
Dim, through the misty panes and thick green light,
As under a green sea, I saw him drowning.
In all my dreams, before my helpless sight,
He plunges at me, guttering, choking, drowning.
If in some smothering dreams you too could pace
Behind the wagon that we flung him in,
And watch the white eyes writhing in his face,
His hanging face, like a devil's sick of sin;
If you could hear, at every jolt, the blood
Come gargling from the froth-corrupted lungs,
Obscene as cancer, bitter as the cud
Of vile, incurable sores on innocent tongues,
My friend, you would not tell with such high zest
To children ardent for some desperate glory,
The old Lie; Dulce et Decorum est
Pro patria mori.

Siegfried Sassoon

Before the war Sassoon was a well-to-do cricketing and hunting man who could afford to have no job. He joined the army on 3 August 1914, the day before the declaration of war.

He wrote prolifically throughout the war and is best known for *Before Arras*, written in 1917. At the time Sassoon was in hospital in London undergoing enforced treatment for shell shock, which was thought to be the only reason why a long-serving, decorated officer recommended for a VC would write an open letter announcing his refusal to obey orders in future. In fact Sassoon returned to the trenches to be with his friends, survived and lived until 1967.

The General – Before Arras – 1917

"Good-morning; good-morning!" the General said
When we met him last week on our way to the line.
Now the soldiers he smiled at are most of 'em dead,
And we're cursing his staff for incompetent swine.
"He's a cheery old card," grunted Harry to Jack
As they slogged up to Arras with rifle and pack.
But he did for them both by his plan of attack.

Suicide in the Trenches

I knew a simple soldier boy,
Who grinned at life in empty joy,
Slept soundly through the lonesome dark,
And whistled early with the lark.

In winter trenches, cowed and glum,
With crumps and lice and lack of rum,
He put a bullet through his brain.
And no one spoke of him again.

You smug-faced crowds with kindling eye
Who cheer when soldier lads march by,
Sneak home and pray you'll never know
The hell where youth and laughter go.

Copyright Siegfried Sassoon by kind permission of the Estate of George Sassoon.

APPENDIX VIII

A.P. Herbert

Herbert was a sub-lieutenant in the Royal Naval Division that fought throughout the war as infantry. The division saw service in Gallipoli and in many of the major battles of the Western Front. After the war he became a Member of Parliament and a celebrated humorous writer, with a particular skill in pricking bubbles of legal pomposity.

The Royal Naval Division managed to preserve something of the Royal Navy despite long service as infantry. This did not always endear them to their senior commanders, and the ways of those commanders did not always endear them to the division. In late 1916 and early 1917 Major-General Cameron Shute was one of those commanders who had a particular dislike of the naval ways of the troops under his command and tried hard to instil Army ways into them. His dislikes encompassed the Royal Navy way of saluting, the full beards that many grew, and many aspects of their attitude to trench life. Sub-Lieutenant Herbert wrote of one inspection visit by Major-General Shute:

The General inspecting the trenches
Exclaimed with a horrified shout
'I refuse to command a division
Which leaves its excreta about.'

But nobody took any notice
No one was prepared to refute,
That the presence of shit was congenial
Compared to the presence of Shute.

And certain responsible critics
Made haste to reply to his words
Observing that his staff advisors
Consisted entirely of turds.

For shit may be shot at odd corners
And paper supplied there to suit,
But a shit would be shot without mourners
If somebody shot that shit Shute.

Reproduced by permission of A.P. Watt Ltd on behalf of The Executors of Jocelyn Herbert, M.T. Perkins and Polly M.V.R. Perkins.

215

THE GREAT WAR EXPLAINED

Philip Johnstone

Lieutenant John Purvis, his true name, wrote this prophetic poem in February 1918, almost nine months before the war ended.

High Wood

Ladies and gentlemen, this is High Wood,
Called by the French, Bois des Fourneaux,
The famous spot which in Nineteen-Sixteen,
July, August and September was the scene
Of long and bitterly contested strife,
By reason of its high commanding site.
Observe the effect of shell-fire in the trees
Standing and fallen; here is wire; this trench
For months inhabited, twelve times changed hands;
(They soon fall in), used later as a grave.
It has been said on good authority
That in the fighting for this patch of wood
Were killed somewhere above eight thousand men,
Of whom the greater part were buried here,
This mound on which you stand being...
       Madame, please,
You are requested kindly not to touch
Or take away the Company's property
As souvenirs; you'll find we have on sale
A large variety, all guaranteed.
As I was saying, all is as it was,
This is an unknown British officer,
The tunic having lately rotted off.
Please follow me – this way...
       the path, sir, please,
The ground which was secured at great expense
The Company keeps absolutely untouched,
And in that dug-out (genuine) we provide
Refreshments at a reasonable rate.
You are requested not to leave about
Paper, or ginger-beer bottles, or orange-peel,
There are waste-paper baskets at the gate.

Reproduced by kind permission of the Borthwick Institute for Archives, University of York.

INDEX

Campaigns and battles are not listed in this index, but are generally featured as separate sections within the chapter headings relevant to when they were fought.

Individuals from Great Britain, Empire and Dominions are indexed individually. Others are grouped by nationality.

Battles between British or French and German forces are generally listed in the Contents (pages v-viii), although some unfamiliar ones are included here.

Military ranks are given as they were at the end of hostilities in November 1918, or on death if earlier.

dismissed from Cabinet and
   commands infantry battalion 38
support of tanks 187-88
Currie, Lieutenant General Sir Arthur
   Third Ypres (Passchendaele)
   107-110
   assessment of career 152-54

France
see also French Leaders
   Franco-Prussian War 1, 3, 45
   pre-war and Entente Cordiale 3, 5
   Plan XVII 6, 13, 17, 159
   Battle of The Frontiers 13-4, 167
   leadership 158-59
   memorials 200, 204
   casualties 209, 211
French, Field Marshal Sir John
   Commander-in-Chief 14, 15
   Smith-Dorrien and Second Ypres
   19, 37-8
   Loos, gas and dismissed 39-40
   assessment of career 143-44
French Leaders
   Driant, Lieutenant Colonel Emile
   Verdun 47
   memorial 142, 206
   Foch, Marshal Ferdinand
   pre-war 5
   becomes Generalissimo 125-27
   last 100 days 131, 133-34
   assessment of career 161-62
   Joffre, Marshal Joseph
   Plan XVII 6, 17
   Artois 38-39
   Verdun 47-51, 55
   Somme 61-2
   relieved of command 56
   assessment of career 159-60
   Nivelle, General Robert

   Verdun 55
   Commander-in-Chief and the
   Chemin des Dames 93-4
   assessment of career 160
   Pétain, General Philippe
   Artois 38
   Verdun 51-5
   Commander-in-Chief 94-5
   assessment of career 160-61

Germany
see also German Leaders
   creation 1-2
   alliances 3-4
   Great Memorandum (The
   Schlieffen Plan) 6-7, 9, 13-4, 19,
   25
   mobilisation 9
   advance through Belgium 15-7
   Eastern Front 25-6
   turning point 116
   Kaiser abdicates and Armistice
   140-41
   leadership 163
   cemeteries 195-96, 197, 200
   casualties 210
German Leaders
   Wilhelm II (William), The Kaiser
   background 2-3
   mobilisation 9
   Verdun 55
   abdicates 140
   Bruchmuller, Colonel Georg
   Kaiserschlacht artillery plan 119
   assessment of career 166
   Von Falkenhayn, General Erich
   Verdun concept 44
   downfall 60
   assessment of career 164-65
   Von Hindenburg, Field Marshal

INDEX